ZHELYABOV

This drawing was made during his final trial and shows him when he was angry. But it is the only good likeness that we have of him.

RED PRELUDE

THE LIFE OF
THE RUSSIAN TERRORIST
ZHELYABOV

BY
DAVID FOOTMAN

*History moves too slowly.
It needs a push.* ZHELYABOV.

NEW HAVEN
YALE UNIVERSITY PRESS
1945

COPYRIGHT, 1945, BY YALE UNIVERSITY PRESS

Printed in the United States of America

All rights reserved. This book may not be reproduced, in whole or in part, in any form (except by reviewers for the public press), without written permission from the publishers.

Acknowledgment and Dedication

THE late Vladimir Burtsev, the historian of the Russian revolutionary movement in which he himself played a memorable role, was kind enough to supply me with a number of hitherto unpublished details. I am indebted to Mrs. Harold Williams for the biographical note on her brother, A. V. Tyrkov. Otherwise, apart from the thesis mentioned in the bibliography, this book is based entirely on published material. The task of establishing and tracking down sources has been facilitated by assistance from many quarters. In particular I wish to mention Mr. Boris Nikolaevski, Dr. Rumanov, Sir Bernard Pares, Professor E. H. Carr, Baron Meyendorf, Mrs. Robert Smith, Dr. Rubakin and Professor Svatikov. I am also indebted to the officials of the British Museum, of the London Library, of the Turgenev Russian Library of Paris, and of the London University Libraries. To these and all others from whom I have received advice and encouragement this book is dedicated. In fairness to them, however, I should perhaps state that the sole responsibility for any statement of fact or of opinion is my own.

D. J. F.

BY THE SAME AUTHOR

FICTION

THE YELLOW ROCK
THE MINE IN THE DESERT
HALF WAY EAST [short stories]
PIG AND PEPPER
BETTER FORGOTTEN [short stories]
PEMBERTON

TRAVEL

BALKAN HOLIDAY

CONTENTS

	Foreword	vii
1.	Background of a Revolutionary	1
2.	School and University	19
3.	The Young Crusaders	37
4.	Deadlock	54
5.	Reprisals	71
6.	The New Party	94
7.	The First Attacks	112
8.	The Spring Campaign	128
9.	"Tarass"	146
10.	Organising Revolution	156
11.	The Final Preparations	171
12.	Killing an Emperor	188
13.	The Roundup	202
14.	The Trial of the Six	218
15.	The End	236
	A Revolutionary Who's Who	244
	Bibliographical Note	258
	Index	264

Foreword

THE outstanding episode of the Russian revolutionary movement of the nineteenth century was the campaign of the *Narodnaya Volya* or "Will of the People's" party, which culminated in the assassination of the Emperor Alexander II in 1881. It was in the shadow of this campaign that Lenin and his generation grew up; and it was as one of the last and youngest recruits to this party that Lenin's elder brother met his death in 1887. Now that Western Europe is prepared to acknowledge the importance of the Russian Revolution as a factor in the history of mankind, the time has come for a study of the Narodnaya Volya and of the men and women who composed it. That is the main purpose of this book. It is a biography of Andrei Ivanovich Zhelyabov who, with his alter ego Sophia Perovskaya, was the party's leading figure at the decisive period of its existence.

Zhelyabov was born in 1850, of a family of serfs belonging to a landowner in the Crimea. He was given the opportunity to go to school, and distinguished himself sufficiently to be awarded a stipend to take him to the University of Odessa. He was expelled before completing his course for a demonstration against an unpopular professor. Like many of his generation he became interested in social questions. He held free classes for workmen and endeavoured to spread socialist ideas among the Odessa factory hands and among peasants in the villages. These activities led to his arrest in 1874. He was eventually released on bail. Three years later he was brought to trial and acquitted for lack of evidence.

So far Zhelyabov had been an obscure worker on the fringe of the Russian revolutionary movement. As he himself said later, he could hardly have been counted a revolutionary at all. We have few details of this period of his life, and to make plain the events that followed it is necessary for his biographer to give some account of what was happening all round him. But in 1879 a small group became convinced that their efforts to make headway were hopeless in face of the ruthless suppression of the authoritarian regime, and that their first task was to create conditions in which they could propagate their views. In June a conference was called to decide on a new policy and programme. Zhelyabov took part, and at once became a prominent member of the Narodnaya Volya party which thus came into being. The party's aim was to overthrow the existing Government of Russia, and, in one of their earlier resolutions, the Emperor Alexander II was formally condemned to death.

During the autumn of 1879 and spring of 1880 Zhelyabov helped to organise and carry through a series of daring attempts on the Emperor's life. These attempts failed. In the summer and autumn of 1880 the party was chiefly occupied in endeavouring to create an organisation powerful enough to overthrow the regime. It was Zhelyabov who first realised the supreme revolutionary value of the army and the factory hands in the towns, and his own main task was to rally the soldiers and the workers. Meanwhile the sentence of death against the Emperor had not been rescinded. In November two members of the party were executed; their comrades thereupon decided to wait no longer and preparations at once began for the supreme attempt.

It was Zhelyabov who was their main organiser. By this time he had lost one outstanding colleague and had become the actual if not the titular leader of the little group of young men and girls committed to a relentless war against the Imperial Government. All through the winter the preparatory work was pressed forward. At the end of February Zhelyabov was arrested. But the stage was then set. Sophia Perovskaya pushed home the attack, and Alexander II was bombed to death in one of the main streets of his capital on March 1.*

Perovskaya was arrested on March 10. She, Zhelabov and four of their companions were tried before the Senate at the end of the month. The issue was never in doubt and the prisoners were hanged in one of the public squares on April 3.

The assassination of the Emperor was a resounding tactical success, and marked the zenith of the party's prestige. But the victory was bought at a very heavy price in casualties. There

* March 1 Old Style. March 13 New Style. Dates are given Old Style throughout.

was no one of sufficient calibre to replace the lost leaders. Inattention to details of security and disclosures made to the police by certain of the weaker members led to arrest after arrest. The survivors made desperate attempts to continue the struggle. But one by one they were hunted down. By 1887 the party had been crushed and the Empire settled down to the repressive and reactionary regime of Alexander III.

The collapse of the Narodnaya Volya was thus due to the carelessness of some of its members and to the failure of others to stand up against a drastic police examination; in other words to a breakdown of the human element, which it is the duty of revolutionary technique to avoid. To ascribe their defeat, as has been done, to the choice of terrorism as a weapon is only justified in so far as terrorist activity exposes the human element to a greater strain, and consequently demands a higher standard of conspiratorial technique. The *Narodovoltsi,* as professional militant revolutionaries, were pioneers, and they suffered the fate of other pioneers. They were eager, optimistic and impatient and it was only by bitter experience that they could learn to appreciate the difficulty of the problems they had set themselves.

This book is an attempt to set out how and why Zhelyabov and his friends abandoned their original policy of reform by persuasion to become revolutionary terrorists; and to explain what they did, how they felt, and what happened to them. It is written in terms of personal experience as opposed to ideological theory, not because the story of Zhelyabov and Perovskaya is, inevitably, the great romantic drama of revolutionary history, but because the writer is convinced that to do otherwise would be to put the cart before the horse. We are all of us, revolutionaries and others, human beings first and theorists afterwards; and temperament and emotional experience play a larger part than cold reasoning in our choice of political aims and methods.

This book is concerned with the period of Zhelyabov's life and not with what happened after him. But this much may be said. The struggle of the Narodovoltsi was more than a "mere experiment in self-sacrifice." It was an experiment in total war against the existing social structure and against the vast imperial machine. It was an attempt, by all available means of persuasion and force, to break open for the Russian masses an outlet to a better world. The Narodovoltsi went about the task they had set themselves with an essentially Russian combination of devotion to the cause, ruthlessness in the framing of policy and ingenuity in its execution. They failed. But in their failure they left a lesson for others to profit by. And they did more. Revolution in action needs emotional inspiration—a fighting tradition of daring, self-sacrifice and discipline. This is what the Narodovoltsi provided. As time went on their methods grew antiquated, their political theories obsolete, their habits of thought no longer fashionable. But the inspiration remained. Their lives were a perpetual challenge to young men and women coming after them. They made a saga. That is their great contribution to the cause they had at heart.

CHAPTER ONE

BACKGROUND OF A REVOLUTIONARY

I

WHEN Kviatkovski * was caught and hanged and his friends sat down to write a memoir for the clandestine revolutionary newspaper, they were unhappy to find how little they knew about his early history. At that time the average expectation of life of a fighting revolutionary was about a year. Further casualties seemed inevitable. In order not to be caught out again the editors decided to conform to modern newspaper practice and to prepare their obituaries in advance. They asked the leaders of the group for an autobiographical statement. Zhelyabov's answer has been preserved. It is our sole authority for his family history and early life.

His people originally came from the province of Kostroma in North Russia. They were house serfs, the property of a gentleman named Stein. Shortly after the Napoleonic Wars Stein left the North to settle on an estate he had bought in the Crimea. He did the thousand-mile journey in the leisurely old-fashioned style with a long string of baggage waggons and all his household. The latter included a cook, Zhelyabov, and a houseboy, Frolov, who were the two grandfathers of Andrei Ivanovich, the subject of this biography. Zhelyabov was already married. The party halted for some weeks in the Podolsk province where Stein had relatives, and here Frolov married a free Cossack girl from a neighbouring village. Henceforth, of course, the bride was part of the Stein establishment, and she went with her husband when they moved on to the Crimea.

* Details of Kviatkovski and of other friends and contemporaries of Zhelyabov are given in the Revolutionary Who's Who at the end of this book.

Stein had two daughters who in due course grew up and married. It was then the custom in well-to-do families for house serfs to form part of the dowry. In this way Zhelyabov and his wife were transferred to the Nelidov family who had an estate at Sultanovka, half way between Feodosia and Kerch. The Frolovs went with the second daughter, who married a Lampsi. Lampsi was a Greek from Anatolia. He had set up as a horse-dealer on arrival in Russia and had made money out of contracts with the Russian Army. Having made his fortune he had set about getting admitted to the "class of noblemen," and thus acquired the right to own serfs. Lampsi's wife bore him a daughter who in her turn grew up and married a Lorentsov. Once again the Frolovs formed part of the dowry, and moved to the Lorentsov property at Kashki-Chekrak. Lorentsov was also of Anatolian Greek origin. His father had started, in a very humble way, as a monumental mason.

Both the Zhelyabovs and the Frolovs had families. The Zhelyabovs' girl became a housemaid. The eldest son was put to work in the kitchen. He ran away, lived like a tramp for months and eventually was adopted by a peasant. Two years later the police caught him and brought him back in chains. One of his brothers also did a bolt—he got over the frontier to the Danube country and stayed there. The third brother, Ivan, was put out to a German market-gardener to learn the trade. It was the practice for any gentleman who could afford it to see that a certain number of his house serfs were trained as skilled men. Ivan Zhelyabov was a diligent pupil. He was also well behaved and respectful. On his return he was made head gardener and even at times acted as steward. Nelidov himself was an army officer, at that time serving at Simferopol, and Ivan Zhelyabov was periodically summoned there to present the estate accounts and to receive instructions. On one of these journeys he passed through Kashki-Chekrak, and visited his father's old fellow-servant Frolov. He met Frolov's family and fell in love with one of the daughters.

Shortly afterwards he came to an arrangement with Nelidov by which he went out to work on *obrok*. Such arrangements were fairly common; the serf became entitled to work for his own account, and for this privilege he paid his master an obrok, or fixed annual fee. He was still determined to marry the Frolov girl. Love matches among peasants were then al-

Background of a Revolutionary

most unheard of, and a marriage of serfs belonging to different families presented the gravest difficulties. The permission of both masters had to be obtained and the master of the bride was unlikely to agree to losing one of his maidservants. But Zhelyabov was persistent. At last he secured the consent at the price of five hundred roubles. Somehow or other he managed to get the money together. It was paid over and the mariage took place. It was a huge sum for a peasant at that time. His marriage was the only occasion on which he departed from the strict conventional groove. In the years to come he would sit by the stove in the evening and look across at his wife and refer rather wistfully to the five hundred roubles. In 1850 their first son was born—Andrei Ivanovich Zhelyabov.

II

The agricultural serf, the peasant, had certain traditional rights. He was a partner in the *mir*, or village community. He had his say in the periodic distribution of the communal land. The produce of his allotted portion belonged to him. He had a certain recognised standing. So long as he fulfilled his labour and taxation obligations his personal life was his own. The house serf, on the other hand—unless like Zhelyabov's father he was allowed to go out and work on obrok—was night and day at the mercy of his master. The relationship was inevitably demoralising for both parties. But the house serf had one advantage over the peasant. In the haphazard economy of the average country gentleman's household he usually contrived to get enough to eat.

Contemporary travellers, both Russians and foreigners, in the country districts invariably remarked on the poor physique of the Russian peasant. Almost as invariably they laid the blame on malnutrition. Malnutrition, of course, was common enough in nineteenth-century Europe, but there were various factors to make it especially prevalent in Russia. One of these was serfdom itself. That system had been imposed to bind the peasants to their own locality, in order to prevent the landowning class losing their landworkers and also to facilitate the collection of the poll tax and the supply of recruits for the army. But the attachment of the peasant to his native village entailed, in the course of generations, rural overcrowding; not in terms of population per acre but of population per acre's production. In many districts the soil did not produce enough to ensure a tolerable standard of living all round. Farming methods were primitive; there was no modern equipment, no scientific knowledge, no available capital. The village drink shop and the village moneylender played their natural roles. Malnutrition, ignorance and dirt brought with them epidemics, lung and skin diseases. Statistics for the years 1871 to 1879 show that only 4.5 per cent of all Russians survived to the age of sixty.

The widespread and grinding poverty had, inevitably, its effect upon the relations between the peasants and the other classes. As far as the secular clergy were concerned church endowments were negligible. The parish priest lived on what he could charge for his professional services at weddings, funerals and baptisms; and the continual bargaining, blackmail and trickery that went on between priest and peasant, equally poverty stricken and almost equally ignorant, effectively prevented the Russian Church from exercising moral or educative influence in the villages. For the peasant, God in Heaven was All Merciful, All Powerful and All Knowing, but God's instrument on earth, the parish priest, was just such another rogue and skinflint as himself.

Again the economic factor weighed heavily in the relations between serf and master. Russian landowners were not rich men. There were, of course, the few who splashed their money in the European capitals and created the myth of the wealthy Russian noblemen; there were the few old princely families and there was the Court set, many of whom were of foreign origin. But these together formed only an infinitesimal proportion of the 350,000 "personal nobles" and the 600,000 "hereditary nobles" who enjoyed the right to own "populated lands," that is, to become masters of serfs. The Russian for nobleman is *"dvoryanin,"* i.e., courtier or servant of the autocrat. Ennoblement had originally, in most cases, been obtained through service of the Crown. At one time all commissioned officers, from ensign upwards, and all corresponding ranks in the civil service automatically became nobles with the right to transmit their nobility to their descendants.

The bulk of this huge class was in no way an aristocracy in the European sense. For one thing they had not the money.

The landowners had only their land to make money out of; and few of them, at that time, were either efficient farmers or careful economists. The restriction of the ownership of populated lands to the nobility prevented the purchase of estates by wealthy merchants and precluded any investment of capital in agriculture that this might have entailed. Few of the landowners were free from debt. In 1861, at the time of the Emancipation, two-thirds of all the serfs belonging to private owners were pledged to the State Bank.

Hard times make hard landlords. The poorer proprietor had no possibility of raising the standard of living of his people. Economics were too much for him; he had to exploit his serfs to keep his own head above water. Their lot was all the harder when an exacting German or Jewish steward was employed to run the estate. Otherwise relations were sometimes eased by congenital Russian tolerance and good nature. But there was no real bond of loyalty between master and serf. There was no community of tradition, of education or of interest. The peasant had never been reconciled to serfdom. His traditions went back far beyond the time when it had been imposed upon him from above, and he waited blindly but persistently for the day when imperial justice would restore his land unencumbered. In the seventeenth century under Stenka Razin, and a hundred years later under Pugachev, peasant resentment had flared up in risings that shook the Empire. Both were suppressed, after much bloodshed, but their legacy remained. The governing classes were perpetually anxious lest something of the sort might happen again. The peasants remained bitter and unreconciled; but they had learned that the first man to make a stand was likely to get his head broken.

As to the nobles, their lot of course was incomparably easier than that of the peasants. Together with the other privileged classes they enjoyed exemption from capitation tax, from military service, and from corporal punishment. But the part they played as a class in national affairs was infinitely less than that of the corresponding class in any other state in Europe. Landowners were the agents for the collection of taxes and recruits from their own estates. But that is all they did. There were local "assemblies of nobility," and Catherine the Great, who had initiated them, presumably intended that the local gentry should play their part in local affairs. But there was no tradition of public service; the class of nobles was too large and too heterogeneous to combine even in defence of its own interests. The assemblies of nobility came to serve no other purpose than an excuse for an occasional gathering or dinner. All public business, great and small, was in the hands of the administrative organs of the autocrat.

The Russia of 1850 was an authoritarian state. It is significant that there was no cabinet—only a "Committee of Ministers." A cabinet with collective responsibility might have implied some diminution of the Emperor's power. The Emperor was father of his people, and his people, in imperial eyes, were immature, inexperienced, not to be trusted with any initiative. The French Revolution and the Napoleonic age had opened a new chapter in European history and Alexander I at the beginning of the century had introduced certain reforms. These were not far reaching enough for the more impatient of his subjects. On the accession of Nicholas I had come the Decembrist revolt. It collapsed; but reform and revolution became indelibly connected in the young Emperor's mind, and thereafter he devoted his considerable energy and talent to tightening up the authoritarian hold.

Throughout the century the minutest act affecting the public weal had to be submitted for imperial consideration and sanction. If a widow in Tomsk wished to endow a cot in the local hospital in memory of her late husband, if repairs were required to the chimney of a police station in Bessarabia, an application had to be made through the appropriate local authorities to the competent ministry at Petersburg, and nothing could be done until due authority was received. Such centralisation naturally stifled all initiative of provincial officials, and the ubiquity of state interference necessitated an enormous bureaucracy to keep it going. It was one of the tragedies of the country that it lacked an efficient personnel to run it.

An enquiry in the central provinces in the 'seventies revealed that of all the servants of the State there employed (apart from those under the Ministries of Justice and Education) 2 per cent had been to a university, 6 per cent to a secondary school, 12 per cent to a primary school, and the remaining 80 per cent had had no education at all. Obviously these were not the men to run a complicated administrative machine. Equally obviously the door would be open to graft. In point of fact graft was universal. Official business, from the issue of a passport to the grant of a railway concession, was conditional on the payment of a sweetener to one or more of the individual officials concerned. No provincial doorkeeper was too low to accept a present; and very few court functionaries too high. Official salaries were low, Russians are usually tolerant, and public opinion was not outraged, except in those few cases where the bribed official double-crossed his client. In fact venality was often a blessing; it circumvented the often impossibly complicated regulations and enabled people to get things done. The old-fashioned, easy-going Russian official was everywhere more popular than the zealous and incorruptible German from the Baltic provinces who never took money from anybody and always insisted on full compliance with every letter of every law.

The Romanovs and their advisers were well aware of the shortcomings of the bureaucracy. Nowhere have more elaborate measures been taken to safeguard efficiency and honesty. The repairs to the chimney of the Bessarabian police station would have entailed a whole spate of plans, proposals, estimates, commissions, inspections and reports, all designed to prevent the local police officer and the local contractor from feathering their nests. But in effect the only result would have been to clog up the pigeon-holes in Kishinev and Petersburg, and to give scope to the inexhaustible Russian ingenuity in finding some way round. The checks and cross-checks merely added complications; and graft thrives on complications. The fact was that the officials were too strongly entrenched. They were essential to the autocracy. The autocracy knew it and dared not push them too far.

The officials, naturally, backed each other up. They were all in the game of defending their vested interests against the outside world. No official might be brought to trial without the consent of his superior, and such consent, of course, was very rarely given. And this solidarity was in itself an effective brake on initiative and progress. If a man was too efficient he showed up his colleagues. If he tried to remedy an abuse or push through some reform he was inevitably endangering the traditional perquisites of someone else. Such a man was a menace alike to his equals and his superiors, and all the forces of obstruction and repression were brought to bear to make him toe the line.

This omnipotent, ubiquitous and arbitrary bureaucracy was generally disliked. The peasant retained his veneration for the Emperor, just as he did for God, but he feared and disliked the officials even more than he did the priests; he knew by experience that the officials were more dangerous. The educated classes had no particular veneration for anything—Russians have a highly developed critical sense—but they liked the officials no better. It was the constant preoccupation of a very large proportion of the Empire's inhabitants to keep out of trouble with the police.

Russia of the nineteenth century is the classic example of the *Polizeistaat*. The powers and scope of the police for intervening in the lives of the general public were very wide. An enterprising contemporary newspaper employed a lawyer to make the count and it was found that the laws of the Empire contained no less than 5,075 articles directly concerned with police duties. To enable the police to exercise a more thorough control every inhabitant of the Empire had to be in possession of a police passport. It was essential for any journey. It had to be produced on any change of address. Innkeepers and house porters were under police orders and had to report arrivals, departures, and any special activities on the part of the tenants.

A more formidable institution than the ordinary police was the Third Section of the Emperor's Private Chancery. This comprised the Gendarmerie and the Secret Police. The head of the Third Section was ipso facto member of the Committee of Ministers; his power was probably greater than any Minister of State. The duties of the Third Section were to keep a check on the other government departments, and, especially, to protect the regime from subversive political activity. The Third Section worked in secret, was responsible only to the Emperor, and had full power to arrest, imprison and banish without trial and without published reason.

"Humanity," wrote Pobyedonostsev, who in a later reign was the great apologist of the autocrat idea, "humanity is endowed with a very effective force—inertia. As ballast in a ship, so inertia sustains humanity in the crises of its history." Human inertia and police omnipotence sustained intact the Russian social structure throughout the long reign of Nicholas I. But the shock of the Crimean War revealed the inefficiency and corruption that lay behind that imposing façade. It became obvious that changes must come.

III

IN the eyes of the advanced Russian intellectuals Nicholas I symbolised all that was brutal, archaic and repressive in the regime. The latter years of his reign saw the first wave of political emigration to Western Europe. In 1855 Alexander Herzen, the outstanding figure among these earlier émigrés, was in his new home at Twickenham. One morning in early March he opened the *Times* and read the announcement of the Emperor's death. The news filled him with indescribable emotion. It was, he says, as if a huge burden had dropped from his shoulders. He felt suddenly ten years younger. He scrambled into his clothes and hurried out to apprise his friend Engelson. But Engelson had already seen the *Times* and was on his way to tell Herzen. The two met outside Herzen's gate and turned back into the house. Soon other friends arrived—Russians, Englishmen, Poles, Germans. They embraced each other with tears of joy in their eyes. Herzen sent for champagne to toast the dawn of the new age, and the Herzen womenfolk went to the kitchen to arrange for a huge triumphal lunch.

After the banquet the party went into the garden, which stretched down to the Thames. Some ragged little boys were playing by the river, and Herzen, still unable to contain his jubilation, called them up and harangued them. It was a great occasion, he explained, a day of triumph, his and their great enemy, the Emperor Nicholas, was dead. He pulled out all the silver in his pockets and told them to buy sweets. The lads, bewildered but responsive, began to cheer: " 'Ooray, 'ooray, Impernickel is dead!" The cheering attracted other children. Herzen's guests all emptied their pockets and soon there was a large crowd on the towpath. Everyone was shouting and singing. Bottles of beer were handed round and someone called up a barrel organ. Dancing and jubilation went on for hours.

As long as Herzen lived in Twickenham, whenever he went for a walk small boys would pull off their caps and greet him: "Impernickel is dead. 'Ooray!"

IV

SULTANOVKA is about a hundred miles from Sevastopol, but Zhelyabov's autobiographical statement makes no mention of the Crimean War. His childhood memories begin when he was nearly five. By this time other children had arrived, and to ease the congestion in the cottage he was sent to his Frolov grandparents at Kashki-Chekrak. He was there for four impressionable years.

Old Frolov had been granted his freedom as a reward for long service, and lived with his wife in a cottage at the back by the hen yard, some way from the big house and the village. The younger Frolovs were all servants in the big house. Lyuba (Andrei's aunt) was a sewing maid; an uncle was a footman. Lorentsov was a hard master. There was a certain Dmitri, called "One-and-a-half" Dmitri because of his huge size, who acted as bailiff and executioner. The peasants were terrified of him. From time to time the small boy would see his uncle taken off to the stables to be flogged and heard him screaming.

Grandmother Frolov was still proud to have been born a free Cossack. She taught the child Cossack songs and told him endless stories about her village. All through his life he was very conscious of his Cossack blood. But it was old Frolov who had the greater influence. The old man was very tall, very gaunt and very solemn, with a long, grey beard. He was a sectary and extremely pious. Zhelyabov afterwards believed that he was slightly touched. He could read the old church script and possessed half a dozen holy books. He was devoted to his grandson and the two became inseparable. They went for walks together, went to the forest to cut wood, sat outside the cottage door on summer evenings. All the time the old man busied himself with the child's education. When Andrei went back home he could read church script and knew the whole psalter by heart.

The incident he remembered most vividly in later years occurred when he was seven. Late one evening he and his grandparents were sitting by the stove when Lyuba, the sewing maid, burst in. She was pale, sobbing and dishevelled. There was a rush of questions and incoherent answers. Andrei tried to make out what was happening; then his grandmother noticed him and pushed him into the next room and locked the door.

He stood against the door listening, but there was only a confused noise. Then came footsteps outside, the sound of the cottage door being opened and the voice of "One-and-a-half" Dmitri. Then hubbub rose. Later Dmitri went out again, taking Lyuba with him. The child was very fond of Lyuba. He hammered on the door and shouted: "What are they doing to my aunt?" No one took any notice of him. He went on hammering and screaming till he was completely exhausted. At last he fell asleep on the floor.

Next morning Grandfather Frolov was not there. They told him he had gone to Feodosia. Towards evening the child and his grandmother walked out to meet him, as they always did when the old man went to town. About a mile from the cottage was a low hill overlooking a long stretch of the road. They could sit there and watch for the tall lean figure; when he came in sight Andrei would run off to meet him and ask if he had brought any sweets from the bazaar. But this time they waited till sunset and there was no sign of him. It was three days before he came back, and only then was Andrei able to piece together what had happened. Lyuba Frolov had been raped by Lorentsov, and old Frolov had gone to lodge a complaint with the Feodosia police. It was an act of great courage for a peasant at that time. What is more he stayed there till the police sent for Lorentsov. Nothing came of the matter, and Lorentsov does not seem to have tried to take revenge on old Frolov. But the incident left a burning impression upon the child. For the next five years, he tells us, he had but one ambition: to grow up and then come back and kill Lorentsov.

He was still full of fury against Lorentsov when he was sent back home to Sultanovka a year later. His mother was delighted at his spirit. "You aren't a Zhelyabov," she told him. "You're a real Frolov." This was a hit at her husband who was always willing to take the line of least resistance and to see good points in the landowners. She herself hated them. She used to say they were all "beasts and torturers." She was half a Cossack and a good hater.

All the same it was a landowner who gave young Andrei his opportunity. Nelidov by this time had retired from the army and was living at Sultanovka. He was a good master, largely owing to the influence of his wife. The story went round the village that the Zhelyabov child had come back a prodigy of learning and Nelidov sent for him. He gave him a book to read from, but it was in ordinary print and he could only read the church script. However Nelidov decided to teach the child himself; after that every day Andrei went across to the big house for his lesson. Soon he learned to read with ease, and Nelidov lent him books. One memorable day he gave him Pushkin's "Golden Fish." "From that day," Zhelyabov wrote afterwards, "a whole new world was opened up." Meanwhile Nelidov determined to do still more for him. When he was ten he arranged to send him as a boarder to the Junior School in Kerch.

V

EARLY in Zhelyabov's school days came the Act of Emancipation of February, 1861, under which some twenty-two million proprietary serfs and a million and a half house serfs were to receive their liberty. The crown serfs, almost as numerous as the others, had already a more favourable lot, and their freedom was arranged by special measures.

The Act of Emancipation followed on four years of commissions, reports, alternative proposals and of spirited obstruction on the part of vested interests. It was, to some extent, "founded on the fear of catastrophe." Already in 1855 Alexander II had announced to the Moscow nobles that "it was better to abolish serfdom from above than to wait till it abolished itself from below"; and it was largely due to the Emperor's personal initiative that the measure became law. The main issue was the ownership of the land. The proprietors took the line that the land was theirs. Once this was recognised there would have been little opposition to the emancipation of the serfs themselves. Most landowners already realised that hired labour was more productive and economical than forced labour; an emancipated and landless peasantry would have had no option but to offer themselves for hire at cut rates. However one of the main objects of the Government was to establish an order of peasant proprietors; and the peasants themselves were so convinced of their right to ownership that any other solution would have led to trouble. Land on the whole meant more to the peasants than freedom. "We are yours," one of them said to his master, in the late 'fifties, "but the land is ours." The tradition of the ownership of the land

Background of a Revolutionary

by the village community or mir went back centuries before the institution of serfdom. The landowners took the line that the peasants enjoyed the land which they tilled for their own use solely by a favour that had become a tradition. But the peasants had never accepted this argument.

The house serfs, of course, presented no such problem. There was no question of their having any claims. The act laid down that they should serve their masters for another two years and thereafter be free. In the case of the agricultural serfs there was a compromise, embodied in a number of complicated regulations designed to cover the different conditions in the various provinces of the Empire. Part of each estate was set aside to become the freehold property of the peasants (to be held of course communally in the mir). The rest remained for the landlord. But the landlord also received compensation for the area ceded, to be paid off by the peasants in forty-nine annual instalments.

Twenty years later Zhelyabov gave his opinion that the Emancipation was a big step forward. It had given the peasant nothing, economically it was no emancipation, but morally it had meant an advance in his self-respect and that was most important. He might have added, as a revolutionary, that it helped to shatter the peasant's sense of solid permanence and to sharpen his discontent. For the peasants were bewildered. They felt no concern for the moral issue. They realised only that they now must pay annual instalments for land which they had regarded as their own. In many districts they believed the whole thing was an elaborate swindle on the part of the landlords and officials who were frustrating the Emperor's good intentions. A liberal landowner has described the difficulty of explaining the measure to his peasants.

"We are ignorant," they told him. "But we feel things ought to be done just as the Emperor orders."

"But this is what the Emperor orders, here in this document."

"But how can we tell? We can't read."

In some districts there were disorders. In the Kazan province a peasant named Popov started a movement that caused serious alarm. The troops were called out and Popov himself was caught and executed, but there were over a hundred casualties before the movement was crushed.

Things settled down again, more or less. The fact that the soldiers came out and were prepared to shoot convinced the peasants that the imperial edict was genuine. Commissions were appointed to determine the allocation of the land, and intricate and acrimonious negotiations took place in every district. The State stepped in as financial intermediary, issuing long-term bonds to the landowners and collecting the instalments from the peasants. The peasant communes were made responsible for these payments. They also took over the task of tax collection and the provision of recruits. In view of this collective responsibility the communes were given wide powers over their individual members. No peasant, for instance, might leave the district without the commune's consent, and he was bound to return whenever ordered. In many cases the peasant found the communes as hard a master as his late proprietor had been. But this does not seem to have been greatly resented. What the peasant did object to was having to pay the annual instalments, and also the fact that in many cases the land allotted was less than the parcel he had enjoyed before the Emancipation.

It was inevitable that a reform of such magnitude should provoke complaints, and they came from many quarters. Sentimental country gentlemen who prided themselves on the affection and loyalty they felt they had inspired in their serfs were disgusted to find that the latter, as soon as freed, would cut wood in their late master's forests, steal his fowls, and generally become most undesirable neighbours. The advanced intellectuals, on the other hand, were estranged at what they felt to be injustice to the peasants; and the students, who had a grievance of their own in the educational policy inspired by Count D. Tolstoi, proceeded to start demonstrations. In an autocratic state a protest against a government measure is apt to be taken by the autocrat as a personal criticism of himself. Alexander II was hurt and indignant at the popular reception of his first great reform.

VI

HISTORIANS are sometimes inclined to underestimate the influence of human emotion. The emotional factor is of prime importance in considering the imperial Hamlet who was called to put right the state of Russia.

Alexander II was forty-three when the Act of Emancipation was issued. He had been given a Spartan education by his father, Nicholas I. Particular attention had been given to making him a soldier. He felt happy and at home with the army, and to the end of his life he had a passion for parades and reviews. As Crown Prince he had been put in charge of the military academies and had carried out his duties conscientiously. He had also served a long apprenticeship in State affairs, and had represented his father during the latter's travels in Europe.

In private life he was often charming. But he had a violent temper and could be vindictive. He had curious phobias. He could not bear the sight of a woman in spectacles; he would imagine she must be a "Nihilist." He was moody. Sex played an important part with him. In his younger days people who wanted to get something out of him would arrange a shooting party, and a beano at the end with champagne and dancing girls. He grew out of dancing girls; and then for a period he was frequently and violently in love. There was the Irene of Turgenev's *Smoke*. Then there was the Empress, a princess of a little German court whom he insisted on marrying in spite of opposition from his father. Later he was struck by the small daughter of one of the Prince Dolgorukis. He arranged for her education, and, when she was seventeen, took her as his mistress. This was in 1863. She remained with him till the end. In 1874 he gave her the title of Princess Yurievskaya and acknowledged his children by her.* He wished to marry her and waited impatiently for the invalid Empress to die. But the Empress lingered on for another six years, and Court life was complicated by the rival intrigues of the Empress clique and the Yurievskaya clique. The Empress died at last, in the summer of 1880, and the morganatic marriage took place six weeks later.

Thus he solved his major personal problem; but a solution of his political problems was never found. As he grew older his moodiness increased. He suffered from asthma and rheu-

---

* It is significant of the attitude of educated Russians to the Crown that the comment has been frequently made that the Dolgorukis were, after all, of better blood than the Romanovs.

matism. For days on end he would be depressed. He was subject to violent paroxysms of weeping. He became hesitant, would change his mind; he would call urgently for certain papers only to declare when they were brought that the question must be left over for his successor. He sincerely wished to serve the good of his country, but circumstances were too much for him. The old order was dead; the scandals of the Crimean War had showed that change must come, but he did not know where it would lead. Alexander II, like his father, had been alarmed at the revolutionary movements in Europe in 1848. The spectre of the French Revolution was always before his eyes,. He had no examples of successful constitutionalism to follow. Conditions in England were too different to be a guide. Russia lacked an upper class and middle class with administrative gifts and a sense of practicalities who could be trusted to manage an empire for their own ends and keep fanatics and the lower class in check. "I give you my word," the Emperor said to the president of one of the Assemblies of Nobles in 1865, "I give you my word that I would be ready to sign a constitution at once, here, on this table, if I thought it would be good for Russia. But I know that if I did so today the country would fall to pieces tomorrow." It is impossible to prove that he was wrong.

He was cut off from the mass of his people by his background and upbringing and by all the mumbo-jumbo of an Imperial Court. He heard nothing for himself, only what those around him saw fit to let him hear. He was not infallible in his choice of advisers: some were good, some indifferent and some bad, but few stayed with him for any length of time. As an autocrat he was told by his ministers and servants what they thought would please him, and as a human being he believed what he wanted to believe. For him the real voice of Russia was the applause of obsequious assemblies of notables and the thunder of Te Deums in commemoration of his various escapes; discordant notes were merely the growlings of some criminal and perverted sect.

It is doubtful whether his conscience would ever have allowed him to believe that a constitution was good for Russia. Moral conviction is apt to form up behind a vested interest, and for the Romanovs the autocracy was a sacred trust received from God, to be maintained and handed on intact. Opposition was therefore a sin, and an attack against the autocrat was blasphemy. As his reign progressed Alexander II devoted more and more interest to the detective work of the political police. It was not through fear of his own skin; his physical courage was never in question. It was because his conception of political crime had inevitably turned the ruler into a policeman.

VII

THE early years of the reign saw the appointment of innumerable commissions to study the main problems of the Empire, and one by one they bore their fruit. An edict granting a large degree of autonomy to the universities came out in 1863. The following year saw the important institution of the *Zemstva* or local government councils, the scarcely less important reform of the law courts, and a measure designed to expand and liberalise education. Work was also in hand on the Act for Municipal Self-Government (issued 1870) and the Army Reform (1874). These two were the last of the great reforms of the reign. By the time they were promulgated the tide of reaction had already set in.

In 1862 came the great fire at the Apraxin Dvor in Petersburg. Its origin has never been cleared up, but it was ascribed at Court to the work of revolutionaries. A few months later there was an attempt to assassinate the Grand Duke Constantine, the Emperor's brother and Regent of Poland. In January, 1863, the Polish rebellion broke out.

The rebellion was a fiasco. The Russian garrison remained loyal. There were no concerted outbreaks within Russia itself. There was desultory guerrilla fighting for some weeks in many parts of Poland, but the insurgents were never in control of any key position, and never in such force as to attempt a pitched battle. In May the rebellion had petered out, and the Russian authorities started their reprisals. Extreme oppositionists made what they could out of Russian atrocities in Poland as propaganda for the revolutionary cause in Russia itself; but this agitation had little effect. National feelings had been stirred, and the congenital lack of sympathy between Russians and Poles prevented popular opinion in Russia being roused by purely Polish grievances. The main effect, in Russia, of the

Polish rising was as an irritant to the Emperor personally and as a tonic to those at Court who were advocating a strong hand. The Third Section got busy. Advanced journals were suppressed and their contributors arrested. In April, 1866, the student Karakozov, made an attempt to kill the Emperor. The attempt failed and he was caught, tried and executed. His act was the end of the impetus towards reform from above.

CHAPTER TWO

SCHOOL AND UNIVERSITY

I

FOR the first three years of Zhelyabov's school days the curriculum evolved under Nicholas I was still in force. The system was strictly authoritarian. The spiritual welfare of the pupil was the first consideration to which all others were sacrificed. In 1840, for instance, medical manuals were forbidden to include any matter which "might offend the instincts of decency and modesty." At the beginning of the century education had been exclusively classical. But after the Decembrist rising it was felt that many passages in Greek and Latin literature might have an unsettling effect on the young. Care was taken first of all to exclude works extolling political liberty and denouncing tyranny, and in 1850 even moral philosophy and metaphysics were ruled out as "of no practical value to young people acquainted with the principles of Christianity." In their stead chemistry and algebra were introduced as politically blameless.

In 1864 came the reform of the schools. The teaching of both classical and other subjects was modernised. For the first and last time during the century the use of foreign text books was permitted. This liberal interlude lasted a bare seven years, so that only those of Zhelyabov's generation were able to benefit. As the Nihilist movement spread young people turned to materialism with a passionate and fanatical devotion. They began to contrast the pure and eternal laws of science and mathematics with the tyrannous obscurantism of Church and State. This made authorities such as Count Tolstoi turn again to the classics; but the curriculum of the classical schools was largely confined to Greek and Latin grammar.

Zhelyabov's autobiographical fragment stops short on his departure from home. We know little about his school days.

We hear of him as tall for his age and "thin as a post." We know he was very poor. But that did not mark him out at school, for most people in Russia were poor, and it was an exception for parents to give their children pocket money. The atmosphere among the boys was democratic. Zhelyabov struck up a life-long friendship with one Misha Trigoni whose father was a general and whose mother an admiral's daughter. This lady had democratic sympathies; she read Herzen and had a photograph of Garibaldi. It was probably young Trigoni who made the first advances, for Zhelyabov still had his hatred of the Lorentsovs and their caste. There is evidence, in his later life, that his own serf origin formed a complex which he never entirely got rid of. He was a sensitive boy. The other boys noticed that he used to flush when the headmaster—a hard-bitten old Swiss—addressed him in the familiar second person singular.

He was an omnivorous reader. Mayne Reid and Fenimore Cooper were then the rage of Russian schoolboys. The vogue of Jules Verne was just beginning. No doubt at Kerch there were tattered translations which passed from hand to hand. Zhelyabov was not a model pupil. We hear of him as ringleader in all the games and as frequently getting himself and other boys into trouble. In the long summer holidays he went back home to his family, now emancipated. There he went out with the others to work in the fields and learned to be a practical farmer. It was there too, when he was sixteen, that he had his first big adventure—his fight with the bull. He heard his mother screaming in the next field. He dashed to the hedge, and saw her running for life with a bull after her. He pulled a stake out of the hedge and went for the animal. He hit with all his force at its forelegs; the bull crashed over and both mother and son got away.

As he grew older he became interested in politics and social questions. There is no record of his reaction to the Polish rebellion. But it is unlikely that a Russian schoolboy, especially one with Cossack blood, would have overmuch sympathy with the Poles. But three years later he was already an enemy of Tsardom and the Karakozov attempt stirred him. In after life he told his friends of his excitement at hearing the news, and his sorrow that the attempt had not succeeded. After the attempt the pupils of all schools in the Empire were marched off to church to a Thanksgiving Service for the Emperor's safety. The service was interminably long and the boys had to be rebuked for fidgeting.

In some schools at this time the elder boys formed secret political societies and smuggled in prohibited books and pamphlets. There is no evidence of anything of this sort at Kerch. Zhelyabov's revolutionary urge found its sole expression in long discussions in the school yard and the dormitories. All this time he was working hard, if intermittently. He was a good scholar and on leaving would have won the Gold Medal, the highest distinction of his year, but for his tendency towards practical jokes and lack of respect for authority. As it was he got the Silver Medal, the second prize, which still carried with it the right of automatic entry into the civil service with a definite rank or *chin*. Zhelyabov, however, was ambitious, and elected to go on to the Novorossisk University at Odessa. He was enabled to do so by a grant of thirty roubles a month from a legacy bequeathed by one Luludaki, a local merchant, to assist poor students of the Feodosia district. His grant worked out at fifty cents a day—about double the wage of an unskilled labourer. It was enough for a student to live on; in fact many of his contemporaries had less. The university agreed to accept him as one of those students "whose exemption from the payment of university fees is justified by their poverty and their disposition towards study." He was duly entered in the Faculty of Law.

II

DURING Zhelyabov's first term at the university the Nechaev affair came to light and caused a sensation all over the country. Nechaev himself has been a puzzle both to his contemporaries and to posterity. Dostoevski wrote one of his big novels round him, but failed to bring the portrait to life. Vera Figner, in 1883, considered that of all the politicals then in prison his release would be the most valuable for the cause. A modern authority has called him "a swashbuckler, a liar and a cad." There is much to support this latter view. But in any case the Nechaev affair is a milestone in Russian revolutionary history.

Nechaev was of peasant stock. His father had been a serf near Vladimir, a hundred miles northeast of Moscow. Nechaev himself was born in 1847. He went to the village school; managed to acquire a secondary education; came to Petersburg when he was twenty; attended some lectures there and was admitted to a teacher's training college. Our first personal glimpse of him is in December of 1868 as a member of a small group of students who met to study contemporary "advanced" literature. One of their favourite authors was Louis Blanc, and as Nechaev knew very little French the reader had to translate into Russian as he went along. Their reading prompted them to appoint themselves a self-styled "Secret Revolutionary Committee." The leading spirits were Nechaev and Tkachev (who afterwards went to Switzerland where he founded and edited a Jacobin newspaper). They drew up a programme, of which the key phrase was: "Social revolution is our final aim. To bring this about we consider political revolution our only effective means."

In January and February, 1869, delegates went to Moscow and other university towns with the idea of forming branch committees. But the conspirators were inexperienced. The authorities got onto their track. Two or three arrests were made and Nechaev himself was summoned to the police.

Two days later Vera Zasulich, then a girl of seventeen, received an envelope through the ordinary post, with two enclosures. One of them read:

"I was walking in the Vasilievski Island this morning and I passed the police cart they use for the transport of prisoners. As it went by a hand appeared at the window and threw out a piece of paper: and I heard a voice: 'If you are a student send this on to the address given.' I am a student and I felt it was my duty to fulfil this wish. Destroy my note."

The other enclosure was in Nechaev's handwriting:

"They are taking me to prison. Which prison it is I do not know. Tell the comrades I hope one day to see them again. May they continue our work."

Vera Zasulich told the comrades. Not long afterwards rumours began to circulate that Nechaev had escaped. A few weeks later they were confirmed by definite information that he was at Geneva. Nechaev in the eyes of all his friends had won his spurs as a hero of the revolutionary movement.

It was not till long afterwards that it was realised that the whole thing had been a ramp. Nechaev had never been arrested at all. He had seen that his position was hopeless and so had not answered the police summons. Instead he composed the two notes for Zasulich and slipped away to Moscow. There he remained in hiding for a fortnight and thought things over. He came to the conclusion that to have hope of success a revolutionary movement must have a big name to back it and also funds. He determined to get both. He left Moscow, managed to cross the frontier, arrived in Switzerland at the beginning of March, and made himself known to Michael Bakunin at Geneva.

The meeting was an instant success. Bakunin had been established in Switzerland for some years as a major prophet of world revolution. His writings had a big influence on the youth of his day. The power of his personality on those whom he met was remarkable. But as a conspirator he was both a megalomaniac and an amateur; as an organiser he was incompetent; in money matters he was—to put the best light upon it—unreliable. Great as was his power of inspiration his actual achievement in the cause of revolution had been nil. He was himself, when he paused to think, conscious of this. In the spring of 1869 he was without a personal following, almost without personal friends, and out of touch with any serious revolutionary organisation.

This last is what Nechaev set out to supply. He brought with him a circumstantial (and imaginary) account of the imminence of revolution in Russia and of the power and influence of his Secret Committee which was to direct it. Bakunin believed him implicitly. He was an optimist and he wanted to believe him. His delight was all the greater as he had remained very much the Russian at heart, and Nechaev was the first contact with his native land he had had for years. He had long preached that the Russian peasant would lead the world revolution. Nechaev's story proved to him that he had been right.

Bakunin, however, was not of the type to allow the other man to do all the talking. To match Nechaev's Secret Committee he revealed, in the strictest confidence, the existence of a World Revolutionary Alliance, and a few weeks later solemnly admitted his new friend to this mythical body by the issue of the following certificate:

"The bearer of this is one of the accredited representatives of the Russian Section of the World Revolutionary Association, No. 2771.

Michael Bakunin."

This document was dated May 9, 1869, and bore the stamp: "Alliance Révolutionnaire Européenne, Comité Général."

Whether Nechaev believed in Bakunin to the extent that Bakunin believed in Nechaev will never be known. He probably believed in him to some extent. It was, after all, in conformity with his own ambitions to do so. The two had much in common, though the younger man possessed the stronger personality. In any case, having established their World Alliance and their Russian Section, they proceeded to give their movement a literature. For some weeks they collaborated in brochures, proclamations and finally the notorious Revolutionary Catechism. These documents are consistent in language, tendency and tone:

"Day and night he [i.e., the revolutionary] must have but one thought—implacable destruction.

"We devote ourselves exclusively to the annihilation of the existing social system. To build up is not our task but the task of those that come after us.

"Brigandage is one of the most honoured forms of Russian national life . . . the brigand in Russia is the true and only revolutionary.

"Thought has value for us only if it assists us in our work of radical and universal extermination. . . . The study of revolution in books will inevitably bring the student to a state of revolutionary impotence. . . . It [i.e., revolution] will only come as the result of practical effort, of attempt after attempt directed to one and the same end—implacable destruction.

"Karakozov was merely the prologue. Now, friends, let us start the drama."

The organisation was established; it had been provided with a creed and a programme. It now remained to find funds. Some years previously a wealthy Russian of Utopian aims had handed over to Herzen the sum of £800 to be used in the cause of social progress. This sum was still intact. Nechaev heard of it, and persuaded Bakunin to demand from Herzen that the sum be handed over. Herzen had long since lost his last illusions about Bakunin, and the little he had seen of

Nechaev he had not liked. But he was an old man and an invalid. He was too tired to embark on a new polemic. He compromised. Half the sum, i.e., 10,000 francs, was entrusted to Bakunin who passed it on (or most of it) to Nechaev. The latter's mission abroad had now been successfully accomplished and in August he left for Russia. The Russian police were aware of his activities in Switzerland and were on the lookout for him. To return undetected was a matter of some difficulty. Bakunin however introduced him to some Bulgarian revolutionaries who in turn passed him on to Bucharest, and from there he was smuggled over the frontier.

By the end of August Nechaev was in Moscow again. He got into touch with three or four students, former acquaintances of his, showed them his credentials from Bakunin and formed them into the Moscow Group of the Russian Section of the World Revolutionary Alliance. The Russian Section, he explained, was ruled by a Secret Committee, whose orders were to be obeyed immediately and unquestioningly. In point of fact this committee was as mythical as the World Revolutionary Alliance. But the fiction served to establish the personal ascendancy of Nechaev (who was, of course, the sole link between the committee and the Moscow Group) and enabled him to maintain a firm discipline, the lack of which, as he realised, had been the main cause of failure of previous revolutionary movements. Nechaev had a dominating personality. His claims and statements were at first accepted without question. The main task of the Moscow Group—as indeed of the Russian Section—was to prepare the country for the world revolution, due to break out on February 19, 1870. But progress was slow and the confidence of the young revolutionaries began to falter. One member asked for permission to resign. Nechaev agreed on condition that the youth disguise himself as a policeman and blackmail a mutual acquaintance in Petersburg for a large sum. This was done and in consequence Nechaev acquired not only the money but the means of blackmailing the waverer for ever afterwards. As time went on the group noticed that whenever an internal disagreement was referred to the committee for decision, the committee invariably endorsed the views of Nechaev. Finally, early in November, one of the members, Ivanov, began to demand tangible proof that the committee actually existed. This left

Nechaev with the alternative of admitting his deception or of removing Ivanov. He chose the latter. He called together the other four members of the group and told them the committee had evidence that Ivanov was in touch with the police and was about to betray the organisation; the committee accordingly had condemned him to death and had ordered the group to carry out the sentence. The members, all except one, demurred. Nechaev insisted. It was essential for his hold over them that they should be associated in the murder. Eventually he carried his point. On November 21 Ivanov was enticed into the cellar of the Agricultural College by means of a story that a printing press, which could be used for secret revolutionary purposes, was buried under the floor. There he was met by the rest of the group and done to death at Nechaev's orders.

On November 25 the police discovered the body and started a hunt for the murderers. Nechaev disappeared, managed to cross the frontier and joined up again with Bakunin in Switzerland. They resumed their co-operation. On Herzen's death they approached his executors for the remaining half of the £800 and succeeded in getting it. But before long they quarrelled, as was inevitable in view of their temperaments. In 1872 Nechaev was arrested by the Swiss police and extradited to Russia to stand his trial for the murder of Ivanov. There was no yellow streak about Nechaev and his trial was a stormy one. He declared the killing of Ivanov to have been a "purely political matter." He denied the competence of the court and refused to answer questions put to him as "the accused." He defied the judges and was finally dragged from the dock shouting "Down with despotism." He was sentenced to imprisonment for life.

But this is anticipating the course of events. Although Nechaev got over the frontier, the police laid their hands on Ivanov's other murderers and also on a number of other young people involved in the conspiracy. Their trial did not take place for nearly two years, but enormous interest had been aroused and all sorts of rumours came into circulation. Young people with active or latent revolutionary sympathies were all on the side of Nechaev. They were still convinced of the authenticity of his escape earlier in the year. They were quite ready to believe that Ivanov was in fact a traitor and that his execution had been justified. It was only after the trials that

School and University

they began to realise the elaborate swindle that had been put across.

A fellow-student has described the strong impression that this affair had upon Zhelyabov. He was not concerned with the ins and outs of the affair and did not try to assess the exact role played by Nechaev. What struck him most was that at another university a real revolutionary organisation had been founded and run by students. He went round to all his friends discussing the possibility of doing something of the sort at Odessa. But his friends were more mature or more prudent. They were ready to abuse the Administration and even the Emperor, but they were not ready for action. And so the project fizzled out.

III

THIS same contemporary has left us a picture of Zhelyabov in his university days. During his two years there he only had one suit, bought off a stall in the Greek bazaar. It was very tight and short in the sleeves and the trouser legs. On its third day it split under the arms and repairs never seemed to be permanent. Zhelyabov was an eager, rather coltish youth, full of vitality, who could never do anything by halves. There were swings in the public park, and it was always his ambition, unless or until his partner protested, to swing up over the crossbar. It was the same at the improvised student dances; he swept through the room like a tornado. When they started to sing he sang louder than any, though seldom in tune. But people liked him.

When he had any money he gave it away, and when, as often happened, the Luludaki executors were late in paying out his stipend he used to live on one bowl of soup a day from the Kuhmisterska. This was the canteen—there was one in every Russian university—assisted by private donations and sometimes even by official funds, where impecunious students could get cheap meals. It often came to be the unofficial centre of the student's life. The Odessa Kuhmisterska was a big room, well warmed in winter. It was organised by the students themselves. They took in newspapers and had a small collection of books. Zhelyabov read them all and any others he could get hold of. He made the Kuhmisterska his headquarters and sat up half the night there, drinking tea and arguing with his fellow-students about the new social theories of Owen, St. Simon and Fournier. These discussions would not have been approved by the authorities; but in 1869 the police at Odessa seem to have taken their political duties easily. The local chief of the Third Section was tolerant and humane. Meanwhile the new railways had opened up South Russia and Odessa was at the zenith of its first boom as a grain port. The town was growing fast. Greeks, Jews and Armenians were crowding in and setting up new businesses. Everyone was making money. The police were making money too, and had little inclination to bother about the Kuhmisterska.

Zhelyabov's earlier biographers repeat a legend that from the beginning of his undergraduate days he kept himself by giving private lessons and that he sometimes earned as much as 150 roubles a month. There is no concrete evidence of this. His name is not on the list of students authorised by the university authorities to give lessons; and he could certainly have got on the list if he had wanted to. His stipend gave him enough to live on and we can accept it that he was content with that. Throughout his life he never took much thought of personal comfort, or paid attention to things that can be bought with money.

The fact that this legend arose is proof of how little is known of his student days. We have, however, two stories which have the ring of truth. A girl who knew him wrote afterwards:

"I had bad news from home and was very depressed. Andrei Zhelyabov met me in the street and asked what was the matter. I told him I had had bad news. 'Well,' he said, 'I myself make it a rule not to worry over any personal trouble for more than three days. I worry hard for three days and get all my worrying over. Try it yourself. You'll be happier.' "

Then in the long vacation of 1870 he got a post as tutor with a rich family at their country house near Simbirsk. His pupil has left a short account of this episode. The first two or three days were difficult. Zhelyabov aired his views at the family dinner table as if he were at the Kuhmisterska at Odessa. The head of the family, an autocrat of the old school, was appalled. So was his sister. Russian tolerance and Russian hospitality were put to a strain. But within a week, although Zhelyabov went on talking, the situation had eased, thanks to his gift of making people like him. The old gentleman still growled and called him a Jacobin and a gallows-bird, but the hostility had gone and he liked to have him there. So did the aunt. His pupil had been won over from the start and the young sisters and the girl cousins quarrelled as to who should sit next to him. Conversation often turned on books and we have a record of Zhelyabov's literary judgments at the age of twenty. Pushkin he considered to be too much the mere artist to be in the first rank; he preferred Lermontov. Byron was a very great poet, and his masterpiece was *Cain*. Victor Hugo, Heine, Dickens, Thackeray and Longfellow were all approved. Of Shakespeare it was more difficult to speak; it was impossible to judge him by reading the plays. One had to see them on the stage.

IV

THE year 1871 was an exciting one for the politically minded undergraduate. There came the news of the Paris Commune. In the same year American competition in the grain trade first made itself felt, and Odessa was hit by the slump. Workmen were laid off in hundreds, employers cut the wages of those they kept, labourers and landless peasants crowded in from the surrounding villages in the hopeless quest to find a livelihood. There were demonstrations and disorders, finally culminating in Odessa's first serious pogrom. No lives were lost, but over a thousand Jewish shops and dwellings were broken up and looted.

We have no conclusive evidence of Zhelyabov's attitude at this time. Chudnovski, who was then living in Odessa and knew him personally, has stated that he strongly disapproved of anti-Semitism. But this was years afterwards, when Chudnovski was an émigré in London and intent upon convincing middle-class English intellectuals of the tolerance and liberalism of the Russian revolutionary movement. Against Chudnovski we have the evidence of the Rabbi Ben Ami who declared that during the pogrom Zhelyabov was "particularly violent in his denunciation of the Jews." We must leave the case as not proven, with the balance of probability on the side of Ben Ami. Zhelyabov's birth and background were likely to make him support what he would feel to be the cause of the Russian workman and Russian peasant as against the Jewish moneylender. It is perhaps significant that later on Zhelyabov never chose a Jewish colleague to work in any enterprise which he was personally directing.

In any case whatever part he may have played in the disorders of 1871 he did not incur the disapproval of the university. The payment of his stipend had always been irregular and in the early summer of 1871 it ceased altogether. Zhelyabov complained to the university authorities. The university had no means of forcing the Luludaki executors to pay, but at the next meeting of the council it was decided that in view of Zhelyabov's "excellent behaviour and studious disposition," he should be allotted twenty roubles a month from university funds until the difficulties over the stipend were cleared up. The university records show that this was paid out regularly until his expulsion.

It is now for the first time that we hear of Zhelyabov taking part in any clandestine activity. Count Tolstoi's new curriculum for schools was promulgated in the summer. The progressives were exasperated and at Odessa a small group of students, including Zhelyabov, determined on counter-action. They arranged to hold free secret classes, for all young people who cared to attend them, in those subjects most affected by the new regulations. These were Russian, French, German, physics, algebra, geometry, history and geography. The arrangement was not only an attempt to thwart the intention behind an unpopular measure: it was also an outlet for the urge, then just becoming so strong among Russian students, to be of service to their fellow-beings. The classes were arranged in five groups. The eldest pupils were from seventeen to eighteen, and the youngest just beginning to read and write.

A certain Anastasia Schechter, aged fourteen and a half, attended Zhelyabov's class on literature and the Russian language. It was, she recorded afterwards, the great event of her week. All his life Zhelyabov made a big impression on the men and women he had to do with. He was a fine-looking youth, tall, very powerful and with a forceful personality. But his manner was simple and friendly. In spite of his shabby clothes the effect on the girls in his class was overwhelming. He would read a poem or piece of prose and then explain it. He read them Pushkin's "Winter" and told them of the struggles of the peasants when cold weather came after a bad harvest. He read them a translation of Hood's "Song of the Shirt" and explained what it meant to have to work in a factory or on piecework at home for a hard employer. "Never again," Anastasia Schechter declares, "could I think of peasants or workmen in the way I had before."

Zhelyabov, of course, was consciously propagandising; and most of his pupils joined up afterwards with some branch or other of the movement. Nine years later Schechter was a member of the *Cherni Peredel,* the rival wing, and attended in Petersburg a secret joint meeting with Zhelyabov's Narodnaya Volya. Zhelyabov himself was present and spoke, and she describes her thrill when he came up to her afterwards and said: "I know you. We were in Odessa together. My name's Zhelyabov." He stopped chatting with her for several minutes and pulled her leg about her party's policy. "It's work in the towns that matters now," he said. "In the country if the police see a new face they lock him up." Schechter asked him to come and see her and he said he would. "But he never came," she writes rather wistfully. "Probably it was because I was a member of the Cherni Peredel." A more likely reason is that he had far too many other matters to attend to.

V

THE expulsion of Zhelyabov from the university was ultimately due to a trivial incident in which he was not concerned. That the affair developed as it did is no great credit to any of the parties to it. It was from first to last a matter of face. Russian students or most of them were sons of parish priests or impoverished small gentry; they lived from hand to mouth while completing their course, and had no great prospects of a career when it was over. But in spite of this, or because of it, they were intensely jealous of their dignity and corporate standing. As to Zhelyabov, his crusading spirit was already strong; and it was a heady experience for a youth of twenty-one to find himself a leader of a big movement. The story, which, incidentally, is an illustration of the working of the government machine, can be reconstructed from the Odessa University archives.

The trouble began on October 16, 1871, in the classroom of Professor Bogishich. Bogishich was a Czech, brought up in the Germanic traditions of discipline current in the universities of the Austrian Empire. He had no great experience of Russians. On this particular day he saw a student, one Baer, lounging in his seat. He stopped his lecture and said: "Do you think you are in a drink shop? If you can't behave you can get out." Baer began to make some explanation. Bogishich shouted: "Silence! Get out!" and hustled him out of the room. The other students afterwards said that he kicked him, but this Bogishich denied. In any case Baer left the room and the lecture proceeded.

Bogishich was next due to lecture on October 20. No students appeared in the classroom, but a crowd of them collected in the passage outside and hissed him as he went by. The matter was reported to the vice-rector, and it was arranged that the rector should meet the students concerned on the following day. He arrived to find a mass meeting. He asked the students to appoint their spokesmen and disperse, which they did. Zhelyabov was one of the delegates. He was not in Bogishich's class, and this was his first appearance in the affair.

The delegates had their talk with the rector and as a result went off to call on Bogishich. They found the latter reasonable and conciliatory. He told them it had been a misunderstanding, partly due to his not realising that the Russian word *kabak* (drink shop) had undesirable associations; in any case he had not intended to hurt anyone's feelings, and he was prepared to say as much at his next lecture on the 23rd. The students were satisfied, and it seemed the incident was at an end.

But it was not. Bogishich thought the matter over and concluded (no doubt rightly) that he would be expected to make a formal apology with consequent loss of face. On the 23rd the classroom was crowded but the professor did not appear. Instead, he sent a message that he was sick. There was an uproar; Bogishich had broken his promise. The students all assembled in the big hall, and when the vice-rector arrived there Zhelyabov was at the rostrum haranguing the crowd and declaring amid tumultuous applause that it was a matter of principle for the whole body of undergraduates that satisfaction be obtained from Bogishich. The vice-rector threatened to send for the police and the uproar increased. Eventually the students

School and University

left the hall, but they collected in little groups in the university courtyard and in the town, shouting "Bogishich must go" and singing a ribald song that someone had extemporised.

It might have been expected that even at this stage the matter was one which the university could have handled by itself. But the authorities were rattled. It happened that the Emperor was shortly due to pass through Odessa and this added to their sense of responsibility. A meeting of the University Council was called and sent a request to the Governor General asking for special police measures; in particular for steps to ensure that no meetings of students took place in private houses in the town. The council also decided to summon a university court to try the ringleaders, to cancel all lectures till the court proceedings were finished, and to make a formal expression of sympathy and regret to Bogishich.

This was duly reported to the local director of education at Odessa who in his turn informed his Minister by telegram. On the same day, October 24, Count Tolstoi telegraphed back:

"Approve decision of council. Request Governor General take immediate and strictest measures. Students expelled from university to be banished immediately from Odessa."

On the 25th Tolstoi telegraphed again:

"Holding of court and execution of its decisions to be carried out immediately. Students expelled from university, however great their number, to be banished from Odessa. No lectures to be held till this is done. Report to me by telegram."

The university court held its first session on the 25th and continued to sit till November 5. There were innumerable witnesses to be heard, professors, students, university officials, anybody in the town who had any evidence to give concerning student demonstrations and meetings. In the town and even among the university professors there was a good deal of sympathy for the students. Colonel Knoop, the Odessa head of the Third Section, deplored the expulsions that he foresaw would be made.

"The ultimate responsibility for the disorders," he reported to his chief in Petersburg, "must rest with Bogishich . . . but the result will be that a number of young men will be deprived of their means of earning a living and their minds will be turned against the Government—all the more so as they will feel they have been made to suffer unjustly. Surely it would be sufficient to reprimand them for their improper choice of tactics."

On November 5 the court made its decision, and on the 9th it was confirmed by the University Council. It was milder than had been anticipated. There were certain minor punishments, one student was expelled for one year "with the right to attend other educational institutes," and two (including Zhelyabov) were expelled for a year with no such right. These three were automatically banished from Odessa.

On November 11 Zhelyabov and his two colleagues were arrested. The court's decision and the order of banishment were read to them, and they were taken to the port under police escort and put on board the steamer for Kerch which was due to leave that afternoon. A crowd of sympathisers came down to see them off, and police reinforcements were called up to maintain order. But it was foggy and the sailing was postponed till the following morning. One of Zhelyabov's friends in the town, a man of standing and substance, offered to stand surety for him if he were allowed to come on shore and spend the night at his house. The authorities agreed. But they were taking no risks and police were posted outside to limit the number of visitors who called to see him. Next morning Zhelyabov was escorted on board again, loudly cheered by a huge crowd of students and townsmen, and the boat sailed. The local newspapers were instructed that no account of his send-off was to be published.

On November 14 town and university were plastered with placards demanding that Bogishich should leave Odessa. The police made enquiries but never discovered who put them up. On November 15 Bogishich did in fact receive the offer of a post in the University of Warsaw. He was by this time only too anxious to leave Odessa, but the Ministry of Education refused to sanction the transfer and ordered him to stay where he was. On November 15 classes were resumed, and Bogishich held his first lecture on the 17th. The lecture passed off without incident. A report on the whole affair was submitted to Petersburg by the Odessa director of education, and in December it was shown by Tolstoi to the Emperor. The Emperor wrote "Good" in the margin.

Meanwhile Zhelyabov had been duly conveyed by the police

to his village. A fortnight later he presented a petition to the local police authorities in which he emphasised the poverty of his family and the burden imposed on them by having an extra mouth to feed; he therefore asked permission to live in Feodosia where he could keep himself by giving private lessons.

The plea of poverty was doubtless exaggerated. There is evidence that the Zhelyabovs, by peasant standards, were fairly well to do. It is more likely that his real motive was to avoid the monotony of village life in winter, when there was no work to be done on the land, and also to get on with his studies. Lack of books and lack of privacy would have made this difficult in the cottage at home.

His application was granted and he went to Feodosia. In July of the following year he wrote to the university, asking for certain certificates to enable him to take up the question of his stipend with the Luludaki executors. The university authorities sent him what he wanted. It is perfectly clear that for their part they were prepared to let bygones be bygones. Indeed the vice-rector had seen him before he left Odessa and had told him they would be glad to have him back in due course.

Early in August Zhelyabov sent in his application for readmission to the university, accompanied by certificates of good conduct from the chiefs of police at Feodosia and Kerch. At the same time he asked to be allowed to sit for the examination for third-year students, which shows he had been working while at Feodosia. His application was approved by the University Council and passed, on August 21, to the director of education for endorsement. The director referred the matter to Petersburg, and replied on September 22 that the Ministry had instructed him to point out that the term of expulsion had been for one year, that a whole year had not yet elapsed; in view of which "and also of the necessity for preserving the student body from undesirable influences," it was not possible to sanction the proposal contained in the application.

The University Council returned to the charge. On September 25 they applied for authority to admit Zhelyabov on November 8, i.e., exactly one year after his expulsion. Again there was a month's delay while the matter was referred to Petersburg. Finally on October 25 a ruling came that the regulations governing the university provided only for the admission of students at the beginning of each scholastic year, and that in consequence a proposal to admit, or re-admit, a student in the month of November could not be entertained.

That was the end. Zhelyabov took no further steps. In July, 1873, he asked the university to send him back his papers.

CHAPTER THREE

THE YOUNG CRUSADERS

I

IT IS important for an authoritarian regime to be able to appeal to the young. The middle-aged, in years or spirit, will play for safety and swim with the tide. There is little danger of their making trouble. But the young and adventurous must be given some outlet for their emotional urge. The tragedy of the Romanovs was partly due to their incapacity to solve this problem, or rather, perhaps, to their failure to observe that it existed. Pobyedonostsev, the mentor of Alexander III, reviewed his generation and remarked with regret that "the minds of men had lost the faculty of recognising their own ignorance and the capacity to learn, that is, to submit to the Law of Life." It is the language of an old-fashioned parent whose children are reaching the difficult age. The Imperial Government was strictly paternal, and throughout the century the regime and the advanced intellectuals regarded each other with mutual incomprehension. Time and again appeals were launched from above to rally to the support of "the established religion, the existing social structure and the institution of private property"; and it caused pain and surprise when earnest young agnostics, with no property and a strong disapproval of the existing social structure, failed to make an adequate response.

Russia of the 'sixties and 'seventies offered an unlimited field for service. The great reforms had opened up enormous scope for agricultural improvements, education and public hygiene. The Empire was acquiring vast new territories in Central Asia and the Far East, all awaiting development. It is idle to speculate what would have been the result of an intelligent attempt to make use of the energy and devotion available. That the spirit of service was there is shown by the way young people volunteered for the Turkish War. All they wanted was a lead from the Government. But no such lead ever came. The imperial system was such that it could only demand blind obedience to the Administration. And for the young intellectual to enter the government service seemed merely to become an impotent cog in a sinister and inefficient machine.

There remained, of course, commerce and industry. The Tsarist regime was a liberal one as far as business was concerned. The rate of industrialisation from 1860 onwards was remarkable and those who took advantage of it made large fortunes. But this field did not supply an emotional outlet. Business remained predominantly in the hands of the merchant class. Money-making as such made no appeal to the young people who eventually turned to political agitation. In fact, as soon as the uglier side of industrialisation became apparent —and, owing to the freedom and encouragement accorded to employers, it was uglier in Russia than in most countries—big business attracted their hostility just as much as the Administration.

The system of Nicholas I had effectively crushed, among young intellectuals, all devotional loyalty to the autocratic machine or to the Emperor as its head. Religion, among the intellectuals, had gone by the board and the Church was regarded merely as a cowardly and obsequious servant of the Administration. An emotional outlet was found, in the early decades of the century, in a blind admiration for Western civilisation. But Russian aptitude for devotion is accompanied by an ingrained critical sense. In the 'forties and 'fifties the Western idol was seen to have its feet of clay. Attention was turned to the jobberies and intrigues of Western parliaments, and, in particular, to Western factory conditions. Meanwhile a German baron of the name of Haxthausen had been studying the Russian peasantry and published in 1847 the first authoritative treatise on the Russian peasant commune.

This work made a great impression upon Russian intellectuals. It was, they felt, a proof that the seeds of the millennium were to be found not in the West but in their own hitherto neglected country. There was a sudden and remarkable revulsion of feeling away from Western "progress." Russia, it was claimed, must avoid altogether the bourgeois industrialism of England and France by passing directly from the autocracy of today to the free federation of peasant communes of tomorrow: and the world would follow Russia's lead.

Such, very roughly, was the main thesis of Herzen. He foresaw no need for violent revolution; once given the vote the Russian peasant would vote himself into Utopia without more ado. But Herzen's influence came to an end with the Polish revolution. He had backed the Poles and thus lost the sympathy of the liberals; and he was too moderate in method for the extreme socialists. The eclipse of Herzen marks the end of the old alliance between liberals and socialists. Thereafter there were two distinct currents, one aiming at constitutional development and the other at revolution.

A tougher race of intellectuals arose in the 'sixties. Herzen and his like were dismissed as "Oblomovs." Oblomov is the name of a character in a novel by Goncharov, a humane, cultured, easy-going and ineffective gentleman. The young men of the 'sixties declared war upon such well-meaning futility. It was the age of Nihilism. "Nihilist" has been used as a term of abuse for the Russian revolutionaries by their opponents, but in point of fact there was never a political creed of that name. Nihilism is a slang term for an attitude of mind, for that passion for debunking which was the reaction against the easy acceptance of ideals of progress.

"Man is an animal." "Photography is higher than Art." "The belly is the centre of the world."

Such were typical maxims of what Pisarev described as "the thinking realist." "We must destroy," he said, "all that can be destroyed. If anything is any good it won't be broken. Otherwise the sooner it is destroyed the better. Hit hard in all directions. It can't do any harm."

But these "thinking realists" were none the less romantics at heart. They were imbued with a *Weltverbesserungswahn;* they dedicated themselves to the service of their fellow-beings and they pursued their aim of a socialist Utopia with a devotion in which a sense of practicalities played little part. *Chto Dyelat?* the novel of Chernishevski which appeared in 1864 and at once became a revolutionary bible, is at least as remarkable for its sentimental emotionalism as for its "realist" ideology. This emotionalism became part and parcel of the revolutionary movement of the succeeding age. Kravchinski, not a mere dreamer but a practical terrorist, tells us that when he visited a clandestine printing press he entered "with the subdued feeling of a worshipper entering a church." We can well believe him.

Chernishevski and Pisarev were both arrested when the reaction set in, and the journals to which they contributed were suppressed. As the hand of the Administration became heavier those young people who could afford it took to going abroad to complete their studies. Girls went as well as men. The decisive part played by young women in the movement has occasioned some surprise to those unacquainted with Russian life. But blind submissiveness to the male has never been a mark of Russian ladies. We have the case of Vera Figner, who as a minor found difficulties in getting a passport for abroad and so ordered a young gentleman of her acquaintance to marry her. She took him with her to Zurich, endeavoured to train him up as a revolutionary, and, on finding him an incorrigible moderate, divorced him.

In the early 'seventies Zurich University was the Mecca of advanced young Russians. At that time their source of inspiration was in the writings of the leading Russian émigrés (Marx was still regarded mainly as an economist) and the three apostles of the Russian Revolution were conveniently established in Switzerland. Bakunin was preaching his doctrine of "implacable destruction." He exhorted his disciples to proceed at once to the Russian countryside and instigate revolts. He harped back to the days of Pugachev. He ignored the fact that since those days modern firearms, railways and the telegraph had made it infinitely easier to suppress a peasant rising. He was convinced that the peasants were only waiting for a lead, and that local movements would soon take on the proportions of a general revolution. This revolution in its turn would lead on to a world order of loosely federated free peasant communities.

Lavrov doubted the imminence of a successful revolution. In any case, in his view, revolution was not the work of an individual or a group but of "a whole row of historical processes." He warned his pupils against trying to hasten it by artificial means; also against regarding themselves as leaders. By doing so they "would only be giving the people another set of masters." His disciples should first complete their own studies so as to fit themselves for the part of educators of the people. Meanwhile Tkachev, the former associate of Nechaev, took a more realist view. He disbelieved in the practicality of a general rising, and he had no desire to wait for a whole row of historic processes: he believed in an attack on the State by a centralised and disciplined body of professional revolutionaries. But the students did not want to give up their belief in the peasants' own capacity for revolt, and did not want themselves to impose a dictatorship. Tkachev's following was very small.

II

MEANWHILE in Russia itself the populist movement was growing. Some of its adherents belonged to the most distinguished families of the Empire. Sophia Perovskaya's father, for instance, had been Governor General of Petersburg for three years. In 1866, after the Karakozov affair, he was dismissed. As Governor General he had enjoyed unlimited credit and run up huge debts, and his dismissal brought a crisis in the family fortunes. Sonia and her mother went to live on the family estate in the Crimea. The general stayed on in the capital. This parting was in many ways a relief, for the family atmosphere was not happy. The father was a tyrant and a bully. There were continual quarrels, and the child always took her mother's side. She came to hate her father; this hatred became the decisive psychological factor in her development.

In 1869 the home in the Crimea was sold. Mother and daughter went back to join the father in Petersburg. The former friction started again; but in the summer the general fell ill, and was taken by his wife and his other daughter to do a round of European resorts. Sonia went to stay with friends, and through them first came in touch with the advanced intellectuals. In the autumn her parents came back again. After those months of comparative freedom it was hard for her to go back to the old life. She declared her intention of living on her own and studying. Her father was furious; but she persisted and in the end forced him to let her take out a passport. Once she left home there is no record of her ever having seen her father again; when she called to see her mother she came up the back stairs. Her mother wished to make her a small allowance. But she was too proud to live on her mother, and managed to earn some money by copying and translation work. Some of the time she lived by herself, some of the time with friends. She attended a course to qualify as a school teacher and passed the examination. They did not, however, give her a diploma—probably because she was politically suspect. In the end she went to stay with friends at Tver, took the course again and this time got her diploma. Meanwhile she had joined up with the Chaikovski Circle, the first and most famous of the secret cultural and philanthropic societies of the 'seventies.

This "circle" like all the others of its kind had started as a group of young people who met from time to time to read books and hold discussions. It had originally no political aims. But it was an age of heart-searching among the educated youth. They had, they felt, received their privileges at the expense of their poorer compatriots. It was now for them to make some return. They started to hold classes for factory workers. These had to take place in secret. An imperial edict of 1862 had forbidden such activities as being "likely to undermine faith in the Christian religion and in the institution of private property, and to incite the working classes to revolt." Inevitably the circles took on a political tinge. The members studied the works of the émigré writers, and, according to their conviction or temperament, became Bakunists or Lavrists. Joint meetings were sometimes held where the rival theories were debated. It was easy, a follower of Lavrov wrote later, to tell the two factions apart. The Lavrists were "more carefully dressed, cleaner and tidier; they spoke better and their hands were whiter." Circles sprang up in every large town in the country and the movement gained in intensity as well as in numbers. The spirit of *Narodnichestvo* arose, derived from *Narod* (people), and defined by an English authority as "a love and reverence for the working classes of one's country, coupled with an altruistic desire to serve them." There came the urge to "cease to be champions of the people in theory alone."

In 1873 the Imperial Government, warned by their secret agents of what was happening at Zurich, issued an order forbidding girl students to study there. It solved the problem which was worrying so many of them, namely whether to finish their studies or to return at once and start on their mission among the peasants. The girl students went back to Russia and many of the men went with them. At home they met their young compatriots whose spiritual development had been proceeding on parallel lines: and suddenly there flared up the astonishing movement of the "Going to the People" (*Hozhdenie v Narod*). Hundreds, thousands perhaps, of youths and girls left their homes, assumed false names and papers (because they knew the police would be after them) and went off to be among the common people. Kravchinski, who was then an artillery subaltern, and threw up his career to join the movement, says: "They went out as bearers of a revelation rather than political propagandists. It was as if a voice resounded throughout the Empire, calling on those whose souls were not yet dead to serve the cause of the people and of humanity. They heard the call, felt the shame of their past, abandoned homes, riches, honours and family. They threw themselves into the movement with a passionate enthusiasm, with an ardent faith that knew no obstacle and counted no sacrifice . . ."

III

It was in no sense an organised movement. It had no plan of campaign. It had not even unanimity of aim. The young Bakunists hoped for an early general rising; the Lavrists hoped to prepare the way for social evolution; a large number, with no special political label, wished merely to do what they could to further the peasant's material and moral well-being. But for all of them it was a voyage of discovery. Thanks to the rigid class system of Russia few of them knew anything of peasant conditions and peasant mentality; and they went among the people to get to know them, to help them, and to bring them the glad tidings that better times were at hand. They had no inkling of the peasants' inherent suspicion of strange people and strange doctrines, and for most of them their mission was a series of bitter disappointments.

The experiences recorded by Debogori-Mokrievich in his memoirs are typical of many. Debogori-Mokrievich was the son of a small landowner in the southwest Ukraine. He completed his studies at Kiev and there became a convert to the new ideas. While still a very young man he and two others went on a pilgrimage to Switzerland to see Bakunin. On their return to Russia they found the police were after them. In 1873 Debogori-Mokrievich was living with Stefanovich (who later played a big part in the movement) and three other companions in one of the poorer quarters of Kiev, endeavouring to learn a handicraft. Then their friends began to "go to the people" and a few months later they were unable to resist the urge to set out themselves. They had no definite programme; only they must make for some district where the local authorities were not likely to recognise them. They fixed on Zhmerinka as their starting point. They made out false passports. They went to a stall in the second-hand market and bought the oldest clothes they could find. Two of the five had learned some shoemaking so these two brought their tools. After buying the tickets their total funds amounted to six roubles each. It was a night journey, and they settled themselves to sleep on the floor, under the seats of the compartment, as peasants did. Every two hours or so an inspector came and kicked them up and made them show their tickets. It was their first experience of travelling as members of a non-privileged class.

"Next morning," Debogori-Mokrievich writes, "we arrived at Zhmerinka and looked for work. We got a job loading railway sleepers on to trucks. Four of us carried them up and the fifth arranged them in the truck. We worked there for a week, earned a little money and determined to go farther. But it would have looked suspicious for a party of five to go about as shoemakers when they only had tools for two. We had to find some other disguise. We realised then that we should have thought this out before leaving Kiev. One of us happened to see a little party of dyers going through Zhmerinka, and we decided to be dyers. This was all the easier because Vasya's mother had a dyeing business, and Vasya knew something about it and promised to teach us. Meanwhile Sh. had begun to lose heart. He told us he could not stand the physical hardships, and wanted to go back to Kiev. We got very angry. Sh. tried in vain to persuade us that he would be of more use to us in Kiev and begged us to keep in touch with him. We kept repeating 'He who is not with us is against us'—meaning, of course, that anyone who did not go with us to the people was our enemy. It was a sad parting. I can remember Sh. now as he stood with his head down while we told him what we thought of him. When he said goodbye his hands were quivering."

So Sh. returned to Kiev and Vasya went off to his mother's to get some dyes. In due course he came back and the four of them set off on foot with their sacks on their backs. So as to look more realistic they stained their clothes, hands and faces with dye. To their great gratification some peasants they met on the road actually took them for dyers. They were held up in one village by the local police official who inspected their passports. It turned out that they had dated one of them 1804 instead of 1874: but the mistake was put down to the supposed office of issue in Kiev, and they were allowed to go on.

"The first few days we made Vasya give us dyeing lessons. We did not make very good progress. However, after a few days we went to the cottages to get work. At first we were shy about it, but later on, when we noticed the peasants never gave us anything to dye, we were more insistent. We took every chance we could to start conversation with them. We ourselves were too blindly assured of the imminence of the revolution to notice that the peasants had not nearly as much of the revolutionary spirit as we wanted them to have. But we did notice that they all wanted the land to be divided up among them. They expected the Emperor would give an order, and then the surveyors would come and the land would be divided up. Sometimes peasants asked us if we had heard of the distribution having already started in any other district. One peasant went so far as to say he would not think of buying land now, when it was so soon to be divided up. All of them expected that the Emperor would give the order. Most of them imagined he would have had it carried through long ago if he had not been prevented by the big landowners and the officials—the two arch enemies both of the Emperor and of the peasant. . . .

"We covered about twenty versts a day and spent the nights in the villages. The peasants did not want to let us stay the nights in their cottages; quite obviously they did not like the look of our dirty, ragged clothing. This was the last thing we expected when we first dressed up as workmen. We knew how suspicious peasants were of anyone dressed like the middle or upper classes, and we supposed that the poorer we looked the more they would be inclined to trust us. We were quite wrong. They were everywhere mistrustful, and were so unwilling to let us in (I suppose they were afraid we should steal) that it became more and more unpleasant trying to get quarters for the night. Sometimes we asked at ten houses and were refused at all of them.

"Quite often we slept out in the open. It was rainy weather, and time and again I woke up in the middle of the night shivering from cold and damp. Sometimes we had to spend a whole night out in the rain. The cheap boots hurt our feet, S.'s feet were sore and bleeding all over. Every three or four days we took a day's rest. Now and then we stayed several days in one place, if we could find an abandoned cottage with no windows and a broken roof which the peasants did not mind us using. We would get straw and spread it on the floor. It seemed a perfect luxury to be able to stretch our limbs out and rest. Our excuse for these long stays was that we were trying to find work. Vasya got the dyes ready; and Stefanovich or I would go round the village and try and get the peasants to give us work. But they never gave us any. If ever they had anything they wanted dyed they used to take it to someone they knew in the nearest town. For food we sometimes boiled ourselves a sort of porridge. More often we just had bread and bacon.

"All this together—the bodily fatigue, and the poor food, and especially our false position with the peasants, their mistrust of us which made us always have to be on our guard—it all had a very depressing effect, particularly on people like S. who perhaps had too idyllic a conception of the peasantry. He left us and went to his relations beyond the Dnieper. . . . So we lost our second comrade."

Hundreds of young people all over Russia, who had set out with radiant enthusiasm, were by this time going back disillusioned to the towns.

IV

MEANWHILE the movement was engaging the attention of the authorities. Count Pahlen, the Minister of Justice, endeavoured to sum up the situation in a confidential memorandum. He had, he wrote, discovered traces of these subversive activities in no less than thirty-four of the provinces of European Russia. He considered them to be the work of a number of secret illegal societies in existence throughout the Empire all "acting on a definite and carefully thought-out plan towards the destruction of the existing social structure." The grave danger was involved that "in spite of the vigorous measures of the authorities certain groups may still be undiscovered and engaged on the continuation of their work." He was forced, further, to come to the conclusion that one reason for the wide spread of the movement was that it was not meeting with a sufficiently firm resistance on the part of the educated classes. Cases had been noted of "men of ripe age and respectable position acting with apathy, if not with sympathy, towards individuals whose grave potential danger to society and to themselves they appear to ignore." Finally, it was the parents who were largely to blame. The youth of the country was "not receiving that basic moral education which only the family can give," and was not being "grounded at an early age in the principles of respect for religion, for the family, for individual rights and for the institution of private property."

While Count Pahlen was thus diagnosing the ultimate causes of the movement the police were taking action. Secret agents were kept busy. Anonymous denunciations were followed up. Correspondence in the post was scrutinised. There were surprise house searches in the middle of the night. Hours were spent in the examination of prisoners. The young people were easy game for the police. Those of them that wished to overthrow the Government had no inkling of how to set about doing so. They were naïve and inexperienced in revolutionary technique. They had no knowledge of how to live and work as "illegals," i.e., with false identity papers. In the years 1874 and 1875 political arrests could be numbered by the thousand. Some of the prisoners were released on bail and kept under police observation. Some were exiled to Siberia or the northern provinces by administrative process. The rest remained in prison till the authorities could make up their minds what to do with them.

V

We have few records of this period of Zhelyabov's life. He was too obscure to make much impression on his contemporaries; and later on, when he was a revolutionary leader, he seems to have spoken little about these earlier years. They were ineffective, and on the whole unhappy. It is possible that he wanted to forget them.

He had, of course, no incentive to "go to the people." He was himself of the people, a peasant, brought up in a village among peasants. He knew how the peasants thought and what they wanted. He had no illusions of the imminence of a general peasant rising. Already he considered the factory workers to be the more immediately important factor in any social change. But his views and aims were not yet formulated. He was not a revolutionary. He was merely a young man who had read a good deal of advanced literature and had a keen emotional sympathy with the peasants and workers, but had not yet made up his mind what part he was to play to help them.

In the autumn of 1872, when his year of banishment expired, he came back to Odessa. His friends there regarded him as something of a martyr, and public opinion had mostly been on his side in the Bogishich affair. He had not much difficulty in making a living by giving private lessons. It is probable that he was able to send money home to his family. He resumed touch with his friends in the Kuhmisterska, and through them he met members of the Volkhovski Circle, the most important of the advanced groups in Odessa. They were Lavrists and busied themselves with smuggling in forbidden literature and holding secret classes for factory workers. The aims and work of the circle attracted Zhelyabov. After a time he was given to understand that if he wished he would be accepted as a member. Membership of the circle was, of course, illegal, and it was a big decision for a young man to take. Zhelyabov went privately to one of the leaders and put his case up to him.

"What would you do yourself if you had responsibilities towards a family you were very fond of—if you had a father and a mother partly dependent on you and if you knew that by joining an illegal society you ran a real risk of no longer being able to help them?" His friend with all the pedantic austerity of a young revolutionary replied that the cause of the masses should come first. Zhelyabov asked for time to think it over. Three days later he came back and said: "I would like to join you if you will have me." For the first time he had committed himself.

Zhelyabov was never prominent in the Volkhovski Circle. We hear of him "listening with extreme diffidence" to the older members. Possibly the Bogishich affair had lost him some of his self-confidence. In any case, soon after he joined he left Odessa and was away for nearly a year. He got a post as tutor in the family of a certain Yahnenko, a wealthy business man and municipal councillor. Yahnenko had a country house and a sugar factory a few miles from Kiev and Zhelyabov joined the family there. He got into touch with some of the factory hands, but little seems to have come of it. He may have been restrained by loyalty towards his employer. He visited Kiev from time to time and his friends in the Volkhovski Circle gave him introductions to the Lavrists there. In this way he met Breshkovskaya, Stefanovich and Debogori-Mokrievich. In a letter written seven years afterwards he recalls a meeting in Kiev "in a room behind a shoemaker's shop with a party of elderly (very elderly) Nihilists sitting round and asking what was to be done."

But that year his private affairs left him little time for social questions. He fell in love with Olga Semenovna Yahnenko, his employer's younger daughter. In the summer of 1873 they were married. Zhelyabov does not seem to have met any serious opposition. The son of a peasant was not, of course, an ideal match, but Yahnenko prided himself on his liberal and democratic ideas. In any case Zhelyabov was presentable. He had brains and personality and in spite of his earlier *gaffe* at the university he might be expected to make a career—especially with an influential father-in-law behind him. Furthermore Olga Semenovna was very much in love.

The bride was barely twenty. We hear of her as a girl whom everybody liked and who was always ready to like everybody. She was pretty, affectionate and musical. The family were proud of her voice. Her father had arranged for her to have lessons from the best music teacher in Odessa and she was in demand to sing at evening parties given by their friends. She herself enjoyed these little gaieties. But she was essentially a domesticated girl. All she wanted was a settled home with a grand piano, babies, and a husband she could be devoted to.

There were signs, if she had cared to see them, of the difficulties ahead when they moved back to Odessa in the autumn. Zhelyabov took on the post of teacher at the Odessa Municipal Poor House. We have no details of this appointment. Possibly he got it through the influence of his father-in-law; and probably after turning down a number of more promising openings which the Yahnenkos had suggested. The salary was very small and he insisted on living on that and on any casual supplements from his private lessons. He told his wife that they must arrange their lives so as to be of help to the common people; and in order to please him she herself went through a midwife's course.

Zhelyabov held secret evening classes for working men. We have no details of them, except for one anecdote which illustrates how hard it was for the young missionaries to instil their ideals into their disciples. Zhelyabov asked a workman, his most promising pupil, what he would do if he had five hundred roubles. The answer was "I would go back to my village and set up as a moneylender." Before long he found other interests besides his classes. Early in 1874 he joined a new group with headquarters in a suburb of Odessa. The central figure was one Makarevich, who established himself in the guise of a shoemaker. The group smuggled in prohibited literature from abroad and engaged in social propaganda in the neighbourhood. But their activities did not last long. The Odessa police soon came upon their traces. Makarevich was caught and put in prison. A few weeks later Zhelyabov was arrested. He disclaimed all connection with any subversive activity and denied that he knew Makarevich. The police had no definite evidence against him. They searched his house but as nothing suspicious was found there they let him go. But shortly afterwards the post office intercepted a cyphered letter in Zhelyabov's handwriting addressed to Madame Makarevich. The cypher was a simple one and the police were able to decipher it. Zhelyabov had written:

"In case of your arrest you should get your parents to go bail for you. Some remarkable developments are about to take place which I cannot explain to you in writing. But money is needed . . ."

The letter went on to explain how the money could be sent, and gave directions for addressing a reply.

Zhelyabov was re-arrested. At the police station he admitted writing the letter and produced an elaborate explanation. He said that though he had never met the husband he had known Madame Makarevich in her school days at Kerch. She had, of course, been greatly distressed at her husband's arrest, and had written to him as her only friend in Odessa to find out what her husband had said to the examining magistrate, so that, in the event of her own arrest, her story would be consistent. Zhelyabov added that he sympathised with her position, but in order to find out what she asked he wanted money to entertain the prison officials.

The only witness the police could find was a certain Evgenia Petrovna whom Zhelyabov had indicated in his letter as the post box for further correspondence. She explained that Zhelyabov had asked her if he might have his love letters sent to her address. That was all she knew.

Colonel Knoop, of the gendarmerie (who had taken the students' part in the Bogishich affair), was satisfied with Zhelyabov's version. He reported to Petersburg:

"Zhelyabov can in no way be convicted of belonging to the Makarevich circle. . . . He has explained the whole situation with great frankness. His part in the affair is due solely to his chivalrous interpretation of the calls of personal friendship. His personal character and his social position—he recently married the daughter of a highly respected municipal councillor—make it extremely unlikely that he could be guilty . . ."

Knoop went on to report that he had sanctioned Zhelyabov's release on a bail of two thousand roubles.

Petersburg answered by telegram:

"Zhelyabov is to be re-arrested at once."

And so, on November 11, Zhelyabov was arrested a third time and committed to prison. "It was then," he said afterwards, "that I became a revolutionary."

He was in prison four months. During that time the police were unable to discover any further evidence against him, and in the end Colonel Knoop had his way; Zhelyabov was released in March on a bail of three thousand roubles.

VI

DURING the two and a half years that he was out on bail he took no active part in the revolutionary movement. He was under constant supervision by the police. Moreover, his father-in-law had gone bail for him, and his sense of family duty would not allow him to take risks. It was an unhappy period. The post at the poor house had come to an end with his arrest, and Zhelyabov and his wife had to live on what he could make from casual lessons. There was friction with Yahnenko, who though a liberal was also a business man, and began to regard his son-in-law as a failure. The young people were miserably poor. Zhelyabov became moody and depressed. We hear of him forbidding Olga Semenovna to go out and sing at her friends' parties. He could not, he said, allow his wife "to delight the ears of plutocrats."

In 1875 the Slavs in Bosnia and Herzegovina revolted against the Turkish Government. The rising attracted interest and sympathy in Russia. Local committees were formed to help the insurgents, and we hear of Zhelyabov collecting funds and organising the despatch of volunteers and supplies. He wished to go out to the Balkans himself, but being still on bail he was not allowed to leave Russia.

We have some record of his other doings. He developed an interest in chemistry, and talked to one of his friends, Semenyuta, about taking lessons. Semenyuta told him straight out that he was too impatient and too clumsy with his fingers: he would never be any use at it. All the same Zhelyabov went ahead and took a course in explosives. The course was an expensive one and ran him into debt.

He made friends with the local fishermen. The sea always had an attraction for him. One of his great pleasures was to go out with the fishing fleet and stay away for days.

They used to dynamite the fish. We hear of Zhelyabov's "joy and excitement" when a charge went off. He used these expeditions for trying out his knowledge of explosives. At least once he nearly blew himself up.

He also made friends with young officers, of both the army and navy. A naval lieutenant once took him on a cruise in his mine-layer. As soon as they had got over their suspicions of his socialist ideas he always got on well with members of the fighting services. There was nothing of the bookish intellectual about him. As for the officers, except for the Guards Regiments, the Russian officers were mostly recruited from the poorer gentry and had little sense of caste. A few of them were interested in social questions, and with these Zhelyabov could talk openly. Once, at the end of a long and intimate discussion, an artillery officer confided his ambition to send in his papers and to devote himself entirely to the social movement. Zhelyabov dissuaded him. "Stay where you are," he said. "You will be of more use to us in the army."

Zhelyabov was not always in Odessa. He paid two visits to Kerch. In 1876 he was with his wife at the Yahnenko sugar factory when their first and only child (a son) was born. But most of the summer months when there was work to be done on the land he spent in his parents' village. He liked farming; or perhaps it was that his restlessness and vitality could in this way find an outlet. He worked sixteen hours a day. His physical strength and capacity for work became a byword among the neighbouring peasants. Olga Semenovna went with him to the country. Tikhomirov, who only met him after he had finally parted from his wife, tells us:

"From what Zhelyabov said himself his domestic life seems to have been fairly happy. He did not regard himself as capable of being overwhelmingly in love. But he was fond of his wife and he valued her affection for him. He had in some ways the ideas of the class he sprang from. Women, in his view, were not there for romance but to produce children and to be working partners. The basis of marriage was not love, which he often made fun of, but family duty, for which, like all peasants, he had great respect."

Olga Semenovna made a gallant attempt to adapt herself. She practised her midwifery and thus added to the family's scanty income. She even went out with the others and worked in the fields. But, as she afterwards admitted, every now and then she would think of her grand piano at home and go and hide in the bushes and cry. There is no doubt that she was very unhappy; and very likely Zhelyabov got rather tired of her.

CHAPTER FOUR

DEADLOCK

I

THE crusade of 1873 and 1874, the Going to the People, collapsed. The young crusaders were disillusioned and gave up the struggle, or were caught by the police and sat in prison awaiting their trial. The few survivors were driven underground. But while the counter-campaign of the police was thus far successful, it was singularly ineffective in crushing the revolutionary spirit. Modern authoritarian regimes have a short way with their opponents. The Tsarist Government was too humane, or not sufficiently realist. The White Terror of the middle 'seventies terrorised only the timid, who in any case were barely worth terrorising. The more resolute were merely shown the error of their tactics, and turned their attention to new means of continuing the struggle.

In one important respect the police campaign was of help to the cause of revolution: the prisons became a breeding ground for full-fledged revolutionaries. We have recorded Zhelyabov's admission that his spell in prison was a turning point in his development. His case was only one of many. In Russian prisons of that time complete solitary confinement * for politicals awaiting trial was almost unknown. Although locked up in separate cells for the night prisoners could meet and talk in the prison yard during the day. Even when this

* The Russian temperament is gregarious; and for most Russians to be cut off from contact with their fellow-beings is a very serious hardship. The late Vladimir Burtsev, who came to London after his escape from Siberia in 1888, and was subsequently convicted for what the English courts regarded as an overzealous defence of the Narodnaya Volya, told me that, in his experience as a "political," most Russian prisons were greatly preferable to the deadly monotony of Wormwood Scrubs. Russian prisons, of course, varied. The Peter and Paul Fortress and Schlusselburg were notorious. Of the twenty revolutionaries in the Who's Who at the end of this book who were sent to one or other of these prisons, fourteen died in the early years of their confinement.

facility was denied they found some means of communication. They could shout across from window to window, sometimes talking in code to prevent the sentries from understanding. Warders might sometimes be bribed to pass notes. A prisoner could tap, in code, on the wall of his cell to the prisoner on the other side. If there was a waterpipe within reach the range of this telegraphy was greatly increased. In all contemporary accounts of prison life we hear of a continual rapping out of code messages all day and all night. Young politicals sometimes spent years in prison awaiting trial. They had nothing to do but brood over their grievances. It was in the prisons, and nowhere else in nineteenth-century Russia, that extremists could spread their propaganda at their leisure and convenience and in complete security among the most susceptible of listeners.

Kibalchich is an outstanding example of the influence of prison life. He was the son of a village priest in North Russia. He was born in 1854. When he was seventeen, two years before the usual leaving age, he was head boy in his school and awarded the Gold Medal. He went to Petersburg and entered the Engineering College; after two years he changed his mind and transferred to the Medical School. The crisis in his life came in 1875 when he spent the summer vacation with a relation in the country near Kiev. There he made friends with some neighbouring peasants. One of them could read and Kibalchich lent him books. They were all books approved by the censor except one, a naïve little story of socialist tendency called *A Tale of Four Brothers*. The vacation came to an end and he went back to Petersburg.

Meanwhile the *Tale of Four Brothers* passed from hand to hand and finally reached the parish priest, who got alarmed and went to the police. An elaborate investigation was started, and at the end of three months the ownership was traced back to Kibalchich. He was summoned to the police and his rooms were searched. There two trunks were discovered; they were opened and found to be full of prohibited books and pamphlets. Kibalchich explained that he had been asked by a friend to store them and had no knowledge of their contents. This was palpably true, as he would otherwise have got rid of them before going to the police station. But he refused to disclose the name of his friend and was therefore sent to prison pending further enquiries. He was in prison awaiting trial for nearly three years.

One of his fellow-prisoners has left an account of him. He was very earnest, very naïve, fond of long doctrinaire discussions with his fellow-politicals. He made two or three attempts to expound his ideas to the common prisoners as well, but they thought he was mad. He lived in a world of books and abstractions. The other prisoners were intensely excited at the Zasulich affair when it came, but Kibalchich took it calmly. He was studious. He taught himself German, French and English, and read all the scientific books he could get hold of. One day a fellow-prisoner told him it had once been suggested that the revolutionaries should make use of explosives. Kibalchich at once became more animated than his friend had ever seen him.

As the prison grew crowded strict supervision by the authorities was made more difficult. One of the guards was squared and agreed to carry notes between the male and female wards. There was soon a regular post. One day Breshkovskaya, in the women prisoners' wing, received a very long, naïve and academic letter from Kibalchich. She had never heard of him and made enquiries. Her friends told her he was a well-meaning youth but of no importance. She answered him, and a correspondence started. His letters were passed round to the other girls and became a standing joke. They served as comic relief from the rigours of prison. Breshkovskaya kept up the correspondence so as not to hurt his feelings. But as time went on she noticed him growing more and more preoccupied with the idea of terrorist action. In the last letter she had from him, just before her transfer to another prison, he wrote: "I give you my word that I shall devote all my time and all my powers to helping on the revolution by terrorist means. I possess a certain amount of knowledge which will enable me and my comrades to exploit my capabilities in the cause of revolution. Very possibly it will require years of study before my knowledge is sufficiently complete to be of real help. But anyhow I shall go on working until it is."

His last few months in prison were devoted to the intensive study of modern explosives.

II

THERE WERE, as Count Pahlen had feared, a number of participants in the "move to the people" who had escaped both arrest and disillusionment. They were still far from unanimous in their aims and programmes. But they all began to realise, to a greater or less extent, the causes of their failure hitherto.

They recognised that their conceptions of peasant mentality had been false. They saw that the peasants were by no means ripe for the revolt, that they still had a superstitious veneration for the Emperor, and were attached to the idea of private property. They had discovered that Bakunin's doctrinaire pronouncements would not stand the test of experience. Bakunin's stock slumped accordingly, and it was years before any émigré writer again had real influence on the revolutionary movement within Russia.

The surviving Narodniks accordingly modified their tactics. They continued with their move to the people, but no longer as amateurs. Now when they learned a handicraft they took care to learn it well enough to earn a living. Instead of pretending to be shoemakers or carpenters, they became in fact shoemakers and carpenters, settled down singly or in small groups, opened workshops and plied their trade. Some took employment in factories; there were fewer of these, for not many of the young people could stand up to the hard physical work for any length of time. Some took minor posts in the administration, in the municipalities of country towns or as clerks to village communes. Some became village school teachers or *feldshers*.* But in each case their intention was to settle down more or less permanently in the position chosen so as to acquire a wide range of personal contacts in the locality; to get a thorough personal knowledge of the peasants and workmen with whom they lived; to acquire a personal influence over them; to foster their spirit of revolt; to encourage strikes, demonstrations and demands; and thus to prepare the way for a new adjustment of the social order.

At the same time the police campaign had shown them that they must reckon with the relentless hostility of the authorities.

---

* A feldsher occupied the lowest grade in the medical profession. He was not a qualified doctor, but had to pass an elementary medical course.

In order to survive they must master some degree of conspiratorial technique. Forged passports must be well enough forged to deceive a police officer. One must be able to spot a police agent, to realise when one was being followed, to throw the detective off the scent. Little tricks were learnt by hard experience. A man for instance who thought a sleuth was after him could make sure by turning round and staring after every girl that passed. If the police were in full chase there was sometimes a chance of escape by crying "Stop thief!" raising a hue and cry and disappearing in the general confusion. Cyphers came to be used for correspondence, and later on as the police acquired the knack of decoding cyphers the revolutionaries made experiments in secret inks. Those letters of the missive that contained the real message were underlined or ticked in lemon juice or urine: when the paper was warmed these marks became visible. An elaborate system of signals was evolved. Warnings were disguised as ribald scribblings in public lavatories. Flats where revolutionaries could receive visits from their colleagues were always chosen so as to have a window visible from the street, and a prearranged all-clear signal would be set up there. It might be a lamp, a bowl of flowers or a special adjustment of the blind or curtain. If there was any suspicion of trouble the all-clear signal was removed. In case of emergency, such as a police raid, the window glass was broken.

III

By the end of 1876 groups were working in all the larger cities of the country. In Petersburg Plekhanov, the Natansons, Alexander Mihailov and their circle decided that the time had come to set up an organised party. They accordingly formed themselves into the *Zemlya i Volya* (Land and Freedom) secret society. In December the society sponsored a demonstration of workmen and students in the Kazan Square. It was poorly attended but so drastically suppressed by the police as to give valuable publicity to the cause. Zemlya i Volya grew into a revolutionary organisation of some importance.

The name was copied from a secret society of the 'sixties; it was justified in that land and freedom remained the two great objectives. The main principle of the party was that the existing social structure was based on the exploitation of the weak by the strong: it must therefore be replaced by a system under which all land should pass to the collective ownership of peasant communes and all factories and mines to guilds of workers. The statutes of the party provided for a General Council, the supreme authority, and a small elected executive or Administrative Centre. Under the Centre came the various sections, the Section for Peasants, the Section for Workers, the Section for Youth (i.e., students) and the *Dezorganizatorskaya Grupa*. This last, the "Disorganising Group," was to rescue comrades from prison, to deal with spies and traitors, and generally to afford "protection against the arbitrary conduct of officials." It was the first time in the history of the movement that any group had formally implied approval of violence; and it is a sign of the growing exasperation at the policy and methods of the police.

The Zemlya i Volya played an important part in Russian revolutionary history. But it was never a nation-wide party. The General Council never met and the Administrative Centre was never elected. The society remained a group of young revolutionaries based on Petersburg. They were in friendly contact with similar groups in other towns, but there was no effective central authority and no co-ordination of policy or tactics. It became obvious almost at once that there was little cohesion even within the group at Petersburg. The provision of the Disorganising Group had been largely due to the influence of Valerian Osinski, the son of a wealthy landowner in the South. But he soon realised that his Petersburg associates were not yet ready for drastic action, and he left them for the more congenial atmosphere of Kiev.

IV

THE Zemlya i Volya, though lacking in cohesion and discipline, was rich in personalities. Plekhanov became an international figure. Alexander Mihailov died young; but while he lived he exercised an even greater influence on the movement.

When the Zemlya i Volya came into being Mihailov was only twenty. But he had matured early. In his last year at school he had organised a little group of his schoolfellows for the distribution of forbidden literature. They even had their own "secret newspaper." When he went on to the Technical Institute at Petersburg he organised a similar group on the same lines. But the authorities suspected him and he was expelled. This was towards the end of 1875. He went to Kiev and joined up with the local group. But while Osinski was to find the Petersburg comrades too slow and too cautious, Alexander Mihailov was estranged by the slap-dash methods of the Southerners. "Everybody here is a general," he complained. "There are no private soldiers." After a few months he left Kiev, and subsequently spent his time in Petersburg, Moscow and the Volga provinces. He was for several months in a settlement of Old Believers near Saratov and acquired a profound knowledge of the doctrines and ways of life of the sectaries.

In Petersburg he attached himself to the clique that later grew into the Zemlya i Volya. He became devoted to Olga Natanson. This was the one romance of his life. It was entirely platonic. His principles would not allow him to approach a married woman, but he never forgot her and he never cared for anyone else. He was not the type to be involved in passing affairs. "I can't understand," he said, "how people can have sex relations unless they are in love. It seems to me repulsive." Apart from Olga Natanson all his emotions went into the cause. Zhelyabov, who afterwards came to know him better than anyone else, once said of him that he was by nature a poet; that his love of meticulous order and organisation amounted to an "artistic passion." It has been suggested that he would have made an ideal Minister of the Interior in a revolutionary government. He assigned himself the role of watching over the security of members of the party. Once he took a room opposite the Secret Police Headquarters and spent three months with his eyes glued to the window, so as to get to know by sight all the secret police agents and their various disguises. He was insistent on all the comrades being on their guard against "the Russian nature"—i.e., against laziness, carelessness and the tendency to gossip. He himself had the very un-Russian proclivity, when a colleague called to discuss business, of pouring out one glass each of whatever refreshment he happened to have, corking the bottle up again, putting it back in the cupboard and getting straight down to business. Whenever he called on friends he would proceed to go over their home from the point of view of security, inspect the entrance, the warning signals, the manner of storing revolutionary documents, and would make such outspoken criticisms that his hosts were apt to resent them as personal attacks and be disconcerted to find that "Cato the Censor" proposed to share their meal as if nothing had happened. He was an adept at throwing police sleuths off the scent. He got to know Petersburg like the palm of his hand. He knew all the blind alleys, all the hidden passages, all the three hundred odd tenement buildings with a means of egress at the back. He compiled an exhaustive list of sympathisers ready to hide fugitives; he knew the advantages and disadvantages of each individual shelter. He deplored the inveterate tendency of young intellectuals to want to dress the part, and insisted on party members dressing like ordinary individuals and not wearing the long hair, Scotch plaid, high boots and dark spectacles that had come to be the conventional habit of the Nihilist. He would never accept excuses. A comrade once complained that the task allotted was bad for his eyes. Mihailov said: "Carry on till you're blind and then retire." He spared himself as little as others. Over his bed there hung a text: "Do not neglect your duties."

V

IN ONLY one instance was it possible to start any serious movement among the peasants, and that was only made possible by methods which the great majority of the Narodniks found repugnant. The days of Nechaev were over. The aim of the younger generation was to deserve as well as to acquire the complete confidence of the people they had set themselves to serve. But in spite of land-hunger and discontent the peasants had far too great a fear of the authorities and far too high a veneration for the Emperor to be induced to act. Without some deception they would never move.

Stefanovich was the originator and organiser of the "Chigirin affair." After his first journey to the people he had returned to Kiev. In 1875 there had been some unrest in the Chigirin and Cherkassi districts. The police had rounded up certain peasants whom they suspected of being involved, brought them to Kiev and kept them there under observation. Stefanovich got into touch with these peasants and managed by dint of infinite patience and trouble to convince them that he was the Emperor's secret representative. By February, 1876, he had secured their confidence and left Kiev under the pretext of going to report in person to the Emperor.

Deutsch and Bokhanovski were Stefanovich's chief associates in the conspiracy. Debogori-Mokrievich, his companion in the Going to the People, also played a part. In the early spring Deutsch went to Switzerland and got busy with one of the émigré printing presses there. In November Stefanovich came back to Kiev. He brought with him an elaborately printed document, with a gilt border and magnificent seals and the signature of Alexander II at the bottom, in which the Emperor declared his wish to have the land divided up among the peasants, and recommended the latter, for this purpose, to enrol themselves in a Secret League. The Emperor, Stefanovich explained, had wished to distribute the land at the time of the Emancipation; but he had been prevented by the big landowners, the Crown Prince and the officials, who had suppressed the Ukase containing the imperial edict. His Majesty's one hope was in the loyalty of his peasants, who must accordingly organise themselves into a secret federation sufficiently powerful to overthrow their common enemies.

Besides the "Golden Charter" Stefanovich produced printed statutes for the Secret League. Each member must swear an oath of loyalty to the Emperor. Each must pay a monthly contribution of five kopeks. Each must provide himself with a pike or other weapon in preparation for the coming struggle. To give away the secrets of the league was punishable with death, and it was incumbent upon every member to kill a traitor without compunction. Each section of twenty-five members was to elect its section leader. Twenty section leaders elected a hetman. The hetman's duty was to maintain contact with and take orders from the "Imperial Commissar," i.e., Stefanovich himself. The whole movement which, Stefanovich explained, had its ramifications throughout the Empire, was to be directed by the "Committee of Imperial Commissars, consisting of individuals appointed personally by the Emperor, Alexander Nicolaevich." All orders issued by a commissar were to be obeyed implicitly. Disobedience was punishable by death.

The peasants were appalled at this evidence of the impotence of their Emperor. But the magnificent manifesto appealed to their respect for print, and the "commissar's" explanations stilled their suspicions. Early in February, 1877, some of them left Kiev for their villages to start recruiting. They soon reported that the peasants would not believe them and demanded that Stefanovich should come in person. For the moment he remained in Kiev, but sent out a retired non-commissioned officer (a peasant himself and a firm believer in the league) with printed copies of the statutes. This had its effect. Two hundred and fifty peasants declared themselves convinced. They met one night in early March in a lonely field, and with a candle, a cross and a Bible they made their oath and chose their section leaders. At Easter Stefanovich himself made a tour of the district. He brought with him the Golden Charter, and this so stimulated recruiting that the league before long had nearly nine hundred members.

Stefanovich called a meeting of the twenty-eight section leaders. The ex-non-commissioned officer was elected hetman. Some of the section leaders still harboured suspicion, and they wanted Stefanovich himself to take the oath; but when he did so they were satisfied. They asked for money to buy their people arms, and Stefanovich gave them a thousand roubles. He took care to hand it over not as a gift from the Emperor (which would only have encouraged demand for more), but as a loan from a branch of the league in another province. The date of the general rising was fixed for October 1, after the harvest.

In May rumours spread around that something was in the air; a little later the police got hold of some lists of members and a number of peasants were arrested. A special commission with a general as chairman came down to the village concerned to investigate. But the peasants refused to talk; there was no further evidence, and the commission decided that the local police were making a mountain out of a mole-hill. In general the peasants showed themselves well aware of the dangers of leakage. They knew their own weaknesses. In some villages they even insisted on the drink shop being closed. They exhorted each other to keep their womenfolk from gossiping, as the women knew all about the league and had themselves given their oath. The parish priests were regarded as the great danger as far as the women were concerned, and horrid stories went round of priests who plied the younger women with vodka to make them talk.

But the women were not to blame for the eventual collapse. The hetman (the ex-non-commissioned officer) embezzled some of the funds. Stefanovich sent round two delegates to inform the section leaders. The delegates stopped for the night at a village tavern, got drunk, and proceeded to try and recruit a soldier whom they met there. The soldier reported to his officer and was told to pass himself off as a willing recruit. Before long the authorities had enough evidence to start making arrests. On September 4 they caught Stefanovich in one of the villages together with Bokhanovski and Deutsch. They found on them the manifesto, some copies of the statutes, printed forms for the oath and lists of the various officers and members. The rest was easy. The police made a general roundup and preparations were made for a spectacular trial to give all possible publicity to the swindle that had been perpetrated on the peasants.

VI

THE outbreak of the Turkish War in the spring of 1877 brought a new factor into the atmosphere. There was at first a burst of patriotic idealism. The liberation of the Balkan Slavs was a cause that appealed to Russian youth. Most of the revolutionary groups lost, for the time, some of their members who volunteered to serve in the fighting line or in the hospitals at the front. This movement would have been more considerable still if the Government had taken steps to encourage it. But no steps were taken, and in time the first enthusiasm died away. There came rumours, soon to be confirmed, of scandals over army contracts. There were stories of incapacity in the High Command, of needless sufferings by the rank and file, of useless slaughter in front of Plevna. War weariness set in, just as in the Crimean War, and with it resentment against the authorities responsible. The revolutionaries had ammunition for their propaganda. Osinski and his friends amused themselves by going out at night and plastering Kiev with false communiqués of Russian disasters. Ultimately the humiliating Congress of Berlin only served to increase public unrest and dissatisfaction.

Deadlock 65

During this time the revolutionaries were especially concerned with the fate of the colleagues in prison awaiting trial. Some of the latter had been confined for three years or more, and confinement was having its natural effect. Prison conditions were hard. The prisoners became defiant, unruly and difficult to handle. Of the prison officials a few had a streak of sadism, and a great many more were anxious not to prejudice their careers by getting a reputation for being soft. There were ugly incidents. In July of 1877 General Trepov, the Chief of Police, visited the Preliminary Detention Prison. One of the politicals did not stand up to greet him, and Trepov ordered the lad to be stripped and given one hundred lashes in the prison yard. The general public were shocked at the ferocity and doubtful legality of this punishment. Among the revolutionaries tempers rose to boiling point. We hear of a meeting of the Zemlya i Volya called in Petersburg. Alexander Mihailov turned up, pale and set and stammering. "The requisite measures have been put in hand," he said. That was all; he would not give any explanation. What had happened was that Mihailov had got in touch with Osinski at Kiev, and Osinski had taken full responsibility for seeing to the "punishment" of Trepov. Action, however, had to be postponed until the big political trials were over. They did not want to prejudice the prisoners' chances.

This flogging was not the only incident. There were demonstrations and hunger strikes, countered by repression and punishments, one of which was confinement in dark cages over the latrines where the stench was such that few could remain conscious for more than eight hours. Revolutionary writers assert that during this period seventy politicals died in prison before they came to trial. This figure may be exaggerated, but the number was certainly large.

In the late autumn of 1877 the trials at last began. The Going to the People had resulted in many hundreds of arrests, but the majority were dealt with by administrative process. In the end only 243 young people were involved in the two great trials, the Trial of the Fifty in Moscow, and the Trial of the 193 in Petersburg. In each case the prisoners were determined that the trials should give that publicity to the cause which a tied press and a restriction on free speech had so far prevented. They meant, in Plekhanov's words, "to stage a duel between the Administration and the Revolution." The authorities on their side took what steps they could to discredit their opponents. They held a good card in one Gorinovich. He had worked as a Secret Police agent in Kiev in 1876 and had been responsible for a number of arrests. But the revolutionaries identified the traitor, and it was decided to finish with him. They lured him to Odessa, enticed him out at night to a railway siding and set on him with knives. When they had done they rubbed lime in his face to prevent the body being identified and left it, with a ticket pinned on the breast: "This is what happens to spies." But Gorinovich was not dead. He recovered, and the police were able to bring him into court with half his face burnt away, as an atrocity exhibit.

Even so the authorities were anxious about the moral effect of the trials. They took elaborate precautions to minimise publicity. Special restrictions were put on the press. The number of accused and witnesses made it easy to plead lack of space in the court. The public were only admitted by ticket, and it was ensured that only suitable persons received them. But Osinski, who came to Moscow for the Trial of the Fifty, conceived the idea of forging tickets. The first day he packed the court with a hundred of his friends; the second day he wanted to reduce the proceedings to a farce and distributed a thousand tickets. However, the police caught him and locked him up till the trial was over.

The accused at the Trial of the Fifty made the most of their opportunities.

Bardina said:

"Our movement can perhaps be suppressed for the moment, but it will only rise again with greater force. The nation will awake, and take vengeance for what has been done to us. Persecute us if you like, as long as you have the power, but we have the strength of right, of truth, of historic progress, of thought and reason, and that you cannot fasten with your bayonets!"

Alekseev, a factory worker, created an uproar. He spoke of the Emancipation of 1861. "And nowadays," he said, "if we go to our employer and ask for a rise in pay, they accuse us of making a strike and banish us to Siberia. That means we are still serfs. If the employer turns us out and we ask for an account of wages due, they call out the soldiers and turn us out of the district. That means we are still serfs. We can look to no one to help us except the young intellectuals—"

The presiding Judge: "Silence!"

Alekseev (shouting): "But they will march with us until the day comes when a million sturdy workmen clench their fists—"

The Judge: "Silence, I said, silence!"

Alekseev (shouting still louder): "And despotism will be pounded to dust!"

VII

THE Trial of the 193, in which Zhelyabov was involved, took place a few weeks later. He was summoned to surrender to his bail in September and transferred to the Petersburg Preliminary Detention Prison where he spent the four months until his release. The atmosphere within the prison was embittered. There had been mass protests and demonstrations over the flogging affair, and Trepov, to enforce discipline, refused to allow the prisoners to exercise together. He caused little pens, some ten yards by three, to be put up in the prison yard, and the prisoners were taken out to exercise one by one. Thereupon the prisoners refused to leave their cells. Zhelyabov, on arrival, did not know of these arrangements. His first day the warder asked him if he wished to take exercise. He thought it was a curious question, and went down to the yard with the warder. Then a prisoner shouted at him from a window.

"Who are you?"

"Zhelyabov."

"A political?"

"Yes. Awaiting trial."

"Why are you taking exercise? We don't!"

Zhelyabov went straight back to his cell, and there voices shouted to him from other windows to explain the position.

As the time drew near for the hearing there were discussions among the prisoners as to whether they should plead, and thus take the opportunity of expounding their views, or whether they should refuse to plead, with the idea that such refusal would be a more effective protest against the arbitrariness and irregularities of their arrest, detention and trial. In the end 120 of them, including Zhelyabov, decided not to plead.

His fellow-prisoners included several who afterwards became his colleagues in the front rank of the revolutionary movement. There was Perovskaya. She had been arrested in 1874, released on a bail of five thousand roubles, and had spent the intervening period in the Crimea with her mother on a small estate of the latter's which had escaped the wreck of the family fortunes. There she had studied medicine. She worked as a nurse in the public hospital at Simferopol and received her diploma as feldsher in 1877. Kibalchich was also involved in the Trial of the 193. So were Yakimova, Grachevski and Langans. But they had none of them, as yet, attained any particular importance or prestige. The outstanding figure among the 193 accused was undoubtedly Myshkin. Myshkin was the son of a non-commissioned officer and by trade a printer. As early as 1873 he had been engaged in the secret printing of illegal literature. A year later he became an illegal. In 1875 he conceived an idea of rescuing Chernishevski from his place of exile and set off for Eastern Siberia. He arrived at Irkutsk, got himself an officer's uniform and forged papers, went on the fifteen hundred miles to Viluysk, where Chernishevski was detained, and demanded the exile from the local police. It was an ingenious plan but Myshkin had no escort of soldiers with him—he had not sufficient funds to provide for a bogus escort—and that made the local authorities suspicious. They temporised and sent to Irkutsk for confirmation. The trick was discovered. Myshkin put up a fight when they tried to arrest him. But he had to surrender and was kept for two years in prison awaiting trial.

Myshkin was one of those who had determined to speak. He started off to expose the aims and ideals of the movement. The court pulled him up on the grounds that these general considerations were irrelevant to the charge against him. He then complained of ill-treatment from the police while in custody. The court ruled that such matters were outside their jurisdiction. Finally Myshkin lost his temper.

"After all these interruptions from the bench," he said, "I have one, presumably my last, statement to make. I am now convinced that my comrades were right when they refused to plead. It is clear to everyone that the truth cannot be told here and that any attempt by any of the accused to speak frankly will be promptly suppressed. I can say, and I have every justification for saying that this is not a court, it is a farce. It is worse—"

The presiding judge rang his bell and ordered the prisoner to be removed. Myshkin however went on:

"It is worse. It is worse than a brothel where girls sell their bodies to earn a living. Here we have Senators—"

A gendarme officer came to the dock, but Myshkin's fellow-prisoners held the bar and would not let him in. Other gendarmes arrived and there was a fight. The prisoners were at last overpowered and Myshkin was dragged away still shouting: "—Senators, out of cowardice and servility and the hope of promotion and decorations, selling other people's lives, selling truth and justice—"

VIII

THE revelations of police irregularities made their impression on the minds of the court. Judicial integrity overcame the fear of displeasing the powers above, and their decision, pronounced at the end of January, 1878, was a mild one. Ninety-four prisoners (including Zhelyabov) were acquitted and the sentences for most of the others were relatively lenient. Only Myshkin was sentenced to ten years' hard labour.

Osinski arrived in Petersburg to organise the "punishment" of Trepov. But before he had made his arrangements a new development occurred. Vera Zasulich, then living in a village under police supervision, had been profoundly affected by the news of the flogging and had formed a plan of her own. On the day the trial concluded she slipped away to Petersburg. She sought an interview with Trepov, pulled out a revolver and shot him. The general fell to the ground badly wounded and Zasulich threw her pistol away and waited quietly for her arrest.

The affair caused a sensation. The man in the street was inclined to take the line that Trepov had got what he deserved. But to the authorities it seemed obvious proof of the need of more drastic measures. The decisions pronounced in the Trial of the 193 were quashed, and the sentences on the prisoners convicted were made more severe. Fourteen of them were sent to hard labour in Siberia instead of Myshkin only. The Emperor expressed anxiety as to the forthcoming trial of Zasulich.

He feared the jury might prove unreliable and suggested a trial without jury. Count Pahlen, however, pointed out that the jury had only to decide on the facts, and the facts were not in question; Zasulich admitted her guilt. He gave the Emperor his guarantee that the verdict would be appropriate.

The trial took place on April 1. Zasulich had a capable and vigorous counsel. He brought out the idealism of his client's motives, and dwelt with great emphasis on the provocation provided by the brutality of Trepov. In this he had so obviously the sympathy of most of those present that the public prosecutor protested that it was Zasulich and not the general who was in the dock. Finally, as a matter of form, the question was put to the jury; and the jury, against all the evidence, brought in a verdict of not guilty. There was an uproar of applause, the judge had no option but to pronounce Zasulich free, and she was carried out in jubilation. A message was rushed to police headquarters and a body of police sent out to re-arrest her. But the crowd would not let them; there was a free fight in the street, and Zasulich was rescued and hidden. A few weeks later she was smuggled over the frontier.

This trial provoked, very naturally, consternation at Court and in the higher ranks of the bureaucracy. Count Pahlen at once resigned, and his successor, Nabokov, proceeded to "clean up" the Ministry of Justice. A project was considered to give the prosecution the right to veto the representation of the accused by counsel. This was dropped. But in May a ukase transferred to special courts all crimes committed against government officials in connection with their official functions, such crimes to include "murder, attempted murder, wounding, all acts of violence, threats or clamour." Existing legislation already provided for the setting up of such courts. Their composition varied according to the gravity of the offence. The most serious crimes would come before the Senate. But all these courts had one feature in common. There was no jury.

CHAPTER FIVE

REPRISALS

I

EARLY in February a small printed notice was posted up on hoardings in Kiev:
"On the night of February 1–2 at Rostov-on-Don, the spy Akim Nikonov was killed. He was executed by us, Social Revolutionaries.

"Last year Nikonov betrayed to the authorities some thirty of his and our comrades. We regard murder as a terrible counter-measure. But the Administration in its oppression of the Russian People is attacking us, the People's defenders, as if we were wild beasts. Thousands of our martyrs lie dying in prison through the treachery of spies. We are now determined to defend ourselves. Those who follow the example of Nikonov will share his fate. The Administration has left us no choice."

The notice bore the seal of the "Executive Committee of the Russian Social Revolutionary Party." In point of fact there was no such body. The execution had been carried out by Osinski and his friends, and it had occurred to them that their manifesto would be more impressive if it bore a seal with that title. So they designed the seal.

There had already been instances of terrorism in the hot-headed South. We have noted the case of Gorinovich. Terrorism had been approved, at any rate by implication, in the statutes of the Disorganising Group. But this was the first time that the revolutionaries had issued a manifesto publicly proclaiming it as part of their policy.

The choice of this method against secret agents was logical. A police spy was, naturally and invariably, a renegade from the ranks of the movement, and once the police had got hold of him there was no converting him back again. The police watch on their agents was too strict and their hold too tight.

A renegade could never afterwards be trusted.* The only infallible method was to kill him.

The decision to kill was, none the less, a big one. Russia of the 'seventies set a far greater value on human life than is the rule in Europe today. The death penalty in the ordinary criminal courts had been abolished for over a hundred years. In spite of Bakunin and Nechaev, in spite of the verbal ferocity of the Nihilists, the mass of the young Narodniks had a sentimental horror of killing. That a section of them ultimately adopted terrorism as a political weapon was due to their exasperation at the methods of the police, an exasperation canalised into reprisals by the influence and example of Valerian Osinski. Kravchinski (Stepniak) who knew him well, has left us a picture of Osinski. He was very much the young aristocrat. He was tall, fair, slight, extremely beautiful and very dandified. "He loved women and was loved by them." His voice was high, rather mincing, and his manner precious. He used to dangle a gold pince-nez at the end of a black silk ribbon. But he was essentially a fighter. He had a horror of treachery and no compunction whatever at the killing of police spies. At the same time he was an incorrigible romantic; the knight errant in him could not rest content with such small game. It was a disappointment when Zasulich forestalled him with Trepov. He looked around for some other enemy of the people. His choice fell on Kotlyarevski, the Kiev public prosecutor. He made his plans in great secrecy with two of the comrades.

Debogori-Mokrievich in his memoirs gives us an account of the sequel:

"On the night of February 23 I was waked by a knock at the window. I asked who was there, recognised Valerian's voice and went and opened the door. It was a damp, cold night and I hurried back to bed and lit the lamp on the bed table. Valerian came in after me, I could hear by the steps that he was not alone. A minute later Ivan Ivichevich and another comrade followed.

---

* There have been cases where revolutionaries have put the screws on a police spy and been able to use him. In 1883 the renegade Degaev, who had betrayed Vera Figner and a number of others, was employed for the assassination of Colonel Sudeikin. But these instances are rare. In any case the ex-renegade can only be used for one particular job and under the strictest supervision. Incidentally Degaev eventually escaped to America under an assumed name and became a professor of mathematics in the Middle West.

"Valerian came to the bed, bent over me and said Kotlyarevski had been settled.

" 'When?' I asked. I felt quite cold.

" 'Just now. We've come straight back.'

"I got out of bed and pulled the curtains closer so that the light should not be seen from the street. I asked how it happened. Osinski told me Kotlyarevski was walking home. They came up to him close to his house and began to shoot. At the first shot he fell, screaming. They fired two more shots and ran off. Ivichevich wanted to go back with a dagger and make quite sure, but the others would not let him. The man was finished and it was dangerous to wait longer.

"I lay in bed thinking, trying to make myself accept what had happened. But I could not, I was shivering and had a feeling that something was pressing on me.

" 'Do you want to stay the night here?' I asked.

" 'Of course. Where could we go? They're watching all the streets.'

" 'All right. We must put the lights out.'

"They spread coats on the floor and all three lay down. I put the light out.

" 'We'll go to sleep,' I said.

"But I could not sleep. My nerves were on edge. I lay and listened. It was quiet in our street, no clatter of horses, no wheels, no footsteps. Time went by. Suddenly in the distance I heard a rumbling like the roll of drums. I thought it might be drummers sounding the alarm. That new unpleasant feeling came back to me. I sat up in bed to listen better. It is hard to describe that feeling: it was fear, but not so much fear of responsibility and punishment as fear and dislike of what had happened.

" 'Valerian,' I whispered. 'Do you hear?'

" 'Yes.'

" 'Like drums.'

" 'Yes.'

"We said nothing more. I listened but I did not hear the rumbling again. It might have been a cart pulling over the cobbles in the Vladimirskaya. The two others were asleep but not Osinski. I was half asleep myself, but all the time I heard him turning as he lay on the floor and coughing quietly."

Next day it turned out that Kotlyarevski had not been killed, or even hit. He had been terrified and had fallen over screaming. The young Kiev terrorists were new to the game; they had not yet the technique. Osinski affected to dismiss the failure with a laugh at Kotlyarevski's cowardice. But three months later the group killed Captain Heiking, the local chief of gendarmerie.

It was Popko who carried out the sentence. He knew Heiking had gone to a cabaret and waited outside. At midnight Heiking came out with a journalist friend. Popko followed them, caught up with them, stuck a dagger into Heiking and ran. The journalist bolted. Heiking lay on the ground bleeding and shouting for help. A passer-by tried to intercept Popko who fired a shot to get rid of him. The shot brought up the police and people from the surrounding houses, and Popko had to fight his way through—killing a manservant and seriously wounding a policeman. In the end he got away. Heiking died of his wounds two days later.

Debogori-Mokrievich writes: "This time, too, just as after the attempt on Kotlyarevski, I had that same oppressive, uncomfortable feeling. It made it clear to me that I myself was no use for terrorist work. It was odd. I had, naturally, never imagined that a revolution would be bloodless—on the contrary I had always thought that streams of blood would flow. But the whole streams of blood shed in a popular rising did not seem to me nearly as terrible as the few stains I saw on the pavement next day."

II

It was not forgotten that the first duty allotted to the Disorganising Group had been the rescue of comrades from custody. Osinski was especially concerned over Stefanovich, Deutsch and Bokhanovski, still in the Kiev prison. They were his personal friends. They were workers of outstanding value to the cause, and their abduction would mean a resounding blow to the prestige of the Administration.

The first step was to get into communication with the prisoners. Fortunately one of the warders could be bribed. The revolutionaries nicknamed this intermediary "The Dove." Apart from his functions as messenger of peace he possessed another quality of the pigeon tribe: he seemed capable of consuming his own weight in food and drink. Debogori-Mokrievich has left us a description:

"The Dove was a fat, stupid, good-natured creature, but he served us well for comparatively little money. When he came with letters to Osinski's room he at once sat down to the cold meal waiting for him. He ate and drank everything there was and then lay on Osinski's bed and went to sleep until the answer was ready. Valerian used to answer the letters in great detail and in very small handwriting on 'conspiratorial paper.' We used a special very thin paper for this purpose to make it easier to smuggle through the prison gates. Everybody was searched when they went through the gates—even the warders. Osinski often spent a whole evening writing his answer. When he had done he woke the man up, gave him the letter and a rouble for himself and sent him off again.

"It was by no means easy to organise an escape from the Kiev prison. For a time we thought we should never be able to do it. It was no use trying to dig an underground passage or bore through a wall. The building was too massive. It was only when we got to know the details of the prison organisation that we were able to work out a plan—on entirely original lines. The warders who looked after the prisoners were taken on locally: they were not part of any police or military establishment. The day warders came off duty at a fixed hour every evening and the night warders relieved them. This gave us the idea of getting the prisoners out of the building disguised as warders. But the head warder, who supervised the relief, would have to be in the secret. At first we hoped he might be bribed. One or two discreet approaches were made to him. But he would not nibble, and we realised we should have to think of something else."

It was in February of 1878 that the first step forward was made. It was of obvious advantage to have a man of their own on the prison staff. Frolenko, one of the revolutionaries, went to the prison with forged identity papers and asked for a job. He was taken on as odd handy man. He showed himself to be intelligent and reliable, and was promoted to be warder in the criminal division. A fortnight later he was transferred to the politicals. He made every effort to gain the confidence of his superiors. He arranged with Stefanovich that he should catch him writing a note to be smuggled out of prison. Frolenko was commended for his zeal, and he reinforced his good impression by the indignation he showed when he found that Stefanovich was not to be punished. (The prison governor had been rattled by the attack on Kotlyarevski and was anxious to give the revolutionaries no pretext for an attempt on himself.)

But Frolenko, however well established, could do nothing alone and the head warder remained incorruptible. By this time it was evident that, if he could be got rid of, Frolenko was well in the running to succeed him; so they endeavoured to bring about his removal. They tried to exploit the governor's fear of offending the politicals. The prisoners invented all sorts of misdeeds on the unfortunate head warder's part and complained to the governor. The head warder was called up, his denials were not accepted, and he was reprimanded and threatened. But he was not dismissed. They hoped that he would at least try and get his own back on the prisoners for these false accusations, and do something to give grounds for a real charge. But he was as patient as he was incorruptible. "Jesus Christ suffered," he said, "and I must suffer too." He was hopeless. And the longer they waited the greater the risk to their attempt. Frolenko's real identity was known to a number of the prisoners. There was the danger that some indiscretion might lead to his discovery.

Osinski finally devised a plan for getting rid of the head warder. Debogori-Mokrievich carried it through. First they made enquiries as to their victim's past. They found he had been formerly employed in a local factory. They knew he was a heavy drinker, and they located his favourite bar. Debogori-Mokrievich in the guise of a gentleman of means and accompanied by a manservant, put up at one of Kiev's best hotels. The "servant" visited the bar concerned and picked up an acquaintance with the head warder. Two nights later he brought him back to the hotel. Debogori-Mokrievich explained that he owned a distillery in the country, that the post of head foreman there was vacant and that he (the head warder) had been recommended for the job by his former employer. The wages were higher than those paid by the prison. The fact of the business being a distillery was also an inducement. The job had to be taken or refused at once, and the head warder took it. He announced his resignation to the prison authorities. He handed his identity papers to Debogori-Mokrievich and received an advance of ten roubles on his wages. He was told to look out for and engage two new hands for the distillery, and to wait in Kiev for his new employer's return at the end of the following week, when they would all travel down to the country together. Upon which the bogus proprietor and his servant drove off to the station.

Frolenko was duly appointed as successor. The governor himself informed Stefanovich of the new appointment, and Stefanovich, to avert possible suspicion, protested the man was a common spy. There was, however, no time to be lost: the distillery story was bound to be exploded before long, quite apart from other dangers. It was decided to disguise the three prisoners as soldiers. Frolenko could only find two military uniforms. The odd man must pose as a workman coming off a job.

The night came. Stefanovich, Deutsch and Bokhanovski put on their disguises and arranged dummies in their beds. But the night warder kept hanging about in the corridor where the prisoners had their cells. Finally Stefanovich dropped, as if by accident, some papers out of his window. Frolenko told the night warder to go into the yard and pick them up and take them to the governor's office. That gave them the time to slip out. The other night warders had been drinking and were asleep. The four men went along the corridors towards the gateway. One of the corridors was pitch dark. Bokhanovski stumbled, put out his hand to save himself and caught hold of a rope. There was a clang. It was the rope of the alarm bell. Down below they heard the sergeant on duty calling out the guard. Frolenko told the others to lie flat in the dark along the wall and himself hurried off to the gate. He explained he had rung the bell by accident. When all was quiet again he went back for his friends.

They had no more trouble. On hearing Frolenko's voice the gatekeeper handed the key out to let him open the gate himself. Two streets away Osinski was waiting with a horse and cart.

That evening Debogori-Mokrievich was sitting in his room:

"Late in the night there was a knock at my window. I went to the door and saw Frolenko.

" 'What happened?' I asked.
" 'They got away.' He came into my room.
" 'How?' I asked.
" 'As we'd planned it.'

"It seemed so simple that I could hardly believe it was true. Frolenko's face showed no animation: only his eyes were very bright. I asked him how far he had gone with them.

" 'Down to the Dnieper. But, my God, that horse you got us. I was hitting him the whole way. He wouldn't go. My arm will be quite stiff. Lend me your scissors, I must cut my beard off.'

"He took the scissors and began cutting at his beard."

Osinski had arranged for a boat, with stores and a change of clothes, and the three fugitives rowed themselves to Kremenchug. It took them a week. They tied up at the bank at night. In the daytime whenever they saw the smoke of a steamer in the distance they pulled in to the side and hid in the reeds. Osinski went to Kremenchug by rail and met them with money and passports.

The unfortunate ex-head warder had his identity papers returned by post, with a note that other arrangements had been made at the distillery, and his services were no longer required. The sum of fifteen roubles was enclosed in view of any inconvenience which he might have suffered.

III

PEROVSKAYA was less fortunate in her attempts to organise rescues. She was one of those acquitted in the Trial of the 193. The police at once tried to arrest her again but she eluded them and became an "illegal." She was member of a group who planned the rescue of Myshkin; the idea was to attack the convoy escorting him to the penal prison and carry him off. But the authorities got wind of the idea and smuggled Myshkin away before the coup was ready.

Perovskaya then went to Kharkov to try to organise escapes from the prison there. She managed to get into communication with the prisoners. She and her associates learned one of the prisoners was due for transfer to another prison and they prepared their attempt. One young man dressed himself up as an officer and went off, with two others as orderlies, in a troika, to intercept the cart with the prisoner and escort. They caught them up some miles out of Kharkov and demanded the prisoner. But the sergeant in charge of the escort was suspicious. Finally one of the bogus orderlies drew his pistol and fired; the bullet grazed one of the horses of the police cart and they went off at full gallop down the road with the revolutionaries after them, shooting. In those early days the revolutionaries were bad pistol shots and seldom seemed able to get hold of good horses. They could neither register a hit nor catch the police cart. They chased it nearly to the next police post, and then a squad of police came after them and they had difficulty in getting back safe themselves. They had to report their failure to Perovskaya and she was furious at this exhibition of male incompetence and cowardice.

She intended to make another attempt; but first she went back to the Crimea to see her mother. The police were watching the house and arrested her. They knew nothing of her Kharkov adventures, but she was a suspicious character, and they exiled her to the Archangel province by administrative process. Two gendarmes escorted her on her two thousand mile journey. She had opportunities to escape between Simferopol and Petersburg, but the gendarmes were "nice," and she did not want to get them into trouble. However they were relieved and the gendarmes on the last lap were less considerate. The party had to spend a night at a small station en route. The stationmaster found them a room. One gendarme lay down at the door and the other at the window. Soon they were both snoring. But they had not noticed, as Perovskaya had, that the door opened outwards. So she opened the door and stepped over the gendarme into freedom. She timed her move as a train for Petersburg was due and climbed onto it. The guard made a fuss at her having no ticket, but she was good at playing the stupid peasant girl and he did not suspect her.

She went back to Kharkov. She was still busy with plans of rescue. Meanwhile she organised a service to smuggle in food and clothing to the politicals in prison, and co-operated with the other Zemlya i Volya adherents in the town. She held meetings for students and for workmen. She went through a midwife's course so as to qualify still further for her work among the people. A contemporary has described her as looking very young for her age with blonde hair and a pink and white complexion. She was serious and meticulous, and indefatigable in her work. She would go to every shop in Kharkov to make sure of getting the best value for what money she had to spend on the prisoners. She had a strong will of her own, and a low opinion of male intelligence and reliability. She was tidy, exact, and punctual, and demanded these qualities from her comrades. If one of them turned up at a meeting in dirty boots he got into trouble. She would have made an excellent governess.

There turned out to be innumerable difficulties in the way of a rescue from the Kharkov prison. She appealed to the group in Petersburg for help and money. They had none to send her and the idea of rescue had to be abandoned. She spent the next few months partly in Petersburg and partly in the provinces, trying to extend the Zemlya i Volya organisation and to overcome the apathy of the peasants. But the police were getting more and more active and work for the cause became increasingly difficult.

IV

THE Zasulich affair opened the eyes of a number of young revolutionaries to the possibilities of revenge on the police. Kravchinski had left Russia in 1875 to go and help the South Slav insurgents in the Balkans. He was still abroad at the time of the attack on Trepov; but it made a great impression on him and he wrote an article extolling Zasulich as a heroine. He returned to Russia in the middle of Osinski's campaign in Kiev. He was indignant at the arbitrary extension of the penalties imposed upon those convicted in the Trial of the 193. Then there occurred ugly incidents in the Peter and Paul Fortress, and a number of politicals imprisoned there went on hunger strike. In both cases Kravchinski considered General Mezentsev, Chief of the Third Section and the Gendarmerie, to be responsible. He conceived the idea of killing Mezentsev and discussed it with Alexander Mihailov. Mihailov encouraged him and offered his help. But it was some time before he could make up his mind.

It was the Kovalski affair which decided him. Kovalski and some fellow-revolutionaries in Odessa had set up a clandestine printing press. In January (immediately after the attack on Trepov) the police had raided them. Kovalski offered armed resistance but was overpowered. In July he was brought up before a special court and sentenced to death. It was the first "political" death sentence within memory, apart from cases of attempts on the life of the Emperor. On July 24 there were mass protests in the streets of Odessa. The police were ordered to fire into the crowd and a workman was killed. Four days later Kovalski was hanged; and in Petersburg Kravchinski and his friends made their final arrangements for Mezentsev.

The attempt was organised by Alexander Mihailov, and in design and execution it was a pattern for an enterprise of its kind. Mezentsev's movements and habits were closely watched before they laid their plans. Kravchinski was the sole assailant. Barannikov, another member of the group, acted as his bodyguard. A third revolutionary was at hand with a horse and trap. This time they did not make the mistake of using an inferior animal. Their horse, "Varvar," had won trotting races and had already done good service to the cause.

At 9 A.M. on the morning of August 4, General Mezentsev, as was his custom when the weather was fine, was walking towards his office with his adjutant. Kravchinski followed him, caught up with him, pushed a dagger into his vitals and ran off towards the carriage. The adjutant gave chase. Barannikov drew his revolver and fired. He headed off the adjutant, but the horse took fright at the shooting and bolted. It was with difficulty that the driver pulled him up, but he managed to do so. Kravchinski and Barannikov jumped in and they all got clean away. Mezentsev died almost immediately.

On the same day a pamphlet was issued with the title "A Death for a Death." It had been composed by Kravchinski himself and printed on the press of the *Zemlya i Volya*. It set forth the motives of the assassination. Incidentally it is an interesting record of Kravchinski's social and political views. "We are socialists," it states. "Our aim is the destruction of the existing economic status and the removal of social injustice. . . . Political forms in and for themseves are to us a matter of indifference. . . . We consider that it is not political slavery that is the cause of the present economic slavery, but the reverse." The pamphlet goes on to set out the various crimes of the gendarmerie against the people and against the people's champions, and to emphasise the personal responsibility of Mezentsev. It concludes with a warning to the Administration: "Do not interfere in our struggle with the bourgeoisie, and we will leave you in peace."

The assassination of the chief of the all-powerful Third Section in broad daylight and in one of the main streets of the capital was the hardest blow that the revolutionaries had so far struck. The Emperor was all the more inclined to feel it as a personal attack on himself since Mezentsev had enjoyed his confidence and friendship. In the first moment of grief and anger he declared that all newspapers throughout the Empire must be suppressed. A meeting of the Committee of Ministers was hurriedly called. They realised that such a measure would only increase the public alarm, but no one wished to argue with the Emperor in his present state of mind. A tame journalist was sent for, and hurriedly composed a special article for *Golos*. With some trepidation the draft was taken to the palace. The Emperor approved, and desired that all the newspapers should publish articles on the same lines. The necessary instructions were given and the newspapers did as they were told.

But more concrete measures were also taken. An edict was published to provide for the trial by a military court of all offences against the State or against State officials. Some time later the procedure of military courts was tightened up. The preliminary examination might be omitted, oral evidence of witnesses became no longer essential, and sentences might be carried out at once, without confirmation from above. In this way a political might be arrested, tried and executed within twenty-four hours.

On August 20 an Appeal to the Nation was published in the *Official Gazette:*

"The Authorities in spite of recent evidence of propaganda of a criminal nature, have shown a remarkable patience. These propaganda activities have been dealt with by the courts through the normal procedure and the Authorities have refrained from taking any special measures . . .

"Their patience is now at an end . . .

"The Authorities cannot and should not mete out to those who deride the law and spurn all that is dear and holy to the

Russian People the treatment they reserve for the loyal subjects of the Russian Emperor . . .

"The Authorities will take action with the utmost firmness and severity against whomsoever may be shown to be guilty of or implicated in machinations against the existing system of government, against the basic principles of social and family life and against the rights of private property as established by law . . .

"The Authorities accordingly appeal to all classes of the Russian People for their unanimous support in the struggle to root out this evil and to save the Nation from the contamination of the most pernicious of opinions and the most appalling of crimes . . ."

In November the Emperor himself, on the advice of Count Tolstoi, made a personal appeal on similar lines at an assembly of the representatives of the various classes at Moscow.

V

THE appeals to the nation fell flat. Their only direct consequence was to provoke a move on the part of the liberals. A certain number of the Zemstva contained a majority of members of progressive views. In these it was decided to make the appeals the occasion for a request for constitutional reform. The Kharkov Zemstvo sent in a petition in which the Emperor was implored to "grant to his faithful subjects what he had granted to the Bulgars"—an allusion to the new Bulgarian Constitution. The petition was not well received. The Minister of the Interior immediately circularised provincial presidents of nobility—who were ex-officio chairmen of the Zemstva—that no motion should be passed by a Zemstvo unless approved beforehand by the chairman. This was followed up by a secret circular that no motion on the lines of that of the Kharkov Zemstvo was to be discussed at all.

The outstanding figure of the Zemstvo of Chernigov was Petrunkevich. This liberal-minded landowner determined to find out at first hand what the extreme revolutionaries were thinking. He went to Kiev, got into touch with the terrorist group and had secret meetings with Osinski and Alexander Mihailov. They assured him that terrorist action had been provoked solely by official arbitrariness and brutality, and that they asked for nothing more than the chance to propagate their views by peaceful means. Petrunkevich returned home and drafted an Address to the Crown to be put to the Zemstvo.

The address emphasized the Zemstvo's devotion and loyalty to the Emperor and the deep concern with which it viewed the recent manifestations of unrest. It went on, however:

"The public can only combat subversive ideas if the public itself has weapons. These weapons are the spoken and written word and freedom of opinion. At present subversive ideas are propagated by a clandestine press and by word of mouth. But public opinion has no means of self-expression . . .

"Such is the position in Russia. With no tradition of respect for the law, with no security guaranteed by the law, with no means to exercise criticism, the general public in Russia is an inert and unco-ordinated mass, incapable of any form of positive action. Accordingly the Zemstvo of Chernigov must, to its great regret, confess itself impotent to take practical measures in the struggle with undesirable social influences, and must bring this fact to the knowledge of the authorities."

The Zemstvo held an unofficial session and approved the Address with only two dissentient votes. It was arranged that Petrunkevich should put it formally to the official session on the following day. That night he submitted it to the chairman. The chairman declared he could not allow the motion to be put as it was contrary to regulations. Petrunkevich asked what law forbade a provincial assembly to petition the Crown. The chairman replied:

"There is no law, but I have instructions from the Minister of the Interior which, for me, have the force of law."

"If there is no law I will put my motion."

"In that case I will take the necessary measures."

When Petrunkevich arrived next day for the official session he found the public had been refused admission. There was a detachment of gendarmes at the door and more gendarmes inside the hall. When the session was opened members protested against the presence of the gendarmes. The chairman replied that they were there at the governor's instructions. Amid general excitement Petrunkevich began to read his motion. The chairman called on him to stop, and, on his refusal, declared the session closed and ordered the gendarmes to clear the hall. Petrunkevich had copies made of the address and sent them to all the Zemstvo in the Empire. The police thereupon arrested Petrunkevich, his Chernigov associates and those responsible for the Kharkov petition, and exiled them by administrative process to the northern provinces. In this way, in the official phraseology, "order was restored to the provinces affected by fermentation."

VI

IT IS reasonable to conclude that the year after Zhelyabov's acquittal was for him a period of frustration and unhappiness. He had seen the collapse of the movement to the people. He had seen the failure of the attempts to make headway in the ensuing years. He had, during his imprisonment and trial, come for the first time into touch with leaders of the movement from all parts of the Empire, and the experience must have been disappointing. There was still no cohesion and little sense of realities. There was no effective counter-weapon against the ruthlessness and vigour of the Secret Police. The Narodniks with their hope of an ultimate peasant rising were, to use his own term, "like fish, beating their heads against the ice."

It is probable that his despondency was increased by a consciousness of his own impotence. Six years before, during the Bogishich affair at the university, he had been a leader. Since then he had done next to nothing and during the years of obscurity his self-assurance had dwindled. It is significant that he made no impression on his fellows at the Trial of the 193. At that time he had little ground for confidence either in the future of the movement or in his prospect of making a personal contribution to it.

In the summer of 1878 Osinski and his friends were the only revolutionary group of real importance in South Russia. They were often in Odessa where Zhelyabov met them. He had not yet committed himself to the approval of terrorism as a weapon. All the same he must have been tempted to adhere to their group. But there was the personal factor. He did not like Osinski. We do not know of any quarrel; probably there was none. Possibly Osinski never realised that anything was wrong. Osinski, the aristocrat, the acknowledged revolutionary leader, doubtless put out his conscious charm and was kindly and condescending. But Zhelyabov, the ex-house serf, with his old hatred of landowners, his egotism, his ambition, his consciousness of personal failure, must have seen the condescension, resented it, and come to hate Osinski; and his dislike opened his eyes to all the amateurishness, the lack of method, the pointlessness that lay behind the courage and idealism of Osinski's crusade.

As always he tried to drown his nervous despondency by hard physical work. In May, 1878, a friend of his had taken a farm near Kamenets-Podolsk. Zhelyabov rented a market garden nearby. His wife and child were with him. They employed no labourers and did all the work themselves. Zhelyabov used to get up at sunrise and work sixteen hours a day. In the evenings he would walk into the next village and talk to the peasants. But he had little success. After the day's work he had no vitality left to propagate the social revolution. The peasants, too, had been at work all day and were too tired to listen. He admitted his failure. "As long," he said, "as the peasant has to work as he does to get himself a crust of bread you will never turn him into a political animal."

In the autumn, worn out and discouraged, he came back to Odessa. He started again on the weary round of trying to give private lessons for a living. He got into debt. The police were watching him but he still managed to hold secret classes for the dock workmen. One of his revolutionary friends, Semenyuta, at last succeeded in forcing him to take a loan of fifty roubles from revolutionary funds to pay off his more pressing debts. Semenyuta was convinced of his potential value to the cause and tried several times to bring him and Osinski together. But Zhelyabov always made some excuse. Once when Semenyuta was persistent he said straight out: "I don't like him. You know I don't like him. He's too finicky. Besides, you'll have all your other grand friends. I'll come some time when there's no one else."

He slept badly and he liked to sit up half the night talking to Semenyuta. We have a record of one of these talks.

"History," said Zhelyabov, "moves too slowly. It needs a push. Otherwise the whole nation will be rotten and gone to seed before the liberals get anything done."

"What about a constitution?"

"All to the good."

"Well, what do you want—to work for a constitution, or to give history a push?"

"I'm not joking. Just now we want to give history a push."

VII

IN THE north Alexander Mihailov became more and more convinced of the efficacy of terrorist action. So did Morozov, one of the editors of the clandestine *Zemlya i Volya* newspaper. He started publishing articles in favour of violence, to the indignation of Plekhanov, who was anti-terrorist. Mihailov found the money to start another paper, the *Listok Zemli i Voli*, where Morozov could develop his views. Round them there formed an inner ring, the "Death or Freedom" group, or "Troglodites," with Kviatkovski, Tikhomirov, Yakimova, Shiraev, Barannikov, Ivanova and Isaev. Kravchinski had to go abroad again, the police were too hot after him, but they looked round for further recruits. One of the first was Kibalchich. Kibalchich, after waiting three years in prison for his trial, was convicted of having had in his possession a prohibited book and was sentenced to two months. He was finally released in June. One of his prison friends put him in touch with Kviatkovski, who advised him to go on with his studies and await events. Kibalchich duly applied for re-admission to the Medical School. His application was still going the round of official pigeon-holes when in August, following the murder of Mezentsev, an edict was issued that all persons who had at any time been "involved in subversive political activities" should be banished from the capital. Kibalchich had the choice of leaving Petersburg or becoming an "illegal." He chose the latter. Kviatkovski and Mihailov gave him enough to live on out of revolutionary funds and he continued his studies of explosives. Later they set him up in a small, secret workshop and he began to manufacture dynamite. Next year the Narodnaya Volya was formed and Kibalchich became its technical expert.

That remained his sole function. He retained his interest in political theory and composed a number of articles on the development of local self-government and similar social and administrative questions. But he had little influence on the policy of the group. His task was to run the laboratories and be responsible for the production of explosive, and this he performed with great efficiency. He did his share of the actual manual work though he was too clumsy to do it well. Shiraev, Isaev and Sukhanov were better workmen. But he was an erudite and resourceful chemist and an admirable laboratory director, and his results astonished the government experts who afterwards examined them.

He lived a quiet, regular life. He insisted on thoroughness and punctuality in the workrooms. Outside he remained to the end earnest, unpractical and somewhat childlike. In many ways he was the stock professor of the comic magazines. He invariably wore an incredibly shabby top hat. He cared nothing about his meals, and had no idea of personal comfort. More than once, when it was his turn to do the marketing, he went into a brown study and spent the money on scientific books instead of on provisions. The girl comrades regarded him as a joke, but he seldom realised they were laughing at him. He took little notice of them except to keep them up to their laboratory work. The only feminine interest he ever had was his ideological correspondence with Breshkovskaya.

Another invaluable recruit was Kletochnikov, a minor official from Penza. At his subsequent trial Kletochnikov gave the following account of his early life:

"Up till the age of thirty I lived in the provinces and consorted with other officials. We spent our time drinking and running after women. This mode of life became disgusting to me and I wished for something better. So I came to Petersburg. But the general moral standard in Petersburg seemed no higher."

It was in Petersburg that he became a convert to the revolutionary cause and asked Alexander Mihailov what he could do to help. The sequel, by a combination of good judgment and good luck, was of considerable importance. Alexander Mihailov suspected a certain colonel's widow of working in with the Secret Police. She let lodgings, going out of her way to attract young tenants, and all of these tenants who had any connection with the revolutionary movement were inevitably arrested. Mihailov told Kletochnikov to take rooms there and watch. Kletochnikov did so, and managed, with some difficulty, to conceal the intense dislike which his landlady inspired in him. He soon discovered she was devoted to cards, and, especially, to winning. He made a point of losing a rouble or two every night. He noticed that she became attached to him. When he complained of being unable to find work and of having soon to return to his home in the provinces she was genuinely distressed. He ascribed his failure to find employment to his loyal conservative views, no longer fashionable in the corrupt and liberal capital. One night he said bluntly that his money was coming to an end and he would have to go home the following week. The widow in her zeal to keep him asked if he knew of any young people with subversive ideas. If he did he might be of interest to friends of hers.

Kletochnikov consulted Alexander Mihailov. They knew of one young revolutionary who was aware that he was being watched already. There being nothing more to give away in his case it was arranged that Kletochnikov should report on him. He did. The widow was delighted. She invited "her friend" round, and the latter, a Secret Police officer, after cross-examining Kletochnikov, engaged him for one month on probation as an outside agent at a salary of thirty roubles. Kletochnikov, after a proper show of hesitation, took it on. The month went by; he produced a number of anodyne reports about the suspect, but he realised that his employer wanted more results; and meanwhile he himself was allowed no opportunity to learn anything about the Secret Police organisation. The experiment seemed doomed to failure. At the end of the month he expected to be fired. But it happened that the Third Section wanted a confidential junior clerk. Kletochnikov's neat and legible handwriting had made an excellent impression. (This was before the days of typewriters.) He had given the impression of being steady and loyal. He was offered the job.

Thus he found himself appointed to the Investigations Department of the Secret Police. His immediate superior, finding him accurate, conscientious and reliable, was only too glad to let him do most of the work. This consisted of copying and summarising the reports sent in by the Third Section's secret agents. Kletochnikov was soon able to give Mihailov not only a complete list of the secret agents in Petersburg but also frequent warning of intended arrests and police raids.

He soon showed his worth. A certain Khalturin, a workman

of peasant origin, made the first serious attempt in Russia to form a trade union, the Northern Workers' Union. He was a man of intelligence and energy and secured some sixty members and a number of sympathisers. His aim was to improve the lot of the workers. He was not a "political." It was not till a year afterwards that Zhelyabov recognised and proclaimed, "In Russia a strike is a political act." Khalturin was opposed to terrorism. "We start a show going," he said, "and then bang—the intellectuals shoot off at somebody and the police are after us." He determined to start a secret workers' newspaper in connection with his union. Press and type were acquired; in December the first number was set up and printed. But before it could be distributed the police made a raid. They captured the press and arrested Khalturin's chief associates. He himself escaped by the skin of his teeth.

Kletochnikov was able to ascertain that it was a secret agent of the name of Reinstein who had betrayed the venture. He reported to Alexander Mihailov, and the Death or Freedom group determined on action. Reinstein was traced to Moscow where he posed as a revolutionary. Two emissaries went down to settle him. Reinstein was wary and it was some weeks before they could act. But at last they lured him to an empty flat, under pretext of a very confidential revolutionary meeting, and there they killed him.

VIII

THE tempo of terrorist action quickened. "We can do anything," Mihailov remarked, "if we are not afraid of death." The next move, early in 1879, came from one Goldenberg, a little Ukrainian Jew. He was sincere and had courage; his defects as a revolutionary were muddle-headedness, excitability and an intense vanity which could not be suppressed. News came from Kharkov of the flogging of students in the prison there, and Goldenberg determined to kill Prince Dmitri Kropotkin, the Kharkov Governor General. First he went to Kiev to get Osinski's backing. Osinski does not seem to have been very sanguine but he took the line that there was no harm in trying. He gave Goldenberg a revolver and money. As it happened it was his last revolutionary act; soon afterwards he was arrested.

Goldenberg went to Kharkov, installed two associates in a "conspiratorial quarter," * and waited for his chance. He followed the Governor General about. Once when the Prince's carriage was waiting outside a government office he got into conversation with the coachman. They discussed the horses, why the Prince was thinking of selling them and what they were likely to fetch. But it was some time before Goldenberg found his chance to shoot. Either the range was too long, or it was too dark; once, in the theatre, he could have shot but he was afraid of hitting the Prince's wife and daughter. At last, on February 9, there was a reception at the new school which His Excellency had consented to attend.

Goldenberg followed him there, but still could not see his opportunity. He went out and waited on a bench in a public park a few hundred yards from the Governor General's residence. It was a still and frosty night. Presently he heard the sound of hooves and saw the familiar carriage and horses. He ran up, caught hold of the shaft with one hand and fired through the window. He had meant to empty his revolver, but the horses bolted and he fell. He went back to the conspiratorial quarter, changed his clothes and slipped out of Kharkov. A few hours later Prince Kropotkin died of his wounds. The whole enterprise, as Goldenberg pointed out afterwards, cost exactly 520 roubles.

IX

GOLDENBERG arrived in Petersburg in a high state of exaltation and declared that he was now ready to kill the Emperor. But the Troglodites had already had two similar offers, one from a Pole, Kobilianski, and one from a Russian, Soloviev, as excitable and as obstinate as Goldenberg, who had just come back from a mission in the villages and was burning to avenge the victims of the Trial of the 193. Mihailov told all three of them to have patience. He himself was then busy with preparations for an attempt on General Drenteln, Mezentsev's successor as Chief of the Third Section. The attempt was made and failed.

* A "conspiratorial quarter" was the temporary headquarters of a revolutionary enterprise. It was a flat or house, taken by two members of the group, a man and a woman giving themselves out as a married couple. It was used for meetings, preparations, changes of disguise, and sometimes as a temporary hiding place. On conclusion of the enterprise it would be abandoned.

Mirski, the assailant, was arrested. Mihailov methodically passed on to the next task, and asked Kviatkovski and Zundelevich to act as a committee and to consider the proposed attack on the Emperor. They gave their opinion that the assault should be made by someone of pure Russian blood; an attack by a Pole or a Jew was likely to be followed by drastic racial reprisals. In any case, they added, Soloviev seemed to them the better man for the task. Soloviev himself was indignant that any other candidate should even be considered. "Only I satisfy all the conditions," he said. "I must do it. This is my work. Alexander II is mine and I will not give him up to anybody." Goldenberg saw the force of the racial argument. He asked, however, to act as Soloviev's assistant, but this was refused.

Throughout March a number of meetings were held to discuss the attempt. The revolutionaries were then, relatively speaking, in funds, and the meetings were held in private rooms in various hotels and restaurants. The first question was whether Soloviev should act alone, or with the co-operation of others. It was decided to let it be an individual effort. His friends would merely provide the revolver and have a horse and cart ready to get him away. The second question was whether the attempt should or should not be made in the name of the Zemlya i Volya. This was an important matter of principle. The society as such, had so far carried out no terrorist action. The *Listok Zemli i Voli* had announced the execution of Reinstein "by order of the Executive Committee." But this "Executive Committee" was a myth. All that there was of it was a seal with that inscription in the possession of Morozov, who was imitating the manifestoes of Osinski at Kiev.

Alexander Mihailov and his group were in favour of having the party committed. He called a plenary session and proposed that the party should assume full responsibility for the attempt. Plekhanov and the moderates were horrified. Popov declared that if the preparations went on they would warn the victim. Kviatkovski asked him if he meant to become a police spy. "If that is a threat," Popov said, "we can shoot as well as you can." At once there was an uproar. Mihailov heard a hammering at the front door. "The police!" he shouted. "Are we going to defend ourselves?" That brought unity; all agreed that they would resist arrest. But it was not the police. It was the porter come to see what all the noise was about.

There was therefore no party sanction, but there was no cancellation of the attempt.

On the morning of April 2 Mihailov took up an observation post with a view of the front of the palace. Alexander II came out for his morning walk. Soloviev ran up and opened fire. The Emperor dodged and ducked: in the words of the official report His Imperial Majesty "proceeded in a zig-zag manner, moving now to the right now to the left." He was too quick for his assailant (who was a poor revolver shot) and escaped with a hole through his clothing. Soloviev was seized and disarmed. Four days later the "Executive Committee" published a manifesto—which was sent through the post to Drenteln and the other officials concerned—giving warning that any attempt to extract information from Soloviev by torture would be punished by death. Soloviev was tried by court martial in May and hanged on May 28.

CHAPTER SIX

THE NEW PARTY

I

THE answer to Soloviev's attempt—the first direct assault on the Emperor for thirteen years—was an imperial edict dividing European Russia into six districts each under a governor general with plenary powers. Plekhanov and his friends regarded this as a set-back to the cause and maintained that acts of violence could only lead to reprisals and alienate moderate opinion. But the terrorists were bent on going further. Terrorism, they insisted, was positive. It was the only means of "waking up the drowsy Empire," of doing away with the fatalism and inertia that were even greater enemies to the cause than the Third Section. It would show the people what the revolutionaries could do, it would inspire an active faith, and it would shatter the prestige of the Administration. Morozov expanded these ideas in a series of articles in the *Listok Zemli i Voli*.

There was thus every danger of a split in the party. In Alexander Mihailov's view terrorism was not the only issue. He considered a new policy was necessary, a new centralised and co-ordinated effort. It was obvious in any case that things could not go on as they were, and it was decided to hold a conference of the party leaders to decide on the future of the movement. After some discussion date and place were fixed for Voronezh at the end of June.

Mihailov foresaw two dangers. The conference might peter out in talk; on the other hand the Death or Freedom clique might be outvoted and be forced to toe the line. He hit on the idea of a preliminary conference of those who shared his views, who could then go on to Voronezh as a compact determined group and override any opposition. He wanted, however, this group to be representative of the whole Empire, not merely of his own little set in Petersburg; he also wanted to reinforce their debating power, for Plekhanov was a formidable opponent. So Frolenko, who had now joined up with him, was sent south to look around for recruits.

There had been heavy casualties among the fighters in the South. Ivichevich and Kovalski were dead. Osinski was in prison, awaiting execution. But there was Kolotkevich at Kiev, who accepted Frolenko's proposals unconditionally. Frolenko went on to Odessa and met various revolutionaries there— including Zhelyabov. No one had thought so far of co-opting Zhelyabov. He was of no standing or importance in the movement. He was a good talker; but hitherto only a talker. He had kept away from Osinski and had argued against terrorist action. But Frolenko happened to meet him and was impressed. He heard stories of Zhelyabov's exploits in his student days. He heard the old story about the bull. He felt, as he said afterwards, "if it comes to fighting this is a better man than we are." He talked to Mihailov who was passing through Odessa and arranged a meeting. Mihailov was also favourably impressed and put the idea to his colleagues when he returned to the capital. They were amazed. "The man," they said, "is a mere Narodnik." But it was finally agreed to invite him on condition that he declared himself ready to take personal part in the assassination of the Emperor. Frolenko put the proposal in those terms. Zhelyabov replied that he was willing to take part in one attempt; thereafter he must retain his freedom of choice. That was enough. He was formally invited to attend the preliminary conference at Lipetsk.

This, as Zhelyabov well realised, was the turning point of his career. It meant a break with the past, a complete abandonment of all his former life. From now on he was an illegal, committed, so long as he lived, to a relentless struggle with the forces of the regime. With his peasant sense of duty he meticulously wound up his private affairs and took leave of his family. He demanded that Olga Semenovna should divorce him. She refused to give him up, and there were entreaties and tears. But his purpose was fixed and he was adamant. He procured a false passport and disappeared. His wife and child never saw him again.

II

The journeys south of Mihailov and Frolenko had not been exclusively to find recruits. There was the question of funds. Mihailov was determined that the new movement to be inaugurated at Voronezh should not start crippled through lack of money. Few of the revolutionaries themselves had private means. Casual contributions were uncertain and precarious. During 1878 the Zemlya i Volya had been largely financed by one man, Dmitri Lizogub, a wealthy young landowner of Chernigov. Kravchinski described Lizogub as "the saint of the revolutionary movement." He was, in fact, a model of humility, austerity and devotion. He accepted gladly any task that was offered him, but was too modest to take a lead. He regarded himself as of value to the movement solely by the accident of his wealth, and anything spent upon himself he considered as stolen from the cause. He would grudge himself five kopecks for tram-fare and his clothes were shabby enough to be a joke even among the revolutionaries.

Though his possessions were large his fortune was not liquid. It consisted of land and not easily realisable securities. There was the further complication of a family trust in which his two brothers participated. He and Mihailov had been working out a scheme to turn the property into cash when, in August, 1878, Lizogub was arrested. His affairs were left in the hands of his land agent, one Drigo. Drigo knew of his employer's relations with the revolutionaries and took the opportunity of his arrest to feather his own nest. In May, 1879, Lizogub was in the Odessa prison and it was to get into touch with him there that Mihailov went to Odessa. Clandestine communication was established, and a power of attorney in Mihailov's favour and a letter of instructions to Drigo were smuggled out. Mihailov went on to Chernigov to tackle Drigo. Drigo was evasive and finally denounced Mihailov to the police. Mihailov was an expert at eluding arrest and succeeded in escaping.* But there was no longer the possibility of laying hands on the Lizogub estate. The attempt had failed.

Simultaneously with the attempt to salvage Lizogub's for-

---

* Drigo, having double-crossed Lizogub and tried to double-cross Mihailov, next attempted to double-cross the Secret Police, with the natural result. He was brought to trial and finished his days in Siberia.

tune Frolenko was organising a more daring and spectacular attempt to secure funds. Unfortunately few details have come down to us. On June 3, 1879, there was stolen from the State Treasury at Kherson the sum of 1,579,688 roubles. A gallery had been driven some seventy feet from a neighbouring house to the cellar where the money was kept. The house in question was found to be full of earth and clay from the gallery. It had been taken in May by a Madam Dr. Nikitin, who had brought with her a cook and a chambermaid.

The scheme had been admirably planned and carried through. Where it broke down was in the get-away. "Madame Nikitin" and the cook were caught and nearly all the stolen notes recovered. The two women were tried by military court at Odessa in January, 1880. But the chamber-maid (Terentieva) got clear with 10,000 roubles, an appreciable addition to revolutionary funds.

III

ON THE EVE of Lipetsk, where the new terrorist campaign was born, Osinski, the leader of the old terrorist movement, met his end. He was tried with a number of others before the Kiev Military Court early in May. Three of the prisoners were sentenced to be shot, the remainder to various terms of hard labour. The death sentences were submitted to the Emperor, who ordered them to be changed to death by hanging. The prisoners were not informed of the confirmation of their sentences. But a few days later Osinski, who was lodged on the top floor of the political wing of the Kiev prison, was transferred to the floor below. He was put in a cell at one end of the corridor. Next to him came Voloshenko, then Debogori-Mokrievich (both of them sentenced to hard labour), then Brandtner, and Sviridenko at the far end.

Two days after the transfer the reason became apparent. The prisoners on the top floor could see over the prison wall to a piece of waste land beyond, and reported that gallows were being put up. They tried to keep it from the condemned men, but it was obvious that they knew. The three said goodbye to their friends on the night of the 12th, before they were locked in their cells. But nothing happened, and on the evening of the 13th they said goodbye again.

The windows of the cells looked out on the prison yard and prisoners could shout to each other through the windows. Opposite, across the yard, was the building of the women politicals. On the right was the main criminal prison.

On the night of the 13th, about an hour after lock-up, Degobori-Mokrievich records that he heard soldiers in the corridor and the opening of Osinski's door. Then Osinski called through the window that there was a sentry in his cell. It was the practice to post a sentry in a condemned man's cell for his last night. The soldiers' steps came back down the corridor past Voloshenko, past Debogori-Mokrievich; but Brandtner's door was opened and then Sviridenko's. These two did not call out a message.

It was a dark night. The prisoners were allowed lamps. Debogori-Mokrievich had not yet lit his. The thin ray of light from the eyehole in the door cut across the cell. The window was open and he swung himself up to the ledge and sat there clinging to the bars. It was a warm night with no wind. There was no sign of life from the criminal prison. They had gone to bed. The politicals were quiet too, all except Osinski, who was shouting in cypher across the yard to Sonia Leshern, one of the girl politicals.

A sentry walked up and down in the yard below. After a while came the sound of low voices from Brandtner's cell. A Lutheran pastor had called to visit him. Finally the pastor went away. There was no sound from Sviridenko. Debogori-Mokrievich could hear the prisoner on the floor above walking about in his cell. Then that stopped. Only Osinski could not be still. He shouted sentences, then cypher figures, then sentences again. Sometimes his voice came sharp and clear, sometimes hollow and muffled; it was obvious he could not sit still at the window, he was continually jumping down to the floor and climbing back again. Then he called to Debogori-Mokrievich and asked him to sing Béranger's "Le Vieux Caporal." Debogori-Mokrievich writes:

"I did not feel like singing. But I felt that if I did, I will not say it would give him pleasure, but perhaps it would distract his mind or make the time pass quicker. So I sang. During the night he made me sing that song three times. It is about one of Napoleon's corporals who was shot for some breach of duty. Poor Valerian. He had always hoped he would be shot like the corporal. He could not bear the thought of being hanged. He had often told me he had a horror of that form of death.

"It was very late. Osinski did not ask me to sing any more. He had stopped talking. The pastor had left Brandtner hours before. There was still no sound from Sviridenko. I sat on at my window ledge. In the cell on the left Voloshenko was walking up and down. Now and then he stopped to spit. Suddenly I heard Osinski's voice: 'Sonia!' Away across the yard Sonia Leshern called back: 'Valerian!' She must have been sitting at her window too. But Osinski only called her name. He did not talk. Everything was quiet again.

"My thoughts went round in my head. It seemed to me impossible that all three were to be hanged. There had been no clear evidence against Osinski at his trial. . . . At last the stars grew dim. It was chilly. Down in the yard the guard was relieved. I heard the clatter of the rifles and the voices. Then once more, silence. I climbed down from the window ledge and lay on my mattress. I was soon half unconscious, but it was not sleep. From time to time I heard the call 'Sonia' and then the answer 'Valerian!' from across the wide, empty prison yard."

In the morning the soldiers came to take the three men to be hanged.

IV

PETER THE GREAT had been the first to take notice of the mineral springs of Lipetsk. He had ordered the place to be made a spa. Hotels were built and public gardens laid out. The local pond was enlarged and embellished into an ornamental lake. After his death the glory slipped away again; but still, every summer, there was a season of sorts and merchants and minor gentry came with their families to take the waters. Since Peter's days pious peasants regarded the place with suspicion. There were no fish in the ornamental lake; too many mineral springs ran into it. But the peasants attributed their absence to the curse of God upon the work of Antichrist.

Alexander Mihailov and Zhelyabov, the Robespierre and the Danton of the new movement, arrived under false names and with false passports on June 13. They took a furnished apartment together and had the opportunity to arrange in advance the course of the congress. Two days later the others began to arrive: Tikhomirov and Morozov, the intellectuals; Barannikov, Kviatkovski, Shiraev and Olovennikova of the Petersburg Death or Freedom group; the Southerners, Frolenko and Kolotkevich. There was a certain danger in so many illegals congregating in one small town. Meetings had to be carefully organised. They went out on picnic parties, and met, as if by chance, in the surrounding forest. One day they went out in boats and met on an island in the lake.

The first meeting was the most important; its task was the formulation of policy. Mihailov at his trial described this in one word: *Narodopravlenie*—the placing of supreme power in the hands of the nation as a whole. It would be preferable to do this by legal means. But in present circumstances legal means were not effective. The party must therefore adopt any means and any weapons that were available; but only so long as the Administration withheld freedom of speech and a free franchise. It was Zhelyabov who developed this thesis.

Purely political reforms, he argued, did not fall within the scope of the Social Revolutionary party. That was the task of the liberals. But the latter had proved to be impotent. At present it was impossible to carry on an ideological struggle. Therefore it was the duty of the Social Revolutionary party to overthrow the Government and bring about a state of affairs in which such a struggle was possible. In other words the first duty of the party was to secure political liberty, and with this end it should unite with all elements capable of political activity.

Zhelyabov went on to review official repression—the arrests, the imprisonments, the banishments, the executions, for all of which the ultimate responsibility must be laid to the account of the Emperor.

"We can only," he said, "attain our end by a resolute attack. . . . A party must do all in its power. If it has the power to overthrow the despot by means of a revolution, it should do so. If it has only the power to carry out the death penalty on him personally, then it must do that. If even this is beyond its strength it must at least make a vigorous protest. But we shall have the strength—make no doubt about that—and the more resolutely we act the sooner we shall have it."

Before the end of the day Zhelyabov had become a leader of the Russian revolutionary movement.

On the previous evening Goldenberg had arrived in Lipetsk and put up at the Hotel Moscow. He did not know where to find the others and so he missed the first day. The others were not sure whether he was coming at all. They did not particularly want him. But he had heard from Zundelevich in Kiev at the end of April that the conference was to be held, and later he had gathered from Kolotkevich that the place was Lipetsk and the date the middle of June. On the evening of the 17th he met the others and so he was able to attend the session of the 18th. This was devoted to the party's new constitution. Zhelyabov took little part in this discussion. It was only later that he realised the necessity of a centralised machine. "At Lipetsk," says Tikhomirov, "he was not yet a confirmed centralist."

The main outcome of the second session was that all present constituted themselves into an Executive Committee, to which it was decided to co-opt Figner, Yakimova, Presnyakov, and Ivanova, and later any suitable candidates who might present themselves. The Executive Committee was originally intended as the instrument of action: policy was to be in the hands of the Directive Committee of three who were also elected. Alexander Mihailov was the obvious first choice. The second was Frolenko *— the most prominent of the Southerners. After some discussion Tikhomirov was elected to the third place. Tikhomirov was of little use as a practical organiser and he had not the nerve of a warrior. But he had the best theoretical brain of the Death or Freedom group and he was good at drafting resolutions and finding formulae. He and Morozov were made joint editors of the party's paper. The two disliked each other, but they were kept in their place by the bigger personalities of their colleagues.

In point of fact it was only the Executive Committee that

---

* Some leading party members have left records allotting the second place to Kviatkovski. The bulk of evidence is against them, including Frolenko and Morozov, the two surviving participants in the Lipetsk conference. But the point is immaterial.

ever counted. The Directive Committee may have met, but we have no record that it did so. Both policy and action were controlled by the Executive Committee.

The rules for this body were drawn up at the second session of the conference. Possible candidates for co-option were to be very strictly scrutinised. Approved candidates were to have the programme read to them paragraph by paragraph. If they did not wholeheartedly approve of any point the reading was stopped and their admission refused. At least that was the rule. In practice, however, Morozov says: "When admitting a new member we never asked his views on socialism or anarchism. We asked, 'Are you ready at once to offer your life, your personal freedom and all that you have?' If he said yes, and if we believed him, we took him on."

In other words it was devotion and discipline that mattered rather than meticulous conformity to one particular doctrine. But a high degree of devotion and discipline was demanded. Membership of the committee was irrevocable. Once accepted the candidate was committed never to resign. He bound himself implicitly and unquestioningly to obey the decisions of the majority of the committee; to admit of no ties of friendship, affection or relationship, and to devote his whole self to the service of the party; to renounce now and for all the future all personal property and belongings and to bring any that he might possess into the common fund. The Executive Committee in itself was to be invisible and intangible. In no circumstances was any member to admit his membership. If necessary he might proclaim himself one of the committee's agents. But if arrested he must deny any connection whatever: he must concentrate on saving his skin. As things turned out this last rule was always broken. In Morozov's words, "the heroic spirit was too strong."

Under the Executive Committee were the rank and file of the party—agents of various grades. The lowest grade was Grade I. It was arranged in that way so that the recruit should not know how many grades there were above him.

And so the conference went on. Outside the sessions we hear of Zhelyabov busy at getting to know his new colleagues who were to be his partners for the rest of his life. We may imagine Mihailov and Frolenko sponsoring their new recruit. One incident has come down to us. One evening the party was walking back to the town and passed a tavern with a peasant cart standing outside. Frolenko betted Zhelyabov he could not lift it by the back axle. He did; and then lifted the cart again with two men sitting in it, while the peasants crowded round and cheered.

On the last day of the conference it was agreed in principle that the Emperor must die. Alexander Mihailov made out the indictment, to prove that the merit of the emancipation of the peasants had been more than countered by his subsequent misdeeds. The decision, however, was only one in principle. Formal sentence of death was not pronounced until two months later when the ways and means were decided on.

The conference was at an end.

V

AFTER the final session Goldenberg left them. Most of the others went on to the official conference at Voronezh. Plekhanov, Aptekman, Perovskaya, Figner and her sister had already arrived. Voronezh was a considerably larger town than Lipetsk, and there was a monastery in the neighbourhood which attracted pilgrims from all over the country. There were also convenient forests for picnic parties. The risk of detection was not great.

Zhelyabov, Shiraev and Kolotkevich were not yet members of the Zemlya i Volya, and the first session was taken up with their election. Then came the serious business. It was Plekhanov's intention to start with a direct attack on the terrorists. He had brought with him a copy of one of Morozov's more violent articles. He read this aloud and asked if anyone present agreed with it. He expected a vigorous disclaimer, but no one spoke. He repeated his question. There was still silence. It was borne in upon him that the general spirit of the meeting was against him. "In that case, gentlemen," he said, "I have nothing more to say." He left the meeting and returned to Petersburg.

The matter was not settled with the discomfiture and departure of Plekhanov. There were still some present who shared the view of the older Narodniks that the party should confine itself to cultural and philanthropic work among the peasants. Such views disgusted Zhelyabov. "And these people

call themselves revolutionaries!" he said. He himself continued to insist on the need for securing political liberties.
"I know a number of peasants," he said, "with intelligence and energy and an interest in village affairs. But as things are now they will never come out in the open. They know they cannot do any good and they do not want to make themselves martyrs for the sake of a dream. They are practical men; they refuse to risk all they have for a will-o'-the-wisp. A constitution would give them the chance to come out in the open—and they would take it. They would have some tangible objective to fight for, and they would be just as stubborn and just as persistent as any of our sectaries have been. That is the way to build up a popular party."

This speech raised an even more controversial issue than that of terrorism. There were cries of horror: the man was a constitutionalist. For there remained the old dislike and suspicion of constitutionalism, and indeed of any "political" as opposed to social activities. Perovskaya, who was annoyed at not having been invited to Lipetsk, was perfectly willing to accept the thesis that the Emperor should be killed in punishment for his misdeeds. She could agree with Zhelyabov that the party had nothing to lose in adopting terrorism; at worst it could only frighten off the impotent liberals. But a Constituent Assembly, in her view, would lead to the assumption of power by a set of wire-pulling politicians and financiers. Her aim was a free federation of free peasant communities: and this could only be attained by a national peasant rising.

Zhelyabov's speech provoked such argument that there seemed serious risk of a deadlock. His Lipetsk friends took him aside and begged him to go slow. After that he did not speak at any further public session and devoted himself to lobbying. He approached individual opponents and tried to convert them to his views. He paid special attention to Perovskaya. It may well be that he already felt a personal interest in her. But he could make no impression and at last gave her up in disgust. "One can do nothing with this woman," he said.

The Voronezh conference ended on a compromise—not so much a working compromise as a formula intended to avoid a split in the party. It was recognised that some form of active struggle with the Administration was necessary. Morozov largely contributed to this decision by reading out the last message from Osinski, in which he called on his survivors to continue the fight. It was agreed that the Disorganising Group should engage in terrorist action, and should be allotted for this purpose one-third of the party's income. Tikhomirov and Morozov were confirmed as editors of the *Zemlya i Volya* paper. Then the conference broke up, and most of the participants went back to Petersburg. When they arrived there they found Plekhanov had collected the support of Stefanovich, Deutsch and Vera Zasulich (who had just returned from abroad), and intended to raise the whole issue all over again. The next two months were spent in inconclusive wrangling.

VI

VERA FIGNER in her memoirs writes:

"My life as an illegal began directly after the Voronezh congress. I went back to Petersburg with Kviatkovski, who took me to Lesnoy, just outside the town, where he and Ivanova were occupying a flat which the organisation had rented. Peasant and working-class women who had anything to do with Kviatkovski always became devoted to him: at Lesnoy we had a German servant girl we could be completely sure of. Our flat was soon the headquarters of the extreme fighting wing. We were all illegals. Lesnoy had the great advantage of having the forest nearby; we could go out as if for excursions and hold meetings under the pine trees where we could see far enough in all directions to make sure we were not being spied on."

Lesnoy was thus the temporary home of the Lipetsk faction. Plekhanov and his allies lived in the town. The joint debates took place in the quarters of one or other member of the rival groups. Sometimes they were held at the lodgings of Perovskaya who had not yet made her decision. Her political convictions still inclined to those of the "villagers," as their opponents called them. But her emotions were all for fighting back against the Administration. "She was," Deutsch writes, "the incarnation of the spirit of revolt. She was determined that official brutalities must not be left unanswered. She never used extreme language. In a soft, small, almost childish voice she proclaimed the necessity of terror."

Deutsch, writing twenty-five years afterwards, divided his opponents into three classes. There were those who, like Perovskaya, favoured terrorism as a weapon of revenge. There were those like Morozov who were terrorists from a natural inclination towards the sensational. Finally there were those like Zhelyabov and Alexander Mihailov who regarded terrorism as the most practical means of extorting political concessions. Of Zhelyabov he writes:

"Tall, magnificently built, broad and with strongly marked features, he was then not thirty but looked older. Just by his appearance he stood out from the rest of us. He was a man who compelled attention at the first glance. I first met him at Perovskaya's. There were ten of us altogether. There was a lively and heated argument on terrorism. Zhelyabov and Plekhanov were the chief protagonists. Zhelyabov spoke quietly, in a low full bass, with determination and conviction, on the necessity of terror. He saw no immediate prospect of success by work among the peasants. He was for concentrating on the more progressive classes. He was all for fighting for political emancipation—a course to which we Narodniks were opposed."

Kovalskaya has left us an account of this same meeting. Zhelyabov turned up late and while they were waiting for him Plekhanov held forth on the manners and behaviour of the new style of revolutionary. He was complacently sarcastic; and Kovalskaya could see Perovskaya getting angry. Kovalskaya herself was one of the villagers and supported Plekhanov. Zhelyabov arrived at last. The meeting began with mutual politeness: but soon the argument started and temperatures began to rise. Kovalskaya had to leave early. Next day she saw Perovskaya.

"I want you to join our group," Perovskaya said. "There's nothing real about your people. We're alive."

"We believe in a proper social revolution—not just making a plot and shooting at people."

"Well," said Perovskaya, "if you ever really start to do something perhaps I shall be on your side."

VII

THESE endless debates and attempts to find some formula of reconciliation exasperated the extremists. Time was passing and nothing was being done. Finally on August 26 the Lipetsk group held a meeting in the forest near Lesnoy. We have no detailed account of this meeting, but it was then that Alexander II was formally condemned to death. It was further decided—Deutsch tells us the proposal came from Zhelyabov—that the sentence should be carried out by blowing up the imperial train on the return journey from the Emperor's summer resort at Livadia in the Crimea.

These decisions brought matters to a head. Thanks to Kibalchich, who had recently been assisted by Shiraev and Isaev, the "terrorists" possessed a supply of explosive. They had sufficient personnel for the task. And it was necessary to go ahead with active preparations, as it was only a matter of weeks before the Emperor's return to Petersburg. Zhelyabov at once went south to make a survey of the railway from Simferopol to Kursk.

The attempt to find a compromise was abandoned.

"Perovskaya and I," Vera Figner writes, "who had hesitated at Voronezh in the hope of maintaining unity, had nothing more to say when our Petersburg friends showed us that everything was ready for action. Finally and definitely we decided on splitting up the Zemlya i Volya. Representatives of the two wings drew up the conditions. We divided up the printing plant, and the funds, which last in point of fact were mostly merely promises and hopes. . . .

"It was agreed that neither party should use the old name. The villagers decided to call themselves the Cherni Peredel (Black Partition, i.e., the partition of the 'black' earth among the peasants). As our first aim was to substitute the will of the people for the will of one individual we took the name of Narodnaya Volya (Will of the People). . . . Morozov said that when we split up the Land and Freedom organisation the others took the land and we took the freedom * . . ."

Figner is not quite correct as regards Perovskaya. She her-

---

* The point of Morozov's little joke is that *volya* in Russian means both "freedom" and "will."

self was at once co-opted to the Executive Committee of the Narodnaya Volya, but Perovskaya was still opposed to the new "political" programme. For the moment she only decided to offer her help for the coming attempt on the Emperor.

VIII

THE debates with the Plekhanov faction did at least give the Lipetsk group the opportunity of clarifying and co-ordinating their own ideas. During the two months Tikhomirov was busy redrafting the programme that had been drawn up by Morozov at Lipetsk. The final version was subsequently published in the *Narodnaya Volya* paper as the official programme of the new party:

"We are, by basic conviction, socialists and Narodniks. We are convinced that only through socialist principles can humanity attain liberty, equality, fraternity, general material well-being, the development of individual personality and uninterrupted progress. . . .

"We find that the people are now in a position of political and economic slavery. . . .

"We find that the existing governmental bourgeois excrescence is maintained solely through the exercise of naked force, through its army, its police and its officialdom, just as, in the past, the Mongol tyranny of Ghengis Khan was maintained. . . .

"At the same time we find that in spite of oppression and persecution certain popular traditions are still alive—the right of the people to their land, communal and local autonomy, the federal principle, liberty of speech and of faith. These traditions are capable of far-reaching development. . . .

"It is our task to free the nation from the yoke of the existing Government, to carry out a political revolution, and to hand over supreme power to the people.

"The Will of the People can be established by the creation of a Constituent Assembly elected by free and universal vote. . . . This, while not the ideal method, seems to be the one most immediately practicable. . . .

"As a party we have our programme which we intend unceasingly to propagate up to the outbreak of the revolution, during the subsequent electoral campaign, and, finally, in the Constituent Assembly itself. Our programme includes the following points:

(*i*) A wide degree of local self-government.

(*ii*) The independence of the mir as an economic and administrative unit.

(*iii*) The land to pass into the possession of the people.

(*iv*) All factories to pass into the possession of the workers.

(*v*) Freedom of conscience, speech, press, of right of assembly, right of electoral agitation, etc.

(*vi*) The existing army to be transformed into a militia.

"With the above aim in view our activities must be developed along the following lines:

(*a*) Propaganda, to popularise the idea of a democratic socialist revolution. . . .

(*b*) Terrorist activity, to remove the most important personalities belonging to the Administration, to protect the party from spies, to inflict due punishment for official excesses and cruelties. This will have as a general aim the weakening and demoralisation of the Administration, the demonstration of the possibility of fighting the Administration, the strengthening of popular belief in the party's ultimate success, and finally the inculcation of a fighting spirit.

(*c*) The organisation of secret societies to be co-ordinated under a central headquarters.

(*d*) The establishment of links and contacts in influential positions in the Administration, in the army, in society, and among the masses.

(*e*) The organisation and successful carrying through of the revolution.

(*f*) Electoral activity in connexion with the composition of the Constituent Assembly."

This declaration was, of course, drawn up in an age with little first-hand knowledge of social experiments. Its authors still clung to the belief that social justice and individual liberty were not only compatible but mutually conducive. They had, however, some experience of revolutionary struggle, and it was natural that they should be more at home in pointing out the way to their goal than in knowing what to do when they got there. A subsequent article in the *Narodnaya Volya* on "The Preparatory Tasks of the Party" would not be out of place in a modern text book of revolutionary technique.

"It is possible that the Government, without waiting for the revolution, will decide of its own accord to yield to the people. This might be described as the natural death of the old regime.

"But in any case the party must take steps to prepare and bring about the revolution.

"It may perhaps be possible to choose a specially favourable occasion, such as a popular rising, an unsuccessful war, state bankruptcy, an international crisis, etc.

"But the party must not count on favourable extraneous circumstances. The party must be in a position to act in the most unfavourable circumstances.

"The party must itself be able to create the opportunity to act and to act successfully. For instance, the opportunity might be created by the simultaneous assassination of the dozen or so individuals holding key positions in the existing Administration. This would tend to induce a panic among the subordinate officials and at the same time would excite the masses. The fighting forces of the party would then seize by assault the main administrative positions and the party would bring into action the great mass of the factory workers, etc. . . . The party must also guard against the danger of the intervention of foreign powers on behalf of the Government.

"The following are therefore the main lines of the preparatory work of the party:

(i) The creation of a central fighting organisation capable of initiating a revolt.

(ii) The creation of subordinate provincial organisations capable of supporting the revolt.

(iii) Measures to ensure the active support of the factory workers in the towns.

(iv) Measures to ensure the active support of the armed forces, or at least to paralyse any assistance they might give to the Government.

(v) Measures to ensure the sympathy and co-operation of the intelligentsia.

(vi) Measures to win over the sympathy of public opinion in foreign countries."

Lenin wrote afterwards:

"It was the supreme merit of the Narodovoltsi that they

tried to unite all discontented elements in their organisation, and deliver a determined attack upon the autocracy. . . . They saw political tasks in their most concrete and practical aspect."

CHAPTER SEVEN

THE FIRST ATTACKS

I

ZHELYABOV completed his survey of the line and made his report. On the basis of the data there provided the Executive Committee decided to organise three independent attacks, to be made respectively at Odessa, Alexandrovsk and Moscow. Zhelyabov had emphasised the particular suitability of the lie of the ground at Alexandrovsk, and he was put in charge of operations there. The Odessa attempt, the first to be made along the Emperor's route, was entrusted to Frolenko, Kolotkevich and Lebedeva.

Figner writes:

"I was not detailed to take part in any of the attempts. I could not bear the thought of moral responsibility for acts that exposed my comrades to the risk of such terrible punishment, so I kept demanding to be allotted an active part. At first they were angry with me for seeking my own personal satisfaction instead of submitting blindly to the orders of the committee. But afterwards they gave way, and sent me to Odessa with the dynamite. . . .

"This was early in September. Of our group only Kibalchich was then in Odessa. He and I found a flat, and we moved in under the name of Ivanitski. Very soon Kolotkevich and Frolenko turned up, and a little later Lebedeva. Our meetings took place at our flat. Kibalchich was in charge of the technical side. Our first plan had been to lay the explosive under the rails in the interval between the passage of two trains. That would have been very difficult—and it seemed better for one of our people to get a job as watchman on the line some way out of Odessa, and dig a tunnel to the railway from his hut. I said I would arrange for the job. Frolenko was to be the watchman—and if necessary Lebedeva would figure as his wife. At first I thought of getting some of my family's friends to recommend Frolenko for the post; but I realised I could not tell them my real motive, and if I did not tell them it would be an abuse of confidence. So I decided to go myself and ask some high official who had influence with the railway administration. I chose Baron Ungern-Sternberg, the future son-in-law of Count Todtleben, Governor General of Odessa. I went to see him and said I wanted a post of watchman on the railway line for my house porter: his wife, I explained, had lung trouble, so he had to get some job out of town. He gave me a note of recommendation to the traffic manager. Ungern-Sternberg, however, did not receive me in the way that a woman of good family expects to be received, and I took care that that sort of thing should not happen again." (It is not quite clear what Figner means by this: perhaps we should remember that she was then young and extremely pretty.) "When I went to see the traffic manager I dressed myself up very smartly, as anyone should who has a favour to ask. He received me with great respect and at once granted my request. Everything was going well . . . but then we heard that the Emperor would not be travelling via Odessa."

The original plan had been for the Emperor to come from the Crimea to Odessa by sea. But he was not a good sailor, the sea was rough and the bad weather looked like continuing. It was decided that he should do the whole journey by rail from Simferopol.

II

WE HAVE several sources from which to reconstruct the Alexandrovsk attempt. Goldenberg in his subsequent statement tells us how early in September he went to Kharkov. For the previous weeks he had been away in the country out of touch with his fellow-revolutionaries. His Kharkov visit was a self-appointed recruiting rally. He approached some student friends there and tried to convert them to the Narodnaya Volya policy. He could not make much impression. A few days later Zhelyabov turned up on the same errand. They held various meetings. One of them was attended by as many as forty students, a bold move in view of the police supervision. Zhelyabov preached his doctrine of absolute war against the Government by an organised combination of all the discontented elements in the country. He preached it with considerable effect, as Goldenberg was generous enough to admit. He describes Zhelyabov as a man of genius.

Towards the end of the month Presnyakov and Barannikov turned up with a hundredweight of dynamite; and Goldenberg for the first time learned of the proposal to mine the Emperor's train. He helped with the arrangements to store the explosive (it had to be kept, of course, in somebody's living room, and there were few of the local students who cared to take the risk). He also helped to make the brass containers needed for the mine. Meanwhile further meetings were held. Deutsch arrived in the hope of winning over the Kharkov students to the side of the Cherni Peredel. There were joint gatherings at which the rival leaders debated their policies. At these, according to Goldenberg, Deutsch was no match for Zhelyabov. All the same the rivalry was a friendly one. It was Deutsch who drew up and had printed a manifesto to be published after the Emperor was killed.

Zhelyabov went off on a preparatory visit to Alexandrovsk and came back to Kharkov. Goldenberg volunteered to take part in the actual attempt. We can infer that Zhelyabov did not want him. Goldenberg went on pressing his services until word came that they wanted more workers at Moscow, so he went to Moscow.

Eighteen months later when Zhelyabov was finally arrested he himself made a full statement of his part in the Alexandrovsk attempt. He explained that consequent on the decision taken on August 26, he, as a South Russian, was instructed to make an inspection of the southern sector and to submit his proposals to the Executive Committee. He accordingly surveyed the line from Simferopol to Kursk and decided the most suitable spot was four kilometres out of Alexandrovsk. The Executive Committee approved and allotted him the necessary funds, explosive and collaborators (i.e, Presnyakov, Yakimova and Barannikov). He worked out the details of the plan with his collaborators during September at Kharkov. He there engaged, on his personal responsibility, two additional helpers —Tikhonov and Okladski. Both were workmen with whom he had already been in touch. These two arrived in Kharkov with no inkling of what was to happen. It was explained to them that "no good could come until another Emperor was on the throne." Soon they were completely under the influence of Zhelyabov's personality, and then were told the details.

On October 1 Zhelyabov went to Alexandrovsk with a passport in the name of Cheremisov, merchant, of Yaroslavl. He gave out that he had the idea of setting up a little factory. Alexandrovsk was a small market town of some six thousand inhabitants and his arrival made a stir. He went round and called on everybody. It is certain that like all the young revolutionaries he enjoyed a leg-pull; and his new role must have been a congenial relief from the furtive existence of an illegal in Petersburg and Kharkov. He made special friends with one Sagaidak, a member of the local town council, who advised him there were better prospects for a tannery than for a soap or macaroni factory, which were the other alternatives. Zhelyabov put in an application to the Mayor of Alexandrovsk for a lease of a site and went off to fetch Madame Cheremisov.

A few days later he came back with Yakimova and their furniture and household effects: also their two employees—Tikhonov and Okladski. They installed themselves in their new home. The town council turned down Cheremisov's first application for a site—he had wanted a plot adjoining the railway line—and there were endless negotiations before the parties agreed on another one, at the far end of the town. There was also a project, which needed much discussion, of fitting up a shop in one of his landlord's houses to sell the tannery's finished products.

Tikhomirov says: "In his role of small tradesman Zhelyabov was inimitable. He completely won the hearts of his new fellow-citizens. His landlord's family was also of Cossack descent, and that at once formed a bond of union. He made real friends with the people, ate with them, drank with them, sang songs, talked incessantly about his tannery."

After the event, it occurred to the worthy townsmen of Alexandrovsk that there had been a great deal more talk about the tannery than actual progress. Indeed apart from the signing of the lease for the site and the payment in advance of the first six months' rent—amounting to twelve roubles—nothing was done at all. But at the time nobody had suspicions. The inception of any industrial enterprise, however small, is usually attended with much discussion. Alexandrovsk was a typical small market town where life moved slowly; and the arrival of a stranger, especially one with plenty to talk about, was in itself an addition to the local amenities.

In point of fact, however, the revolutionaries were working extremely hard. At the point chosen for the mine the railway ran along an embankment seventy-five feet high. Parallel with the embankment and about a hundred yards away from it ran a road. Between the road and the embankment was a deep dip. The plan was to bury two brass cylinders—each containing forty pounds of dynamite and provided with detonators— under the sleepers some fifty yards apart. The cylinders were to be connected with a wire lead, and from each another lead was to be run to a spot on the road. The ends of these were, at zero hour, to be connected with an induction coil and a portable battery.

The mine was to be fired at the exact moment when the coach containing the Emperor was immediately above one of the cylinders. It was calculated that the force of the explosion would be sufficient to send the whole train crashing down the side of the embankment, which in itself would be an additional safeguard of success.

The imperial suite usually occupied three trains, and the task of finding out in which train and which coach the Emperor was actually travelling devolved on Presnyakov. In October Presnyakov proceeded to Simferopol to watch. Barannikov went on to Moscow. Kibalchich paid one visit to Alexandrovsk to bring the induction coil, and shortly afterwards Isaev came over for one day to offer technical advice. Apart from this the venture was entirely the work of the "Cheremisov" household.

At their subsequent trial Tikhonov and Okladski gave an account of how the wires were laid and the cylinders buried. This, of course, could only be done at night. All traces of work in progress had to be covered up before daylight. In view of the approaching transit of the Emperor the authorities were taking special precautions, and a patrol passed along the line every three or four hours.

Zhelyabov, Tikhonov and Okladski would wait till the town had gone to bed and then go out to the scene of operations. Zhelyabov insisted on doing all the actual work himself. The other two acted as sentries, posted a hundred yards along the line in each direction to watch for the patrols. When the patrols approached they took what cover they could lying flat in the mud. It rained incessantly. Zhelyabov had that affection of the eyes which Russian peasants called "hen-blindness"; he could see next to nothing in the dark. Tikhonov had to lead him by the hand to the place of work. Once, when Tikhonov had left him, he lost his bearings completely and stumbled along the embankment as far as Okladski, who thought he was the patrol. On another occasion when the night's work was done he crawled up the line to recall the sentries and found one of them (we may assume it was Okladski) asleep. He shook him to his feet. "In war they shoot a man for that," he said. For a couple of minutes he stood glaring at the man and fingering his revolver. Then he put his pistol back in his pocket and they went home.

The first task was to lay the wires, and as it happened they completed this just in time. The mud and the debris brought down by the rains clogged up the culvert under the embankment, and the water, denied its outlet, formed a deep pool over all the dip between the embankment and the road. The rain continued. It was bitterly cold. The workers were obsessed with the fear that the rain would turn to snow; snow of course would show their tracks up. As it was they came back every night before dawn numb with cold and soaked to the skin. They had little sleep. All day Zhelyabov had to be round with his new friends, discussing the leather business, keeping up his reputation of being good company. He fell ill, but time was pressing and each night he went out on his task shivering and with a high temperature. He had bought a cart and a couple of horses, and when it came to laying the cylinders they took them out on the cart. He would not let the other two touch the cylinders or the detonators. Laying the cylinders was especially difficult because of the patrols. Night after night they had to bring them home again. The rains continued. The whole landscape was a wilderness of mud. Then at last he got one cylinder into position.

On November 16 Presnyakov arrived from Simferopol. He reported that the Emperor was due to pass Alexandrovsk on the 18th. There would be three trains: the Emperor would be on the second train in the fourth coach. Presnyakov arranged to report by code telegram if any change were made at the last minute. Then he went south again.

Zhelyabov gave out to his friends in the town that his wife had to go to her home on family business: possibly he might have to follow her, in which case the tannery must wait till the spring. Yakimova went off with her luggage. On the night of the 17th they succeeded in placing the second cylinder. Climbing up the embankment Zhelyabov slipped and the cylinder slid down the slope into the pool at the bottom. But he fished it out again and put it into position and attached the wires. They went back to the house. There was no telegram from Presnyakov.

Early in the morning of the 18th they harnessed up the horses, loaded the battery and the coil on the cart, and drove out. They connected the wires and waited in the rain. At ten o'clock the first of the imperial trains came into view. It passed. The second train came. As the fourth coach passed over the first cylinder Zhelyabov pressed the switch. Nothing happened. The train clattered on north. The third train came and went. When it had passed the three conspirators inspected the battery and the connections. They could find nothing wrong. They climbed on the cart again and drove back to Alexandrovsk.

There was nothing to be done except salvage the material. The attempt had failed. Zhelyabov was now very ill: besides the fever on him he had the shock of the disappointment and the reaction after the strain of the last two months. But that night all three were out again and gathered up the wires. On the next day, the 19th, the snow came. It was no longer possible to salvage the cylinders. They had to leave them where they were for possible use should the Emperor live long enough to go down to Livadia next year. They waited for news from Moscow and heard that Moscow had been a failure too. Zhelyabov said goodbye to his Alexandrovsk friends. He sold the cart and the two horses. He put the furniture into storage. Tikhonov and Okladski left, and on the 23rd he followed them.

The Executive Committee's technical experts held an enquiry on the cause of the failure. They could come to no conclusion. After this lapse of time we have even less chance of doing so. Vera Figner in her memoirs suggests that Zhelyabov bungled the pressing of the switch. But there is reason to suspect that Figner disliked Zhelyabov, and in any case the expert committee ruled out this possibility. Some of the revolutionaries suggested later that Okladski might have broken one of the wires on purpose. Here again there is no evidence. It is a common tendency to put a failure down to sabotage by traitors. In view of the conditions under which the work was done, the weather, the floods and the police patrols tramping up and down, there seem plenty of more natural causes for a break in the circuit.

III

ALEXANDROVSK never saw the "Cheremisov" family again. But the following March, when the next six months' rent was due, Sagaidak got a letter from Moscow in a not very educated hand:
"Dear Nikolai Afanassievich,
  First of all my warmest greetings to you and to your family and all my good wishes. Did you get my letter from Tambov? I have not heard from you. Things are not going well with me. People say they will do things and then do not do them. We must wait and see what the future brings. Dear Nikolai Afanassievich, I ask you please to go to the town council and pay the twelve roubles for my rent for the coming half year. Get a receipt and keep it for me. Masha [i.e., Yakimova] sends her greetings to you and many kisses to Lukeria Ivanovna. In about six weeks Masha will be having a child and the family do not want her to travel now. Now goodbye and keep well and healthy. Write to me to my address in Tambov . . ."
  "Cheremisov" went on to give directions about the furniture in store, and a number of further elaborate greetings. Accompanying the letter was a money-order for thirteen roubles. The odd rouble was for Sagaidak himself.

IV

ALEXANDROVSK as we have seen was organised and for the most part carried out by Zhelyabov alone. The Moscow attempt was more elaborate. No less than eight members of the Executive Committee took an active part in it,

The chief organiser was Alexander Mihailov. He himself made a preliminary visit of inspection, and then sent Hartmann to complete the purchase of a small house in the Preobrazhenskoe quarter, on the outskirts of the town, near the main railway line from Kursk and the South. Hartmann himself, a North Russian of German origin, had just been co-opted to the Executive Committee. Mihailov promised to find a girl to pose as Hartmann's wife and act as housekeeper. He offered the post to Sophia Perovskaya, who accepted at once. She realised the risks involved, and wound up her affairs in Petersburg. It is significant that she handed over her money, information and personal contacts to the Cherni Peredel and not to the remaining members of the Narodnaya Volya. Then she left for Moscow. The house was bought for one thousand roubles. The former residents were evicted, and Hartmann and Perovskaya installed themselves under the name of Sukhorukov. Alexander Mihailov came back to Moscow and took rooms in the town. Aronchik and Chernavskaya, in the guise of another young married couple, established themselves in a flat which was to serve as conspiratorial quarters. The other collaborators took rooms or put up at cheap hotels; and the work began.

The plan was to drive a gallery from the cellar of the house to the railway embankment some fifty yards away and there lay a charge under the line. The first main preoccupation was not to arouse the suspicion of the neighbours. The house itself was fairly isolated. The quarter was a poor one. The area between the railway and the Preobrazhenskoe cemetery was mainly waste land, rubbish heaps, allotments and little market gardens, with here and there a ramshackle one-storied cottage. The people, market gardeners or else day labourers in factories in the town, were mostly Old Believers who accounted it a sin for a man to shave his beard and thus deface the image of God in which he had been created. They were reserved and intensely suspicious. Hartmann gave himself out to be a workman employed in the town. It was natural therefore that he should not be visible during the day. The main brunt of contact with the outside world thus fell on Perovskaya.

In the middle of October Goldenberg arrived from the South. He reported to Mihailov (whose address he had) and Mihailov took him to the house and set him to work.

"As I was new to it," Goldenberg says, "I did the simple work. I cleared the earth from the gallery to the hatch and from the hatch to the storehouse; and I used to help Perovskaya with the housework."

They were none of them expert miners; and indeed, except for Hartmann, there was no skilled manual worker among them. Their tools were primitive. They had a cheap compass for keeping the gallery straight; as a matter of fact they did not keep it very straight. They had a short pointed "English spade" to pick out the earth at the gallery head, and two shovels to shovel it back. As the gallery advanced Hartmann fixed up wooden rails along the floor and a little truck on wheels, worked by a rope on a pulley, to get the earth back. Presumably it was Hartmann who was responsible for boarding the walls and ceiling.

The gallery was $3\frac{1}{2}$ feet high by $2\frac{1}{2}$ across. Its mouth, in the wall of the cellar, was boarded up to prevent exposure in case a stranger made his way down there. There was a hatch in the boarding to let the workers in and for the earth to be taken out. An iron pipe was installed for ventilation. One man worked at the head of the gallery; another shovelled the earth on the truck. A third stood at the hatch to receive it. A great problem was the disposal of the earth. The capacity of the storehouse was limited. They piled it up in the cellar, put it under the floor boards of the living room. Finally they had to spread it over the yard at night or dump it in near-by rubbish heaps. It was hard work. Morozov cracked up and had to return to Petersburg. The life of a revolutionary intellectual with its lack of air and exercise, frequent lack of adequate food and continual nights of tea drinking and talk did not make for physical fitness. "Grishka [Isaev] the student," says Goldenberg, "was the best worker. Aronchik was lazy; the others would not have him to work with them." The young people were determined not to be taken alive. They had a bottle of nitro-glycerine, sufficient to blow up the whole house, and in case they were discovered Perovskaya was to explode it with a pistol shot.

Those lodging in the town would arrive at the house just before daylight. They worked from six to eight; had tea; then continued till two, which was dinner time. They had a short rest after dinner and then worked on till ten at night. When things were going well they progressed at the rate of one foot per hour of work. There were frequent alarms. They had been working a week when the former occupant came round for some jam which she said she had left in the storehouse. The storehouse was full of earth and props for timbering the gallery. It was impossible to let the woman see it. Perovskaya said she had lost the key. Later she took the jam round herself. A few days afterwards the storehouse caught fire and the neighbours ran across to help. Perovskaya told them that God had brought about the fire, and if it was His Will He would put it out Himself. It was a sentiment that the Old Believers appreciated and she was able to keep them away. Time and again the venture was saved by Perovskaya's quick-wittedness and resource. She did the marketing, and as the quantity of provisions was far in excess of what two young people could consume she had the continual problem of eluding the well-meant interest of neighbouring housewives. People would come to the door and gossip. She found a real if unconscious ally in a cat that had attached itself to the conspirators. She built up an elaborate saga round its appetite, ingenuity, and capacity for breaking crockery. Time and again she averted awkward questions by some story of the cat's latest exploit.

There were other troubles. They came to the base of a telegraph pole and had to deflect the gallery round it. It rained—as it had at Alexandrovsk. Water collected in the gallery and began to rise. They had no pump and no means of procuring one. Incessant bailing doubled the work and brought the workers nearer to complete exhaustion. Finally, owing to the continuous rain and faulty timbering, the roof of the gallery fell in. What was worse was that the subsidence formed a big crater on the surface. There was a rough track along by the side of the line, where the railway patrols used to pass, and the crater was just at the side of the track. Luckily no patrols came along that afternoon and the few passers-by did not appear to notice. That night they filled in the hole. But it made extra work and used up time that they could ill afford, besides adding to the nervous strain. One of the diggers carried a dose of poison so as to be able to commit suicide in case he was buried by another landslide.

They reached the embankment. But here progress was harder than through the soft soil. The embankment was full of big stones. To remove them would entail the risk of another landslide. A subsidence on the embankment itself was certain to be noticed. They determined to buy a drill. But they had no money for it. Funds in any case were running short.

They took the bold decision of mortgaging the house. Hartmann went into the town and found a moneylender, and the moneylender came out with an official of the Housing Department and a gendarme to inspect the property. That was perhaps the most anxious moment of the whole enterprise. But it passed off successfully. Perovskaya bargained hard. They got six hundred roubles and could buy a drill.

The use of the drill led to a modification of their plans for the actual mine itself and they began to fear the supply of explosive would not be enough. They had learned by this time that the Odessa attempt was off, and resolved to get hold of the dynamite at Odessa. Goldenberg was the one who could best be spared, so they sent him to fetch it. Before he left they were discussing their final plans. There was the question of who should have the honour of firing the charge. "I," Goldenberg writes, "gave it as my view that I should be the one to fire the charge, as I had carried out the execution of Kropotkin." But the others did not agree with him. It was decided that Shiraev should press the lever. Shiraev was the technical expert. He did not take part in the digging. His job was to lay the explosive, connect up the leads, see to the detonators and the battery. Perovskaya, in view of her invaluable services during the past few weeks, was allotted the honour of watching through the window and giving the signal at the exact moment. "She told me," Goldenberg records, "how pleased she was at having been chosen to give the signal."

On November 9 Goldenberg left for the South. He may have been a tiresome little man, but he was sincere and wholehearted, and the girls were grateful to him for the help he had given in the housework. Perovskaya found him a pair of warm stockings, and Chernavskaya went shopping and bought him six pocket handkerchiefs. "One of those handkerchiefs," Goldenberg wrote in his depositions, "I had on me at the station at Elizavetgrad. The others I left behind with my other things in Moscow."

Goldenberg duly arrived in Odessa and took over the dynamite from Frolenko. Kibalchich was then in South Russia and since he was in general charge of the party's explosives, Goldenberg wished to meet him and discuss the position at Moscow. They exchanged telegrams but there was a muddle. On the 12th Goldenberg was waiting at Odessa for Kibalchich, and Kibalchich was waiting at Kharkov for Goldenberg. That evening Goldenberg took the train for the North: Kibalchich, a little later, took the train for Elizavetgrad. When he got to Elizavetgrad he found a stir at the station. People were standing in little groups and talking excitedly. Kibalchich caught the words: "A young man with a small but very heavy portmanteau." Goldenberg had been arrested.

On the 14th the party at the Villa Sukhorukov heard of Goldenberg's arrest. On the 17th they got a telegram from Simferopol: "Price of flour two roubles our price four." That meant the Emperor was in the fourth coach of the second train. It is an illustration of the ineptitude of the authorities that so obviously bogus a telegram did not arouse suspicion. On that day the conspirators had a final conference. It was decided that Hartmann and not Shiraev should press the lever: there was the danger of a visit from the police at the last moment and it was safer to have the normal occupant of the house there and not a stranger. All the 18th they hung about waiting for news from Alexandrovsk, but no news came until the evening when they heard the Emperor had arrived at Kharkov. That meant that Alexandrovsk, as well as Odessa, had been a failure. The last remaining chance was Moscow.

V

ON THE morning of the 19th Prince D. D. Obolenski came in from the country to Tula in the hope of a lift to Moscow in one of the imperial trains. The Emperor's passage had disorganised the time table: ordinary trains were running up to eight hours and more late. Obolenski found the police and railway officials at Tula completely exhausted. Rumours had been current that the Nihilists were up to something. Goldenberg's portmanteau full of dynamite was proof of it. The favourite theory was that the revolutionaries would throw a torpedo on the rails as the train passed. There were patrols, house searches, precautionary arrests. Few officials along the line from Simferopol had had much sleep during the past

The First Attacks

week. It was with profound relief that the chief of police at Tula watched the Emperor's train rumble out of his district.

Prince Obolenski was on friendly terms with a number of the Court officials, and had little difficulty in securing permission to travel in the baggage train. Under the original schedule this train should have been the first. But additional cars were attached at the last moment, and owing to the extra load the locomotive was unable to keep to the time table. There were delays at every stage, holding up the whole convoy, and, the Emperor being nervy and impatient, it was decided to alter the order and put the Emperor's train in front.

Obolenski found a number of friends on board. He chatted with them; had something to eat; sat back in his corner and read a book. At eleven o'clock at night the guard came to warn him they were nearing Moscow and he started to get his things together. Suddenly there was a crash. Obolenski was thrown out of his seat. He scrambled out of the coach and walked up the line. Guards, soldiers and railway-men were running up and down and shouting. Everything was in confusion. It was pitch dark and Obolenski tripped over a fallen telegraph pole. He noticed a hole in the ground from which came a thin trail of smoke. Some fifty yards away was a small house. One of the guards went across to it: there was a light burning in front of the ikon, the samovar was boiling and the tea things were on the table but there was no sign of the occupants. Obolenski walked up to the fourth coach. It was on its side, right off the line, a broken mass of iron and timber. No one was hurt. It was a baggage car with no one on it. It was full of jam, being brought back from the imperial estates in the Crimea for the palace in Petersburg. Jam and the broken containers were scattered all over the place. One of the railway engineers appeared and explained that the rain must have loosened the embankment. Obolenski said he smelt dynamite. The engineer maintained it could not be dynamite. All the railway people and police were busy explaining that it must have been an accident: the precautions taken had been such that any attempt by the revolutionaries was quite out of the question. However Obolenski had recently been supervising blasting operations on his estate and recognised the smell of dynamite. He walked to the town, found a cab and drove on to the Kremlin. It was late by this time. The official reception was over and the Emperor and his staff had gone to bed. Obolenski insisted on seeing Count Adlerberg. After some delay the Count appeared, sleepy and incredulous. He held that the matter should be reported to the Governor General, so Obolenski went back to his cab and drove to the private residence of old Prince Dolgoruki. The old Prince was in his dressing gown in the study drinking a final cup of tea. Obolenski was shown in to him and reported that a mine had been exploded under one of the imperial trains. "Never!" said the Governor General. "Impossible." But Obolenski was not to be shaken. At last the old man broke down altogether, and knelt beside the table with the tea-things to offer up his prayer of thanks that the Emperor was unhurt.

VI

ON NOVEMBER 22 the Executive Committee of the Narodnaya Volya issued their first manifesto to the Russian nation:

"On November 19 near Moscow, on the Moscow-Kursk railway, an attempt was made by order of the Executive Committee on the life of Alexander II, by mining his train. The attempt failed. We do not find it necessary to go into the causes of the failure.

"We are convinced that our agents and our party will not be discouraged by this failure. . . . They will go forward with new faith in their strength and in the ultimate success of their cause . . .

"We once more assert Alexander II to be the personification of arbitrary, cowardly, bloody, and ever more violent despotism. . . . He has merited the death penalty by the pain he has caused and the blood he has shed . . .

"But our concern is not with him alone. Our aim is the freedom of the people and the good of the people. If Alexander were to recognise the evil he has done to Russia, if he were to hand over his power to a General Assembly chosen by the free vote of the people, then we for our part would leave him in peace and forgive his past misdeeds.

"But, till then, implacable war.

"We turn to the whole Russian people with an appeal for help for our party in its struggle. It is not easy to fight the entire forces of the Administration. The failure of our attempt on November 19 is in itself a proof of our difficulties. For the overthrow of despotism we need the help of all. This is what we require, and what we expect, from Russia."

There was, of course, no mention of the attempts at Odessa and Alexandrovsk. At that time no one knew that they had been made.

CHAPTER EIGHT

THE SPRING CAMPAIGN

I

WITHIN a week of the failure at Moscow the party suffered a serious casualty. On November 24 Kviatkovski, one of their best political brains and practical organisers, was arrested. He had taken no part in the railway attempts, as there was urgent work for him in Petersburg. By the time Vera Figner went down to Odessa she had grown very fond of him. She arranged that when she left the flat her younger sister Evgenia should move in and take her place as housekeeper. This was done. But an important detail was overlooked, which eventually led to Kviatkovski's arrest.

One of Kviatkovski's tasks was to act as link with the secret printing press. The *Zemlya i Volya* had found by experience that it was best to keep the editorial department completely away from the actual production of the paper. The *Narodnaya Volya* kept up this usage. Tikhomirov and Morozov never went near the address in the Sapernaya where the press was lodged. All communications passed through Kviatkovski.

The first number of the *Narodnaya Volya* newspaper appeared in October. Police headquarters in Petersburg at once issued a confidential circular to officers in charge of police districts to the effect that any officer would be court-martialled if it were discovered through an outside channel that the press was operating in his area. They checked up on all the dealers in newsprint, and as the result was negative they concluded that the revolutionaries imported their paper. (As a matter of fact they used ordinary correspondence paper which they wetted.) Then the police established a special corps of listeners to listen outside windows and on the landings of the big apartment houses for any sound of a press at work.

Ivanova, a girl of twenty-three, was in charge of the press, with one other girl and three men to help her. Special security precautions were observed. They only used the actual press if they were convinced that no listeners were about. Otherwise they smeared the type with ink, laid on the paper, and tapped it down with a brush. This process took a long time and the result was smudgy but at least it made no noise. Press and type, of course, could all be hidden away in cupboards and were so kept unless actually in use. To give the flat an air of greater innocence they employed a charwoman once a week, and made a point of frequently calling in the porter to see to the closet or repair the scullery tap. Ivanova and her colleagues lived under a special discipline. They met none of their fellow-revolutionaries apart from Kviatkovski. They were not allowed to visit theatres, cafés, or other places of public entertainment. One of the men had no identity papers of any kind, and he never left the flat except on the days the charwoman came: then he took a moment when the porter was not looking to slip out, and walked about for a few hours in unfrequented streets. His real name was Lubkin, but none of his companions knew it. They called him "Ptashka." Another of the men had a passport in the name of a government clerk. He went out at the same time every morning as if going to his department, and carried an official brief case. The copies of the *Narodnaya Volya* used to leave the flat in this brief case, and they smuggled in their printing paper by the same means.

The arrangements for the press were well thought out. But early in November a girl student was caught in Moscow with a copy of the paper and admitted under examination at the police station that she had got it from Evgenia Figner. By an oversight Evgenia had been allowed by her comrades to remain a legal, i.e., to continue under her real name. Moscow reported to Petersburg, and the Petersburg police looked up the girl's address in their register and made a raid on the flat. They obtained, as yet, no clue as to the location of the printing press, but they were able to arrest Kviatkovski as well as Evgenia Figner. They also found a supply of dynamite, and, what puzzled them for some weeks, two rough plans of the Winter Palace with curious markings.

Kviatkovski was not the party's only casualty. Three weeks later Shiraev was caught. Zundelevich had already been arrested in the Petersburg Public Library. When Perovskaya came back from Moscow her friends entreated her to go abroad until the police drive had abated. "No," she said, "I will stay here with the fighters." She was anxious to learn what progress the Cherni Peredel had been making during the last few weeks; her sympathies were still with that group if they would only get a move on. But the Cherni Peredel had no positive answer to give her. They had to admit there was no immediate prospect of a general peasant rising: if she would go abroad for some months they hoped that on her return their plans would be more definite. This made her angry, and she went off to see Zhelyabov. The following morning there was a meeting of the Executive Committee of the Narodnaya Volya, and there Zhelyabov announced "with radiant joy" that Perovskaya had asked to be co-opted as a member.

And so on the evening of December 31 when the Narodnaya Volya, like everybody else, relaxed and had their New Year's Eve party, it was Perovskaya, pink and white and looking like a schoolgirl, who presided at the samovar. They all enjoyed themselves. Zhelyabov, we hear, was irrepressible. At that time spiritualism was coming into vogue, and late in the evening someone suggested they should try their hand at table-rapping. The lamps were extinguished and they sat round the table in the dim light of a flickering bowl of punch. The ringleader invoked the spirit of the late Emperor Nicholas I. "Impernickel" was coy and took some time to answer. But he answered at last and they put him the burning question: "In what manner will your son, Alexander II, meet his death?" There was a long wait; then a series of unintelligible thumpings; and then another wait. They almost gave up hope. But at last, suddenly, the following message was rapped out. "Alexander Nikolaevich will die by poison." A slight chill came over the party. None of them seriously believed in spiritualism, but they were young and the omen was unfortunate. There was not and never had been an intention to carry out the attempt by poison. They lit the lamps again and restored their spirits by singing the "Marseillaise."

II

THE two plans found among Kviatkovski's papers were connected with perhaps the most daring and spectacular attempt on the Emperor's life ever sponsored by the Narodnaya Volya, an attempt in which Kviatkovski had been assisting Stepan Khalturin.

Khalturin, as we have seen, had been the founder and prime mover of the Northern Workers' Union. When his organisation was crushed he went through the same psychological crisis as so many other revolutionaries. He became convinced of the futility of the further use of peaceful means. He conceived the idea of killing the Emperor, primarily as a reprisal for the suppression of his union. He discussed the matter with those few ex-members who had escaped arrest. "Alexander II," he said, "must be killed by a workman. We will not tolerate that Russian Emperors should regard the workers as of no account." His friends agreed with him. Khalturin by that time was in touch with Kviatkovski, and he came to him with the proposal to blow up the Winter Palace with the Emperor in it. "A mass assassination," he explained, "is more effective than a hundred single murders." He maintained he could do all the work single-handed. All that he required was a sufficient stock of dynamite.

Kviatkovski, Alexander Mihailov and Tikhomirov, sitting as a sub-committee of the Executive Committee of the Narodnaya Volya, considered the suggestion and decided to approve it. It was another string to their bow should the attempts on the railway line fail. Khalturin was co-opted to the Executive Committee, and Kviatkovski was told off to remain in Petersburg and offer him any help and advice that he might need.

Khalturin, under the name of Batishkov, applied for and obtained a job as carpenter on the imperial yacht. He was an excellent workman and his behaviour was impeccable. He attracted the favourable notice of the household officers, and in October he was transferred to the Winter Palace. At that time, of course, the Emperor was still in the Crimea. Discipline in the palace was consequently slack. Khalturin himself was bewildered at the disorder. The main entrance to the palace was guarded day and night by soldiers and it was difficult even for members of the imperial family to gain admittance. But the back door was always open. Servants and workmen could bring in friends as and when they liked, and even keep them there for the night. Scrounging and stealing were universal; Khalturin himself was forced to steal so as not to attract the attention of his colleagues. In fact at times it was necessary to steal to live, as the payment of wages was very irregular.

"Batishkov" was described in his identity papers as a peasant from Olonetz. Khalturin was careful to play the part. He gaped with peasant bewilderment at the complicated splendour of the capital, and was incessantly scratching his neck, a habit for which he was rebuked by his superiors. He became the clown of the servants' quarters. But clowns are popular and his fellows did their best to teach him some notion of decent behaviour. He took care to make friends in every department of the palace. In his spare time he used to visit them, and so got to know the geography of the building. He discovered that the cellar which served as workroom and living room for himself and two other men was directly under the guardroom, which last was under the Emperor's private dining room.

The failure of the attempt at Moscow on November 19 meant that everything for the moment depended on Khalturin. Kviatkovski started supplying him with explosive. The two used to meet in the town and Kviatkovski would bring little packets of explosive in his pocket, which Khalturin took back and hid under his pillow.

On November 24 Kviatkovski was arrested and his plans of the palace discovered.

Two nights later all the workmen and servants in the palace were waked by a detachment of soldiers. Everybody was turned out of bed, lined up, checked off, and searched. Then the personal luggage was searched. But not the beds. Khalturin's small store of dynamite remained undiscovered under his pillow. But from that date discipline was tightened up. A gendarmerie post was established permanently in the cellar. A strict control over servants and workers was instituted. They were served out with identity discs to be produced whenever they went in or out. In addition they were regularly searched on coming in.

Zhelyabov, who had just returned from Alexandrovsk, took over Kviatkovski's duties and went on with the supply of explosive. Now of course the quantities had to be small enough to be smuggled back in Khalturin's boots or the lining of his coat. Luckily the police patrols knew him and trusted him. It was safe as long as the quantities were very small. But it was slow work. Besides, night inspections and surprise searches became more frequent.

Khalturin continued to play the hick. Petrotski, the corporal of gendarmes in the cellar, was at first amused, and then, like the others, became genuinely fond of the man and tried to teach him better manners. He did his best to stop the neck scratching. He was particularly upset to see Khalturin picking his nose in the presence of an officer. But he appreciated his honest character and noted that he was hard working and likely to end up as a master carpenter. So Petrotski brought his daughter to the palace and introduced her. Later he hinted to Khalturin that the two would make a good match: finally he made the proposal outright. Khalturin was non-committal; but, as he explained to Zhelyabov, this was a gratifying sign that the gendarmes did not suspect him. He obtained a further proof a few days later when the Emperor himself came into the room where he was working. "If only," he said to Zhelyabov, "I had had a hammer." At Christmas he received a gratuity of one hundred roubles.

The arrest of Kviatkovski and the subsequent crop of rumours caused a very natural excitement among the palace workmen. There were discussions in Khalturin's cellar as to the possibility of some terrorist ("socialist" was the term used) forcing his way into the palace. Khalturin took part in these discussions. He asked his friend Petrotski how one could tell a socialist, and the corporal explained that socialists were desperate-looking fellows with wild eyes and ferocious gestures: they were easy to recognise.

Khalturin's health was affected. He was consumptive, and suffered from living in a cellar. In addition there was the strain of having continuously to play up to his part. Sleep was interrupted by the night alarms and searches. The risk of detection grew greater as his store of explosive increased. He had perpetual headaches, and at last realised he was being gassed by the fumes from the dynamite under his pillow. He transferred his store little by little, whenever he was left alone in the cellar, to his box where he kept his spare shirt and few personal belongings. This box was to be the mine. There was no possibility of laying it elsewhere.

III

MEANWHILE the authorities had become suspicious of the flat in the Sapernaya where the printing press was housed. Major Miller, of the Petersburg police, was ordered to carry out a raid on the night of January 17–18. Miller knew that the flat had two entrances. He sent his assistant with a couple of police to watch the back, and came himself to the front door with the rest of his force and the porter. The porter, as instructed, rang the bell. Nothing happened. Then he rang again; a woman's voice asked who was there and he answered, "A telegram." There was silence. (No telegrams were ever sent to this flat so that this answer proved it was a raid; but the police, of course, did not know that.) The porter shouted again for the door to be opened. Then the woman's voice—it was Ivanova's—was heard calling, "Wake up, the police!" Miller told his men to knock the door in. They broke it open and he went through. It was dark inside, but a figure loomed out of one of the rooms and fired at him. Miller—who knew how the flat lay—bolted into the kitchen, and as the shots followed him he ran through the kitchen and out of the back door where he found his assistant waiting. He told him to keep a watch on both front and back entrances while he went for reinforcements.

What had happened inside was that Ivanova had told Ptashka to keep the police out while the rest of them burnt the documents. They packed the stove with manuscripts, passport blanks, government seals (stolen for them by Kletochnikov), lists of associates, lists of police spies. When the stove did not burn fast enough they piled the papers on the floor and set fire to them there. They smashed the windows. Gendarmes posted in the street outside saw smoke pouring out of them and sent for the fire brigade.

Miller was gone about half an hour. While he was away his assistant went down the stairs, round and up to the front. Ptashka had shut the front door by that time, and as the officer tried to open it two more shots came through the panel, wounding him in the hand. The police ran down to cover on the floor below. When Miller arrived with reinforcements they fired a volley through the door. A male voice in the darkness beyond shouted "We surrender"; and then came Ivanova's voice, cursing the men for cowards. The police made a rush. As they reached the hall there were two more shots; then again a shout of "We surrender." The police pushed on and found the two girls and two men. They pressed into the next room and discovered Ptashka lying on the floor with his brains all over the carpet. He had taken two shots to kill himself: the first only grazed the temple, but the second went through his forehead. The police removed their prisoners under escort and proceeded to search the flat. But all the incriminating documents had been burned.

Early next morning Morozov looked down from his flat, and saw Zhelyabov, who had succeeded Kviatkovski as link with the press, hurrying along the street and looking up for the all-clear signal in the window. He had come with news of the raid on the Sapernaya flat. He was afraid he might be too late and that the police might have found Morozov's address and have already descended on him.

Within a couple of months the party got another press going in quarters in the Podolskaya.

IV

KHALTURIN meanwhile continued with his work. By the middle of January he had stored a hundred pounds of dynamite in his trunk. Kibalchich reported to the Executive Committee that this quantity, exploded in Khalturin's box, would be sufficient to destroy the cellar, the guardroom immediately above it and the Emperor's dining room on the floor above that. Accordingly, always provided that the explosion was correctly synchronised with the Emperor's presence, they now had enough and to increase the quantity would merely increase the number of innocent victims. This last argument appealed strongly to the committee. Zhelyabov, who in any case was impatient by temperament, found additional grounds for urging immediate action. He realised the growing risk of detection and he saw Khalturin often enough to appreciate the imminent possibility of his physical breakdown.

But Khalturin objected, with all the suspicious obstinacy of a hard-headed working man opposed to a pack of intellectuals. He ridiculed the idea of his breaking down. He was convinced the police and authorities trusted him and would go on doing so. Finally, the attempt to couple humanitarianism with blowing up an imperial palace was absurd. There were bound to be at least fifty innocent victims in any case. The one essential was to make absolutely sure of success. The parties wrangled inconclusively for some days. Then Zhelyabov made use of a rumour that new quarters outside the palace were to be found for the carpenters, and Khalturin was forced to toe the line. That same evening he fixed up a fuse in an iron pipe that ran up the wall behind his box.

Two conditions were necessary for firing the fuse: the Emperor had to be in his dining room, and Khalturin alone in the cellar below. As to the first, the Emperor dined at half-past five. He was not particularly punctual, but he had usually started by six. The other condition was more difficult. The absence or presence of the workmen depended on the particular job they happened to be doing; but Petrotski, the gendarmerie corporal, had no fixed hours and might be there at any time. Every afternoon for a fortnight Zhelyabov hung about in one or other of the streets off the Admiralty Square. Each time Khalturin walked past as if he did not know him. This went on till February 5.

At the subsequent enquiry Razumovski, one of Khalturin's fellow-workmen, said that at five o'clock on the afternoon of February 5 he, Bogdanov (another workman) and Batishkov were sitting in their cellar drinking tea. They had not bothered to light the lamp. Petrotski was not there. Bogdanov finished his tea and went back to his work. Another workman looked in and asked for Petrotski. They supposed he was somewhere about in the palace. The man then asked why they were sitting in the dark and they explained they were just going back to work. All the same, Razumovski went to light the lamp, but Batishkov told him he had upset it half an hour before and spilled the paraffin. Razumovski wanted a light to find some tools, and Batishkov pulled a candle end out of his pocket and lit it. When the tools were found he blew it out again. Razumovski went off to his work and left Batishkov sitting in the dark.

Another workman said that at a quarter past five he passed the cellar window and looked down. Batishkov was alone there. He had the stump of a candle and was bending over something at the far end of the cellar. But he had his back to the window, and it was impossible to see what he was doing.

A little after six Khalturin met Zhelyabov at their usual rendezvous. This time he said "It's ready." The two turned and walked back to the corner of the Admiralty Square, and looked across to the Winter Palace. It was a dreary February evening. Suddenly at twenty minutes past six there was a terrific explosion and all the lights in the palace went out. People came running from the doors. The guard turned out. Then men with stretchers began to carry out the dead and wounded. (The total casualties were ten soldiers and one civilian killed, and thirty-three soldiers and twenty-three civilians wounded.) Zhelyabov and Khalturin waited as long as they dared in hope of news of the Emperor; but they could not wait long as the police would be combing the streets. When they reached the conspiratorial quarter Khalturin fainted from weakness, exhaustion and nervous strain. As soon as he came to he asked about the Emperor. They could not tell him. He began to rave, said he knew the police were after him, and wanted a pistol to shoot himself. At last they calmed him by saying the house was mined and they would blow themselves up if the police came.

It was not till next morning that they heard that the Emperor was safe. Prince Alexander of Battenberg had arrived in Petersburg in the afternoon and had been received in private audience. The audience had gone on until after the usual dinner hour, and the Emperor was just starting for the dining room when the mine exploded.

Zhelyabov at once began to talk of getting ready for the next attempt. But Khalturin was furious. He maintained that the failure was entirely due to the Executive Committee having refused to follow his advice. He declared that Zhelyabov was personally responsible, and refused to co-operate further with the Executive Committee as at present constituted. It was impossible to pacify him. He packed up and left Petersburg. It was not until a year after Zhelyabov's death that he again took part in the Narodnaya Volya's activities.

V

The blowing up of the Emperor's own palace in the middle of his capital was the most sensational attack that the revolutionaries had launched. The impression created throughout the Empire was immense. The explosion was followed up by a manifesto from the Narodnaya Volya. The Executive Committee expressed regret for the death of innocent victims, but declared the party's intention to go on with the struggle "until the Emperor shall have handed over the task of Government to a freely elected Constituent Assembly." So long as this first step had not been made towards the emancipation of the Fatherland, the party would carry on its struggle to the end by every means within its power.

There were far-reaching repercussions in the inner circle of the Government. Internal unrest had long been regarded as a serious problem. Nearly a year before, in the spring of 1879, the Emperor had appointed a commission consisting of the Ministers of the Interior, Education, War, Justice and Finance, and the Chief of the Third Section, with Valuev, Minister of Imperial Domains, as chairman, to report on the causes of the "rapid spread of subversive doctrines" and to suggest some practical remedy. The commission had already reported that "while refusing to admit the situation as being hopeless it must be recognised as critical; and the danger threatening the Government must not be ignored."

The explosion brought matters to a head. Three days later a meeting was held at the palace at which the Crown Prince, the unremitting opponent of any form of concession, gave his opinion that the cause of the trouble was not the insufficiency of police measures but the lack of cohesion between the various government organs. He proposed the appointment of a Supreme Commission, with an outstanding personality as chairman, who would assume full responsibility for the re-establishment of order. The idea was promptly put into effect. The following day, at a meeting of the six governor generals, the Emperor approved the creation of a Supreme Commission and placed at its head Count Loris-Melikov, Governor General of Kharkov and conqueror of Kars in the Turkish War.

A fortnight later a student named Mlodetski made an unsuccessful attempt on Loris-Melikov's life. Two days afterwards the Executive Committee issued another proclamation:
"With reference to the attempt of February 20, the Executive Committee find it necessary to state that its inception and execution were due solely to private initiative. It is a fact that Mlodetski offered his services to the committee for some terrorist act. But he was unwilling to await a decision and he proceeded to carry through his attempt without the knowledge and without the assistance of the Executive Committee."

VI

WE HAVE it on Yakimova's authority that when Zhelyabov wrote in March to his friend Sagaidak in Alexandrovsk with money for the half year's rent he was still hoping to blow up the Emperor's train there on its way back to the Crimea in the early summer. But in April news came through from the Third Section (via, of course, Kletochnikov) that showed the project to be impossible. Something had occurred which probably contributed more than anything else to the ultimate disasters of the Narodnaya Volya. Goldenberg, in prison, had begun to talk.

The handling of Goldenberg, a brilliant piece of police work, was conducted by a Captain Dobrinski. He possessed in the highest degree the technique of dealing with political prisoners. Of the only two other police officers who had anything like his success, Sudeikin was too oily and Strelnikov too gruff. (Incidentally both of these last were killed in the end by the party's agents.) But Dobrinski's manner had just the right degree of quiet friendliness and frankness. He started by putting Goldenberg in the same cell with another political, one Kuritsin. Kuritsin had turned renegade and was in police employ, but Goldenberg did not know this. Goldenberg talked to Kuritsin and Kuritsin passed on what he said, so that when he began his interviews with Dobrinski, the latter already knew a great deal and managed to persuade Goldenberg that the police knew so much that any hope of success by terrorist action was doomed. He convinced him, too, that he (Dobrinski) was a warm advocate of liberal reforms, and that he had official knowledge that such reforms had already been approved by the Emperor in principle; it was only terrorist activity that was holding them up.

Some time later, when he had got to know his man, he suggested that it was up to Goldenberg to come to the rescue of his country by acting as mediator between the Government and the revolutionaries. Goldenberg fell into the trap. He first asked for an assurance that no harm should come to his former associates. This was given. Thereafter, for weeks on end, he and Dobrinski discussed the possibilities of mediation. In the process all the details of Goldenberg's revolutionary background came out—the attempts on the railway line at Odessa, Alexandrovsk and Moscow; the Lipetsk conference; the killing of Kropotkin; the attempt of Soloviev; Goldenberg's earliest exploits. Names, pseudonyms, addresses and particulars were checked up. As a result the police were able to circulate to their agents a list of over a hundred names and descriptions of political conspirators, and a mass of evidence was handed to the Public Prosecutor's Department to be used as and when required. When he had got all he could out of Goldenberg Dobrinski dropped him, and a subordinate officer took him on. There was no longer the need to keep the farce up. "Remember," Goldenberg said at the end of one session, "not a hair on any of my friends' heads is to be touched." "We don't bother about their hair," said the officer. "We want their necks." Goldenberg thought he was joking.

Not long afterwards Zundelevich was transferred to that prison. He heard from Goldenberg what had been happening and was appalled. Goldenberg refused for some time to believe he had been tricked. When at last conviction came to him he tore his prison towel into strips and made a rope of it, and next morning the warder found him hanging dead from a bar in the window. Kviatkovski passed out a message to his comrades that Goldenberg should not be regarded as a traitor. But the harm had been done. Besides the names, descriptions and evidence, the authorities had acquired a wide knowledge of the party's organisation, scope and methods, and of the identity of the party's leaders. Apart from the intrinsic value of this information the police could and did use it to decisive effect when they had young and inexperienced prisoners in their hands.

VII

KLETOCHNIKOV's report on the revelations of Goldenberg made a big difference to the revolutionary plans. Any further thought of Alexandrovsk was, of course, out of the question. The police had already visited the site and dug up the two cylinders with the dynamite. Indeed it seemed advisable to abandon the whole idea of an attack on the imperial train. The Executive Committee decided early in April that an entirely new scheme was necessary. They worked it out in broad outline, and, at the end of the month, Perovskaya was sent to Odessa with orders to carry it through.

Our knowledge of this second abortive attempt at Odessa is derived from Vera Figner's memoirs and from the depositions made by Merkulov to the police. Figner was then the resident representative of the Executive Committee at Odessa. At that time she was busy on a scheme directed against one of the local officials. She was acting on her own initiative, and, apparently, without the sanction of the Executive Committee. In any case as soon as Perovskaya arrived she dropped her previous scheme. All her energies were required on the new attempt, the more so as the Executive Committee had no funds to spare for the venture, and were relying on Figner to raise the money from her local contacts at Odessa.

The plan was to choose a street on the Emperor's route between the railway station and the harbour; take premises there and open a shop; and then tunnel a gallery from the basement and lay a mine under the middle of the road. It is proof of the efficiency and drive of the two girls that they had raised the money, installed a grocer's shop at No. 47 Italianskaya, and were well under the road with the gallery all within a month. Other members were sent down to help them. Sablin played the part of Perovskaya's husband and proprietor of the shop. Zlatopolski helped with the mining. Yakimova and Isaev established themselves in a conspiratorial quarter where Isaev prepared the explosive. In addition Zhelyabov had sent a note recommending the employment of a young workman, Merkulov, and he was duly recruited. He was a difficult lad and Figner did not like him. He was always complaining and finding fault, and crabbing about the intellectuals' role in the movement as compared to that of the workmen. The others thought that he was working off some complex and tried to humour him.

They had a drill and the actual tunnelling gave no difficulty. The first setback was an accident in the laboratory. Isaev blew off three fingers on his right hand. Yakimova had to take him to the Municipal Hospital. It was an extremely painful wound but Isaev insisted on coming out of hospital almost at once. He was able to go back to his old quarters. Merkulov had been sent to make investigations at the block where he lived, and had reported that none of the neighbours had noticed the explosion. They went on with the work. Time began to press. They could only work at night as by day it would have been impossible to hide their activities from customers in the shop. They dumped the excavated earth in a small room at the back. A rumour came that all houses along the Emperor's route were to be searched the night before he passed. So the earth was packed into trunks and parcels and transferred to Figner's flat. She got rid of it as best she could at night, after her maid had left.

Finally news came that the Emperor would not be passing through Odessa. Figner wrote to Petersburg to propose using the mine to kill General Todtleben, the Governor General. This was turned down by the Executive Committee, for the present mining operations must be reserved for the Emperor. Figner, however, was authorised to organise an attempt on Todtleben by other means. So the grocer's shop was tidied up and all traces of the tunnelling operations hidden. Perovskaya and the others went back to Petersburg. Figner and Sablin stayed on and made various plans for Todtleben. They explored the possibilities of a bomb attack: it was difficult, because no convenient form of hand grenade had as yet been evolved. Then Todtleben left Odessa, and so that project also came to nothing.

Figner by this time was getting tired of the provinces, and applied to the Executive Committee for a transfer to Petersburg. Her application was approved and Misha Trigoni, Zhelyabov's old school friend, was appointed to take her place at Odessa. Figner hurried back to Petersburg; and was duly hauled over the coals by the committee for not having waited to hand over personally to her successor.

VIII

WHEN the Odessa plans broke down the revolutionaries made one further attempt to assassinate the Emperor in Petersburg. It was organised by Zhelyabov and consisted of a scheme to blow up the Kamenni Bridge on the Ekaterinski Canal as the Emperor passed over it on his way to the railway station to entrain for the South.

Our knowledge of this attempt is derived solely from the subsequent court proceedings, in particular from the depositions of Merkulov who, together with Isaev, had returned from Odessa in time to participate. Barannikov, Presnyakov, Merkulov and Teterka were given a rendezvous in a small bar near one of the canals. Here they were joined by Zhelyabov who explained his plan for blowing up the bridge. Merkulov, in his depositions, stated that, in addition, Alexander Mihailov had a scheme for posting four bomb throwers near the bridge in case the big explosion failed. Mihailov himself would have a bomb hidden in his hat. But Mihailov at his trial denied this story and it seems probable that Merkulov was inventing.

A few days later Teterka was told by Zhelyabov to go to a certain address and ask for "the cushion." He did so and "an unknown man" gave him a sack with a gutta-percha container, weighing about seventy pounds. The police were subsequently able to identify this man as Isaev who admitted he had prepared the explosive and containers. Teterka carried the sack to the Petrovski Park where Zhelyabov and Presnyakov were waiting for him. They had a boat on the canal there, already containing a similar sack and coils of wire. All three got in the boat and rowed out to a spot where they could work unobserved. There they attached the wires and rowed back via the Fontanka, the Kryukovi and the Ekaterinski Canals as far as the Kamenni Bridge. When they reached the bridge they let the sacks overboard and fixed the loose ends of the wires to a raft at some little distance up stream.

When the day and time of the Emperor's departure had been ascertained Zhelyabov arranged for Teterka to meet him in the town and bring a basket of potatoes. Zhelyabov was to bring a battery and an induction coil. These were to be hidden in the basket under the potatoes and taken down to the raft. The wires were to be connected and Zhelyabov and Teterka would sit washing the potatoes till the Emperor reached the crown of the bridge, when Zhelyabov would press the lever.

Such was the plan. It was brought to nothing by "the Russian nature" against which Alexander Mihailov was so constantly warning his comrades. Teterka had no watch and turned up late at the rendezvous. They hurried down to the raft, but it was too late. The Emperor had already passed the bridge and was well on his way to the station. He would not return to Petersburg until the autumn.

Two nights later Zhelyabov, Teterka and Barannikov went out in a boat to try and recover the explosive. They failed; their grapnels were unsuitable. So the sacks remained at the bottom of the canal till the police fished them up a year later.

IX

THE fiasco at the Kamenni Bridge was the last episode of the first terrorist campaign of the Narodnaya Volya. The campaign had lasted eight months and entailed the organisation of six attempts. Four of them had failed to materialise, and the knowledge that they had ever been planned was confined to the handful of actual participants and to the members of the Executive Committee. Two attempts had been carried out and had failed. The party had lost its first printing press. Five members of the Executive Committee and some half dozen of its "agents" had been arrested. In addition, thanks to the disclosures of Goldenberg, the police were hot on the trail of Presnyakov and Okladski, both of whom were apprehended in July.

In spite of this the net result of the campaign was a considerable addition to the strength and prestige of the party. It must be remembered that when, on the breakup of the Zemlya i Volya, the Narodnaya Volya came into being, the latter consisted of some twenty young men and women whose aims and views were known only to a handful of fellow-revolutionaries who disagreed with them. Their total resources consisted of, at most, something like $1500 in cash, two hundredweight of dynamite, a printing press, a few personal contacts, and nothing else. But the explosions on the railway line at Moscow

The Spring Campaign

and in the Winter Palace at Petersburg turned this obscure little group into front page news. The Executive Committee became a definite factor in the affairs of the Empire. The attempts organised by the committee convinced the authorities of the impossibility of proceeding along the old lines, and opened the way to the experiments of Loris-Melikov. The party's demands for constitutional liberties won them considerable sympathy in liberal circles. And the sensational attacks on the autocracy made an irresistible appeal to the emotions of youth. The stock of the Cherni Peredel began to slump: doctrinaire socialism and the weary round of uphill propaganda in the villages lacked the glamour of what the Narodnaya Volya were doing. The young party had more recruits than it could properly absorb.

All this is a remarkable example of what can be achieved by terrorist action. But there is another side to the picture. Terrorism, even more than war, requires meticulous training and an iron discipline to enable human nature to support the strain. The human element, without discipline to back it, is uncertain. Enthusiasms waver and ideals become distorted. The young founders of the Narodnaya Volya, outlaws, with no safe base to retire to, living in hiding and chased day and night by the police, had neither time nor opportunity to instil this discipline into their agents. They could inspire devotion, but devotion is not enough. Goldenberg, left to his own devices, was tricked.

CHAPTER NINE

"TARASS"

I

IN THE early summer of 1879 Zhelyabov had been persuaded with some difficulty to declare himself ready to take part in one attempt on the Emperor's life, after which, as he insisted, he was to be completely free to renounce all further connexion with terrorist action. Within a year he had assisted in organising no less than six attacks; he had played the leading role in the execution of two of them, and an important part in a third. He was regarded in revolutionary circles as the leader of the extreme militant wing. One of his old Odessa friends has recorded his bewilderment at this transformation of a peaceful propagandist into a firebrand of the revolution.

But the change is not inconsistent with what we know of Zhelyabov's personality. By temperament he was a fighter. His immediate reaction was always to hit back, not to move into safety or to compromise. As a child he dreamed of revenge on Lorentsov. As a schoolboy the Karakozov attempt filled him with enthusiasm. We have every reason to suspect that his early interest in explosives was not inspired by an academic devotion to science. He must already have realised that violent action of some kind would be needed to bring about the revolution, and that he must prepare himself to play his part. He had no humanitarian scruples. He never spared himself or felt the temptation to spare others.

His early opposition to terrorism was twofold. He disliked Osinski personally and he did not see what practical good could come of Osinski's campaign. Zhelyabov became a wholehearted terrorist, but never an indiscriminate one. He never shared Morozov's belief in terrorism as the supreme remedy for social and political ills. For Zhelyabov terrorist action was one weapon among many. It was a valuable weapon, certainly, but only so long as it formed part of an organised and co-ordinated effort towards a definite objective.

After Lipetsk his former objections were no longer valid. In Alexander Mihailov he found a colleague with whom he could work in complete harmony. The party's aims and programme were his own. And thus there was released that flood of dynamic energy which so astonished his old and new associates. The man himself had not changed, but now at last his abounding vitality could find an outlet. The Narodnaya Volya gave him all that any man of his temperament could ask for—a complete break with the failures and humiliations of the past, a leading role in a movement that had been his dream since childhood, the confidence that his part was well within his powers, and a vast empire waiting to be conquered.

II

WE POSSESS comparatively little material for the private lives of the Narodovoltsi. A strict impersonality was their ideal. Friendship, even within the party was frowned on, in theory at least, as "a violation of social justice," and contemporary records are mostly lacking in the personal touch. In the case of Zhelyabov only two letters have come down to us; both of them deal exclusively with the affairs of the movement. His most intimate associates died with him or soon afterwards, and revolutionary historians have been more concerned with the revolution than with the man himself. Nevertheless we have certain glimpses that are illuminating.

Anna Pribyleva-Korba, a member of the Executive Committee, has recorded an incident in the summer of 1880. She fell ill and was admitted to the Petersburg Public Hospital. There was one other patient in her ward, a young dressmaker's assistant. One day four visitors arrived—Perovskaya, Zhelyabov, Barannikov and Isaev. They were all in the best of spirits and the visit was a happy one. The little dressmaker lay listening to the anecdotes and laughter. When they had gone she turned to Korba.

"Who are these people?"
"They're old friends of mine."

"I've never seen people like that before. How did you get to know them?"

"I've known them for years."

"They're wonderful. I don't know who's the nicest. They're each nicer than the other. They're so clever and so amusing and, well, so good. One can see that they're good. You're wonderfully lucky to have friends like that."

All the time she was in hospital, Korba tells us, the little dressmaker kept harking back to that visit and asking when her friends were coming again.

Zhelyabov's good spirits were not unfailing. At times he was moody and depressed. There is evidence of this in an incident that took place soon after he had got his Workers' Section started. In view of the usual shortage of funds it was arranged to hold meetings for university students to explain the work that was going on and to induce them to subscribe. We have the account of a girl who attended one of these meetings. She was invited by Kokovski, a young student closely associated with Zhelyabov in organising the workers. On this occasion fifteen were present—all legals. A sympathiser had let them use his living room. Zhelyabov as usual was late. He looked tired and dejected. When his turn came to speak he mumbled and repeated himself. Those present who knew him by reputation as the party's great orator and organiser were bewildered. When at last he finished Kokovski got up and tried to salvage what could be salvaged of the meeting.

Suddenly Zhelyabov grew paler. Kokovski broke off in the middle of a sentence and went on to speak about a serial story that was running in one of the papers. The audience looked round and saw the porter at the door. He asked what was happening and the occupant of the room explained it was a nameday party. The porter remarked, "Well, I shall have to tell the police," and left them. There was panic and confusion. The host produced what food and vodka he had in his cupboard. A student went out for beer. The main problem was to get rid of Zhelyabov: if the police found him he was lost and all the others hopelessly compromised. But Zhelyabov refused to go. He was evidently ashamed of his previous performance, and intended to retrieve his self-respect by his behaviour in the crisis. He came to life. He joked, told stories, chatted about his plans. The minutes went by. The others grew more and more apprehensive. Finally Kokovski pushed him into his coat and out of the door. The party listened anxiously for sounds in the passage. If nothing happened for five minutes they could be confident he had got away. The five minutes passed, and the relief and reaction were so great that when at last the police officer arrived he received a royal welcome. They made him join in the party. He became completely drunk and told such disgusting stories that the young ladies did not know which way to look.

Zhelyabov was a hard taskmaster. A few months after his arrest Okladski gave way under police examination and began to talk. He was brought to trial and sentenced, but the farce was not kept up for long; he was released and became a whole-time Secret Police agent. More than forty years later, in 1925, the Ogpu came across his record in the Tsarist archives. The old man was arrested and tried before the Soviet Court, and the few surviving veterans of his revolutionary days were called to testify against the renegade. Okladski told his story simply and without emotion. He described the winter nights at Alexandrovsk when Zhelyabov took him out to the embankment. He looked across the court to Yakimova. "You all think he was a hero," he said. "But he had many faults. He was a complete egoist."

And yet Zhelyabov, like Alexander Mihailov, could show tact and understanding in handling his colleagues. There was the case of Tikhomirov, "Starik" as they called him, who found the life of a revolutionary to be telling more and more on his nerves. Korba has left us an account of a meeting of the Executive Committee in the summer of 1880. At the end of the proceedings Tikhomirov made a speech. He had been tortured, he said, by the thought that his comrades had, and always had had, a far higher opinion of him than he really deserved. He therefore begged the committee to accept his resignation and to absolve him of all further responsibility and obligation towards the party.

Mihailov was the first to answer.

"My dear Starik, if I may say so without being offensive, you are talking rubbish. We all have a high respect for you and your work. It is thanks to you that the party's written propaganda has been so effective. Your help and advice in our committee has been second to none. And since you talk of resignation, I must remind you that you yourself drafted our constitution, under which the resignation of any member is expressly and unconditionally forbidden."

Zhelyabov got up.

"I too am entirely against our friend Starik resigning. I am sure that such a suggestion on his part can only be due to his being physically run down. I propose we send him south on sick leave. Being a Southerner he will pick up more quickly there than in Petersburg."

So Tikhomirov went south to recuperate.

III

WE HAVE record of certain remarks of Zhelyabov which help us to form a picture of the man and of the militant revolutionary.

There was the Revolutionary Red Cross. This was an organisation whose main object was to assist political prisoners and to facilitate escapes. It was in friendly contact with all the revolutionary groups, and the Narodnaya Volya had a representative on its committee. The activities of the Revolutionary Red Cross were, of course, illegal. But they did not entail anything like the risk that attached to the work of the fighting sections of the party, and there was a tendency on the part of certain members to attach themselves entirely to the Red Cross. Zhelyabov at once took a firm stand against this tendency:

"I am not saying anything against the Red Cross," he said. "Apart from its own work it has a value for us as a school for young revolutionaries. One reason why we have a representative on their committee is to see what people they have who might in time be fit to undertake more serious work. But to allow the Red Cross to recruit our own people would merely be to deplete our forces for the real issue. We must not exaggerate values, and we must call things by their proper names. Philanthropy—even revolutionary philanthropy—is philanthropy, and war is war."

Of terrorism he said:

"You can call it the heroic method. But it is also the most practical: that is to say if, an important if, you keep on with it unceasingly. Occasional individual attacks may alarm the public, but they do not effectively demoralise an administration. You must make attack after attack uninterruptedly and relentlessly against one fixed and prearranged target."

One of his colleagues once reproached him for tiring himself out by personally attending to the multiplicity of small tasks that the organisation of a revolution entails. Zhelyabov answered:

"You cannot always tell what is a trifle. It may sometimes turn out—and then it may happen that it is essential to mobilise not only the whole party but also the maximum effort of each individual in the party. And anyhow, it is my nature to go on like that. Besides, people keep coming to me with all sorts of ideas which they try and force on me. It is better if I have my own first-hand impressions of everything and then I can take a line of my own and be sure of it."

IV

AND so we can form some picture of Zhelyabov the man. To his colleagues he was friendly, simple and easy of access. He had to a marked degree the gift of inspiring the devotion and enthusiasm of men and women of very different class and temperament. To Kokovski, the student, he was *the* great revolutionary hero to whom no other could be compared. Rysakov, the artisan, admits that he was "completely dazzled." Sukhanov, the naval officer, felt for him a devotion that was almost fanatical. There are many other instances. But this magnetism of Zhelyabov, coupled with his impatience and a certain lack of discrimination in judging character, was a real cause of danger to the party. Events proved that some of his recruits were only to be trusted so long as he was there to lead them.*

There were probably some among his colleagues on the Executive Committee who did not like him, but we have no evidence of this except in the case of Vera Figner, and then only by implication. It is likely enough that two such domineering personalities would find cause for friction. Figner, we know, was apt to argue back when decisions of the Executive

---

* Okladski, Rysakov and Merkulov were all recruited by Zhelyabov. It is interesting to note that Azev, the notorious agent provocateur of the succeeding generation, who possessed an unattractive personality and made a point of discouraging recruits, had no defections from his Battle Organisation.

Committee did not suit her; and we can be certain that Zhelyabov was relentless in demanding that same blind obedience that he forced himself to observe. All the same Figner in her memoirs calls him "our leader and tribune."

He was an egoist. Tikhomirov tells us he well realised this was his great failing and that his life for those months with the Narodnaya Volya was a constant struggle to keep down his personal ambition, to bend to the will of the majority, to cease to be the man Zhelyabov and be instead the instrument of the Executive Committee. This discipline he maintained to the end. At his final trial, when he was the central figure in the most sensational process of his generation, his attitude was completely impersonal. Throughout his long duels with the prosecution and the court, he was fighting not for his life, for that issue was not in question; not for his honour as a revolutionary leader; not for any personal faith; but for the policy and programme which the party had laid down.

His egoism may well have been the flamboyance of youth. For a Russian he was late in maturing, and it has been said of him that he never really grew up. There was much of the adolescent about him—his impatience, his love of working with his hands, his little vanities. He was inordinately proud of his long black beard. This last was so conspicuous that Alexander Mihailov begged him, for the sake of security, to trim it down. He would not listen. "They can catch me if they can," he said. "But I will not have my beard touched."

He could live for the moment and take all the moment had to offer. But often he was immersed in day-dreams. He loved the water. In his Petersburg days his great recreation was to take a boat and row himself out to the mouth of the Neva: the vast expanse of grey sea and grey sky and flat coast-line moved him to ecstasy. He was profoundly affected by music, especially by the Cossack melodies he had known since childhood. He was an omnivorous reader, especially of poetry and romance that gave him the stuff to feed his day-dreams. A friend once called at his room a few hours after his return from three days and nights of continuous travelling and work. He expected to find him asleep: but Zhelyabov was wide awake, sitting up in bed and finishing Gogol's *Tarass Bulba*. He explained he had picked it up as he got into bed, and had just gone on reading; it was impossible to lay it down. He was completely carried away by the book. The saga of blood and battle and implacable struggle against enormous odds had touched his innermost being. For days he would talk of nothing else. One of his friends took to calling him Tarass and, as the cap so obviously fitted, the nickname stuck. Zhelyabov used many pseudonyms, but to his intimates he remained "Tarass."

V

He was no ascetic like Kibalchich and Alexander Mihailov. It was easy for him to make an impression on the young women with whom he came in contact. He had every natural advantage—his good looks, his magnificent physique, his daring, his prestige, his simplicity of manner, his virility. We are told he took full advantage of his opportunities. It was only towards the end that a new factor came into his life.

He first met Sophie Perovskaya at the Trial of the 193 in the winter of 1877–78 at Petersburg. He seems to have made no impression on her. We can guess, however, that she made an impression on him by the attention he paid to her at the Voronezh conference eighteen months later. It may well be that conscious as ever of his own serf origin he was piqued by her noble birth. But at Voronezh she disapproved of his political theories and would not listen to him. Finally he left her in a huff. But they were still in touch when the party returned to Petersburg, and we find her showing annoyance when Plekhanov saw fit to be sarcastic at Zhelyabov's expense. When she came back from the attempt at Moscow and found that the Cherni Peredel had made no progress towards a general peasant rising, it was Zhelyabov whom she consulted. Next morning Zhelyabov announced, "with radiant joy," that Perovskaya was willing to become a member of the Executive Committee.

In the spring Perovskaya was sent down to organise the mining venture at Odessa. Soon after her return began her close partnership with Zhelyabov in revolutionary work. Together they organised the workers' movement. We hear of their going, with Barannikov and Isaev, to visit Korba in hospital, and of their being in high spirits. Gradually the "self-willed and domineering" Perovskaya, the admitted man-hater, came to realise where her feelings were leading her. She did nothing by halves and her surrender was complete. Figner says that Zhelyabov "swept her off her feet." That summer she was sharing a flat in the 1st Rota Ismailovski Polk with another girl, one Rina Epstein. In September Epstein told the porter she was going to Moscow and left. A few days later Zhelyabov moved in, with a false passport making him out as Perovskaya's brother.

Tikhomirov writes:

"He became intimately associated with Perovskaya and for the last few months they lived as man and wife. Perovskaya was, for him, his 'wife' in the sense in which he understood the term. It meant much to him. He had a very high opinion of her intelligence and her character; as a colleague in the cause he felt she was incomparable. In their circumstances one cannot speak of 'happiness.' There was continual anxiety—not for each self but for the other—continual preoccupation, the unceasing rush of work which meant that they could scarcely ever be alone, the certainty that sooner or later there was bound to come a tragic ending. But there were times when the work was going well, when they were able to forget for a little and then it was a joy to see them, especially her. Her feeling was so overwhelming that in any but Perovskaya it would have crowded out all thoughts of her work."

Again, in his memoir of Perovskaya, Tikhomirov writes:

"In the last year of Sophie's life she fell in love for the first time. It was Zhelyabov. She had always been a strong feminist and maintained that men were the inferior sex. She had real respect for very few of them. But Zhelyabov was up to her calibre. She was utterly in love with him, in a way I never thought could happen to her with any man."

We know nothing of their life together except what came out at their trial. They lived very quietly and modestly. They had no servant. Perovskaya herself did the housework and the marketing. They received no letters and hardly any visitors. They generally stayed at home in the mornings, and went out between four and five in the afternoon. It was often late at night before they returned. Their home was a small one, consisting of two rooms and a kitchen. When the police finally made their raid they found it poorly furnished—like the flat of a minor clerk in a government office. There was a cheap tablecloth on the table, and the windows had muslin curtains.

The cushions were stuffed with straw. The samovar had a broken handle and the knives and forks and crockery were odd pieces from different sets. There were three or four books, novels. One was the recent Russian translation of *Lost for Love* by Miss Braddon.

CHAPTER TEN

ORGANISING REVOLUTION

I

THE appointment of Loris-Melikov was a measure of considerable importance. It would perhaps be inexact to describe him as a liberal. But his regime was very far from that envisaged by the Crown Prince when he originally made his proposal. After some months of office Loris-Melikov explained his policy to an intimate friend. "I have opposed," he said, "the aspirations of the constitutionalists, which for the moment are quite unrealisable in this country. But I am entirely of the opinion that we must listen to the views of sensible and practical men." In other words he wished to do what he could to secure and deserve the confidence of educated public opinion and thus "create a void round the revolutionaries." But he knew quite well that any proposal which might entail the limitation of the imperial prerogative would have no possible chance of acceptance by the Emperor.

Loris-Melikov could show some substantial achievement during his term of office. He managed to get the Supreme Commission abolished and remained himself as Minister of the Interior, with powers, however, that resembled those of a Prime Minister, or rather of a Grand Vizier. He secured the suppression of the Third Section as such. It became, with all its personnel (including Kletochnikov), one of the departments of the Ministry of the Interior. He secured the resignation of Count Tolstoi, the reactionary and unpopular Minister of Education. He produced a greater liberty for the press; and a number of more or less liberal periodicals began to make their appearance. He let it be generally known that his programme for the coming five or six years was to consolidate the activities of the Zemstva; to bring the police under full control of the law; to carry out a certain decentralisation of the Administration; to take measure of public opinion and public desires by special commissions of enquiry; and meanwhile to allow the press to discuss the activities of the State, so long, of course, as it did not "unsettle people's minds by illusory chimeras."

In the public eye this "Dictatorship of the Heart" seemed to have its reward in the cessation of terrorist attempts. As we have seen two attempts were in fact organised, though they failed to materialise. It is however a fact that after the Odessa attempt there was an interlude. None of the survivors of the Narodnaya Volya have attempted fully to explain this lull. But we are justified in assuming that they did believe there was some (though perhaps not a great) chance of the introduction of a constitution, and that they did not want to prejudice the issue by a renewed attack. At any rate in the early summer a meeting of the Executive Committee was called to decide an important point of principle. According to Korba who was present there was considerable discussion and a resolution was finally passed in the following form:

"To avoid anarchy, no attempt whatsoever is to be made to overthrow or to undermine the authority of the Constituent Assembly. In consequence, should the Constituent Assembly decide to maintain the imperial regime, this regime is to be acknowledged and recognised on condition that the party be allowed to continue its propaganda by all normal methods."

It was signed by Zhelyabov, Mihailov, Frolenko, Isaev, Kolotkevich, Barannikov, Korba, Lebedeva, Yakimova and Olovennikova. Figner and Perovskaya were presumably still in Odessa.

But the hope of constitutional concessions was not the sole reason for the lull. Some of the party's most valued members—including Kviatkovski, Shiraev, Zundelevich and Presnyakov—were in prison awaiting trial, and an attempt on the Emperor might make the difference between the death penalty and imprisonment. Another consideration was doubtless the fact that the Emperor had left for his summer resort at Livadia, and to attack him there presented serious tactical difficulties. Finally, as has been shown, the party had started from very small beginnings. So far it was trying to run before it could walk. A respite was urgently needed to absorb new members, collect funds, and build up an organisation on the lines laid down in the party's statutes.

II

FUNDS were always a problem. We find evidence of this time and time again. The revolutionaries were meticulously scrupulous about money. Figner records how Perovskaya came to her to borrow fifteen roubles. She had been ill and spent the money on medical treatment. "It must not," she told Figner, "come out of party funds." She informed Figner that her mother had sent her a silk cloak which she had given the house porter to sell; she would repay the loan out of the proceeds.

There is no evidence that the party kept regular accounts. Burtsev, an outstanding authority, is of the opinion that they did not do so. For the first few months notice of donations received was passed to Morozov who published acknowledgments in the *Narodnaya Volya* newspaper. On the basis of these acknowledgments it has been suggested that the income of the party for the first eighteen months of its existence was 15,000 roubles (or £1,500). All that time there were on an average some twenty members entirely dependent on party funds for their livelihood. We know they lived poorly, but they cannot have lived for less than 30 roubles a month. To keep twenty members for eighteen months at 30 roubles each would cost 10,800 roubles. That left, supposing the estimate to be correct, barely 4,000 roubles for travelling expenses, newspapers and printing, the explosive laboratories and incidentals. Incidentals are always heavy in an illegal secret society. Cabs, for instance, were often necessary to get rid of a police agent. At any moment some large or small expenditure might and often did become a matter of urgent necessity.

Certain members of the Executive Committee, notably Figner and Perovskaya, had monied friends from whom donations could from time to time be obtained. But in the last resort the financial question was bound up with that of popular appeal. The only sound basis was a long list of regular subscribers. This in itself is one of the reasons for the keen rivalry between the Narodnaya Volya and the Cherni Peredel. It was of vital importance to each of the parties to stake out a claim to any subscriptions that might potentially be forthcoming. There was a prolonged polemic between the two factions, and in the end the Cherni Peredel was reduced to a rump. But the issue was not decided by the logic of their arguments. It was the glamour of the Narodnaya Volya's attacks that appealed to the young people's emotions. But in this case emotional enthusiasm provoked only a meagre cash return. For one thing the appeal was felt principally by young students, who had very little money to give. For another the party remained too small and too preoccupied with other matters to organise their collecting service on a proper basis. The problem of finance was a chronic one, right to the end.

III

THE fact remains that the party had bitten off more than they could chew, and they had neither the time nor the personnel essential for the various tasks laid down in their programme. No great progress was made with the enlightenment of public opinion abroad. It was true the Hartmann case gave them a certain publicity. Hartmann had fled to France after the Moscow attempt. Thanks to the revelations of Goldenberg the Third Section were aware of the part he had played, and their agents located him in Paris. He was arrested by the French police at the instance of the Russian authorities, who demanded his extradition. The case became a big issue in French politics and the young Clemenceau and the ageing Victor Hugo showed great activity on Hartmann's behalf. In the end extradition was refused and he was released. Thereafter he became the representative of the Executive Committee abroad. He had neither the education nor the personal contacts for this role. Morozov spent several months abroad in 1880. But Morozov was also unsuitable. As an extreme Jacobin and out-and-out terrorist he was liable to estrange just those elements which the party desired to win over. In the summer of 1880 Zhelybov wrote to the celebrated Ukrainophil émigré Dragomanov—whom he had met seven years before in Kiev—and asked him to take over the task of presenting the party's case in the press abroad. Dragomanov refused: he was too ineradicably opposed to any policy that provided for terrorist action. Subsequently certain letters were addressed by the Executive Committee to other prominent Left Wing personalities, including Karl Marx. Though we know Marx to have been favourably impressed, we have no record of any replies received, far less of any specific results attained. The Narodnaya Volya was essentially a Russian phenomenon. It was neither inspired nor influenced by individuals or happenings abroad, and itself made little direct impression on the development of the social movement in the West.

We have few details of the party's work among the educated classes at home. The academic youth were, of course, naturally revolutionary minded. We know that frequent meetings of students were addressed by one or other member of the Executive Committee. We have evidence of the presence of Zhelyabov and Kolotkevich at at least one student demonstration. But we know nothing of any special organisation of the party set up to deal solely with either the students or the professional classes. There was, however, a close contact with certain of the leading liberal publicists. Figner and, especially, Tikhomirov, were very friendly with Mihailovski and Shelgunov, the respective editors of *Otechestvenne Zapiski* and *Dyelo*. Both these distinguished journalists were in full sympathy with the party's programme for a constitution, and had a high, even exaggerated, opinion of the party's strength. Their collaboration went so far as to allow Mihailovski to contribute unsigned articles to the revolutionary *Narodnaya Volya,* while Shelgunov published in the *Dyelo* a number of articles by Tikhomirov over the pseudonym "Koltsov."

IV

ONE of the earlier numbers of the *Narodnaya Volya* laid down that "if, at the first outbreak of revolt, the party can close the factories and get the workers into the streets in a revolutionary frame of mind, ultimate success is already half assured." Of all his activities the Workers' Section was probably nearest to Zhelyabov's heart. "I am a born demagogue," he once said. "My place is in the street, with a crowd of workmen." He was impatient, always anxious for quick results. He saw no prospect of quick results in a peasant movement. "Our trouble in Russia," he said, "is that we have no Parnell, no Fein. We cannot get any punch in an agrarian movement." The workmen were more venturesome than the peasants (or they would never have left their villages), less tied to the past, less prone to pin their hopes of change to the Emperor's bounty.

The Narodnaya Volya Workers' Section started from zero. Khalturin's union had been broken up. Similar efforts in the big towns in the South had come to nothing. All Zhelyabov had to build on was a short list of names of men who would be likely to listen without giving him away to the police. His personality was his great asset. It is a proof of the way the men took to him that at once they gave him a nickname. His *nom de guerre* in the Workers' Section was Zahar, but the men called him Borodach after his beard. He had his small band of helpers. One of them was Franzholi, an old comrade of the Volkhovski Circle in Odessa who had escaped from Siberia in March of 1880. As things progressed Zhelyabov divided up Petersburg into different districts and put an intellectual in charge of each. Perovskaya had the Petersburg quarter; Grinevitski the Viborg quarter; Kokovski the Vasilievski Island, to be succeeded there when his health broke down by Rysakov. They trained the workmen to take their part in the work of organisation. By the end of 1880, after eight months' effort, there were twenty workmen who could help with the recruiting and the formation of cells in the various factories. All together, by that time, they could claim some 250 members of the Workers' Section in Petersburg alone. In Moscow there were thirty cells with four or five members in each. There were others in Odessa, Kharkov and Rostov-on-Don. In addition there was a large number of workers who knew more or less what was going on and who sympathised, but who had not the courage to join outright.

Frolenko records that Zhelyabov reported one day to the Executive Committee that the workers wanted to have a revolutionary newspaper of their own: the *Narodnaya Volya* under Tikhomirov was essentially an intellectuals' paper. The committee approved of the proposal and allotted the necessary funds. A press was acquired and set up in a flat in the Troitski Pereulok, taken under a false name by Jesse Helfmann. Here they produced at long and irregular intervals the *Rabochaya Gazeta* (the *Workers' Paper*). The press was old and small, and they were doing well when they could turn off sixty sheets an hour. It is significant to note that none of the working-class members were as yet capable of helping on the editorial side. The material was written by Kokovski, Grinevitski and Zhelyabov himself. It is characteristic of Zhelyabov that whenever he could spare the time he would come himself and lend a hand in setting up the type. Perovskaya was another link between Helfmann and her colleagues and party headquarters. She would often call to encourage them and bring news of what was happening in the outside world.

It was on the press in the Troitski Pereulok that Zhelyabov and Kokovski printed, in the autumn of 1880, their Programme of the Workers' Section of the Narodnaya Volya. This document recapitulates in simple language the general aims of the party, and lays down the special tasks of the workers. The workers were reminded that they, together with their allies in every class of society, formed a section of one great party, committed to implacable war against the existing Administration and now gathering strength for a general rising. The workers must therefore form secret cells, recruit new members and keep up the fighting spirit by organising strikes and exploiting every possible cause of dispute between employers and employed. At the same time they must realise that in the last resort the collaboration of the peasants would be a decisive factor, and they must therefore win over to the cause their friends and relations in the villages.

The workers must be ready, when the party gave the signal, to seize the factories and other key points in the large towns. They must assist the party to form a temporary administration to maintain order until such time as the Constituent Assembly had begun to function. If, on the other hand, the existing regime were to grant a constitution the workers must exploit to the utmost any facilities which it gave them. They must return their own deputies to Parliament. They must continue to organise strikes and demonstrations, and exercise an ever-increasing pressure upon employers and the bureaucracy. They must always bear in mind that a constitution would not be the end of the struggle. Sooner or later a revolution would almost certainly be necessary.

A copy of this document was sent to the ageing Karl Marx in Highgate. We have no record of his having acknowledged it. But the old gentleman was highly gratified at the attention, and his copy was afterwards found to be heavily scored with marginal comments and underlinings.

V

In an early number of the *Narodnaya Volya* it was laid down:

"On the outbreak of revolution the importance of the army is enormous. With the army's support we could destroy the government machine without even calling on the masses. But if the army were hostile success would be impossible."

There is reason to believe that it was largely on Zhelyabov's insistence that the party decided to concentrate in the first place on the officers rather than on the rank and file. The inception of the movement demanded men of some education and initiative, men who, above all, could be trusted not to betray secrets. Officers in the Russian Army and Navy mostly came from the poorer gentry, that same class which provided so many of the revolutionary leaders, and which was the most naturally receptive of the new ideas. It will be remembered that in his Odessa days Zhelyabov was on close terms with a number of young officers, and had advised one of them, Aschenbrenner, that he could do more service to the cause by staying where he was than by resigning his commission. That same Aschenbrenner afterwards wrote of his comrades who joined up with the movement:

"Some had the revolutionary temperament. Others were just normal, decent officers caught up by the logic of events. The use of troops for police work influenced their final decision. So did their reading, and also, of course, the personal influence of the revolutionaries."

One of those with "the revolutionary temperament" was Sukhanov, a young naval lieutenant who went through a course in marine mines at Kronstadt in 1878. On completion of the course he was put in charge of the new Naval Electrical Institute in Petersburg. In 1879 he got to know Alexander Mihailov, and, in the late summer, Zhelyabov and Kolotkevich. He accepted their opinions in their entirety—tsaricide and all. When he was tried three years later, the prosecution brought up the question of his oath to the Emperor. He replied: "I made my oath in perfectly good faith and I would have carried it out loyally if circumstances had not led me along another path." As he also said, he "did not bother about dynastic questions." He was taking the path which, in his opinion, led to the greater happiness of the Russian people.

Soon after meeting Zhelyabov he introduced him to some of his brother officers. Zhelyabov was out of form. He talked (as one of them said afterwards) "as if they were a crowd of workmen—sensational demagogic stuff." The meeting was a failure. For the next few months Zhelyabov was preoccupied with attempts on the Emperor. But not long after the Kamenni Bridge affair Sukhanov arranged for some twenty officers, as many as he knew were safe, to come to his rooms one evening. They had no idea what was going to happen. When they arrived they found two civilians, one a tall man with a long black beard. For an hour or so it was an ordinary social evening. Then Sukhanov called for silence. "Two of these walls," he said, "are exceptionally thick. The other two connect with my other rooms. My servant is a Tartar and speaks no Russian. Now, Andrei."

Zhelyabov got up.

"Gentlemen," he said, "our friend here tells me you might be interested to hear something of our activities. I shall be glad to give you a few details. We, Revolutionary Terrorists—"

There was a gasp. This was considerably more than any of the audience had expected.

Zhelyabov went on to make one of the best speeches of his career. He spoke simply and unaffectedly of the sufferings of workmen and peasants. He described the official reaction to any attempt to ameliorate their lot. He asked his audience whether they as Russian officers were prepared to see the Russian people exposed to this treatment without making an effort to help. He made a tremendous impression. It was, of course, too much to expect that all the officers present would at once commit themselves. But that evening saw the beginning of the Fighting Services' Section of the Narodnaya Volya.

The scheme of this was simple. Groups of officers were formed in various garrison towns of the Empire, under a "Central Military Group," which last was in touch with and under the orders of the Executive Committee. Liaison was maintained by Zhelyabov, Kolotkevich and Perovskaya. The revolutionary officers were to concentrate on winning the affection and confidence of the soldiers under them, so as to ensure that the latter would follow them in a crisis. They were not to carry out revolutionary propaganda among the rank and file: this was to be arranged independently, by the Executive Committee, through ex-soldiers and workmen. It was, however, up to the officers to get to know their men, and to indicate which of them should first be approached by the party's agents.

The Fighting Services' Section was a long-range venture. It was not intended to be brought into action until the outbreak of the revolution. To prevent the organisation from being compromised a rule was passed that no serving officer might participate in any of the party's terrorist acts. Even Sukhanov, who had been co-opted to the Executive Committee before this rule was made, was not allowed, in spite of his protests, to do more than help Kibalchich prepare the explosive. In the end, however, he did help to dig the mine in the Malaya Sadovaya, but this was only because they were very short-handed. The wisdom of the rule is shown by the fact that in the police drive of 1881, based on the revelations of Goldenberg, Okladski and Rysakov, the only officer to be arrested was Sukhanov. The Fighting Services' Section remained for the time intact.

Its ultimate downfall came in 1883. By that time the old Executive Committee had been wiped out, all except Figner, and she made a desperate attempt to revive the party by bringing in the officers. It was then that they were betrayed to the authorities by Degaev, himself an ex-artillery cadet. Sixty-six officers were arrested and sentenced, drawn from the garrisons of Kronstadt, Petersburg, Moscow, Odessa, Kharkov, Nikolaev and Tiflis.

VI

THE summer and autumn of 1880 were thus devoted to expanding and organising the party's resources. In October Kviatkovski, Presnyakov, Shiraev and Zundelevich were brought to trial before the Petersburg Military Court. With them in the dock were Tikhonov and Okladski (of the Alexandrovsk attempt), Ivanova and her fellow-survivors of the printing press in the Sapernaya, and six others. The Trial of the Sixteen was the first in which members of the Executive Committee had been involved. The accused did not deny their connexion with the party. Probably they considered that in view of the strength of the prosecutor's case any attempt to do so would be futile. Instead they followed the example of earlier revolutionaries in trying to make the prisoners' bench a tribunal for the propagation of their ideals. Kviatkovski was especially concerned with correcting and amplifying the distorted account of the Lipetsk programme which the police had obtained from Goldenberg. The proceedings terminated on October 30. Kviatkovski and Presnyakov were condemned to death, the others to various terms of imprisonment. The death sentences were carried out on November 4.

These executions had a decisive influence on the party's subsequent policy. It must be remembered that in spite of the state of war between the Administration and the extreme revolutionaries the death penalty was still very rare. Its employment was highly unpopular throughout the country, not merely in liberal circles. There was only one executioner in European Russia, a certain Frolov * of Moscow, and it is significant that when he was not available there was great difficulty in finding a substitute. We know of a case when Frolov fell sick shortly before an execution at Kharkov. The authorities looked for a volunteer throughout the army and police but failed to find one. Then they tried the various prisons. Only one prisoner, a murderer, was willing to undertake the task. His terms were 250 roubles in cash, the countermanding of a flogging on the soles of the feet to which he had been condemned, and immediate transfer to Siberia. His offer was considered, but the authorities received a better one at the last minute from a Novobelgorod peasant who was willing to act for 60 roubles, free transport in a three-horse carriage from Novobelgorod to Kharkov and back, 1 rouble 60 kopeks a day subsistence while absent from home, and twenty-two glasses of vodka immediately before the execution. It was this amateur who somehow or other completed the hanging. But it was a long time before the prisoner was dead.

Vodka formed a recognised part of an executioner's equipment. Frolov's bill for the execution of Kviatkovski and Presnyakov (which incidentally shows a mistake in addition of 40 kopeks) has been preserved in the Russian State Archives. It contains an item of 19 roubles for "incidental expenses"

* He had no connexion with Zhelyabov's mother's family, though the name is the same.

which we can safely take to include alcohol. There was no modern drop platform. The rope was tied in a noose round the prisoner's neck and he hung till he strangled. The bungling of the vodka-sodden executioner often made the process a grisly business, and in the public mind the horror of the penalty itself was heightened by disgust at the way it was carried out.

The execution of Kviatkovski and Presnyakov came as a bitter personal blow to the members of the Executive Committee. For Zhelyabov and some of the others it was the first occasion on which any close friend and associate had met that fate. At the same time it opened up a wider issue; it seemed to show the limits that had been set to Loris-Melikov's "Dictatorship of the Heart," and the prospect of concessions freely granted from above was more than ever remote. The question of a further attempt on the Emperor's life at once became acute, and a full meeting of the Executive Committee was called. Maria Olovennikova has left us an account:

"There was a good deal of argument over the renewal of terrorist activity. It was clear that it would mean that our other activities would suffer: we would have to devote all our resources to terrorism. Mihailov took pains to emphasise the importance of the other sides of our work. So did Zhelyabov. He realised the difficulties we were up against better than anyone else. Tikhomirov as usual agreed with the majority. Perovskaya was all out for terrorism, whatever the cost. So was Yakimova . . ."

The votes of Perovskaya and Yakimova carried the day, and it was resolved at once to start the necessary preparations. "Our girls," Kibalchich wistfully remarked, "are fiercer than our men." But the question at issue was not one of principle but one of time and means and expediency. Zhelyabov himself admitted "The honour of the party demands that the Emperor be killed."

VII

THE death sentences had, indirectly, one other far-reaching consequence. They led to the arrest of Alexander Mihailov.

Mihailov had snapshots of Kviatkovski and Presnyakov and wished to have them copied. There were no photographic experts in the ranks of the party and it was necessary to go to a professional photographer. The police had guessed that was likely to happen, and all photographers were warned and their premises watched. Mihailov noticed there was something suspicious as soon as he entered the shop. He was asked to leave his snapshots and come back in a couple of days. When he went out he saw he was being followed, but he was an expert at eluding detectives and managed to get away. When he told his comrades of his adventure they implored him not to return to the shop. He reassured them. "I am not so mad as to do that," he said. But, incredibly, three days later he did go back and walked straight into an ambush of police.

To the party his loss was irreparable. More than any other individual he was the founder of the Narodnaya Volya. He was probably their best political brain. He was an ideal counterpart for Zhelyabov. The wisdom and circumspection of the one, the drive and resourcefulness of the other made them the perfect combination. Throughout, they worked in complete harmony. Alone of their colleagues they possessed the gift of seeing current issues in their full perspective. But it was not only in the formulation of policy and tactics that Mihailov's loss was felt. He was the guardian of the physical security of the party and of every individual in it. When he had gone there was no one to take his place.

VIII

Shortly after Mihailov's arrest Zhelyabov made one attempt to have the attack on the Emperor's life postponed. His incentive arose from the condition of the peasants in the Volga provinces following on the failure of the 1880 harvest.

As we have seen, the Executive Committee had little time to devote to the peasants. The countryside offered no prospect of an immediate return in a revolutionary sense. The programme of the Executive Committee laid down in general terms that the party should "prepare the ground for the co-operation of the peasantry in a revolt, and in the electoral campaign to follow after the revolt . . . The party must win over conscious adherents among influential peasants. . . . Every member of the party in contact with the peasantry must put himself in a position to defend peasant interests, and must gain himself the reputation of being the true friend of the peasants." Yakimova tells us that certain points of the programme, dealing with the actual organisation of the revolt, were never published. She does not tell us what those were. But it is safe to assume that very little definite progress was actually made.

The crop failure of 1880, however, changed the whole atmosphere of the countryside. Within a few months the price of flour doubled. Subsidiary products such as straw for fodder and dried cow-dung for fuel were marked up fourfold. Peasants, foreseeing that their scanty stocks would not last out the winter, crowded into the towns in search of work. But the drop in the general purchasing power caused manufacturers to be cautious and they laid off a large proportion of their existing hands. The law of supply and demand in a free labour market produced its inevitable result. The daily wage of a port worker in Samara fell from 85 kopeks to 35. In the Saratov area agricultural wages fell as low as 20 kopeks. Epidemics began to appear. As the autumn wore on the party's correspondents in the provinces reported a continual increase of misery and despair.

Zhelyabov was especially affected by these reports. A peasant himself, they meant more to him than they could to any townsman. He realised the moral degradation that extreme want can bring. No doubt, as a revolutionary, he grasped the potential political significance of famine. But according to Korba (who is our authority for this episode) he was more concerned with the urgent need for securing relief measures from the Government. At the end of November he called a special meeting of the Executive Committee. Present were Korba herself, Barannikov, Kolotkevich, Perovskaya, Isaev, Zlatopolski, Yakimova, Langans and perhaps Frolenko (Korba wrote her account many years afterwards, and could not be sure about Frolenko).

Zhelyabov addressed the meeting. He read extracts from the various reports and gave a detailed picture of conditions in the distressed areas. Then he came to the point:

"I consider it essential not to lose the opportunity for action which these conditions offer us. I propose to go myself to the Volga provinces and place myself at the head of a peasant revolt. I am confident that I possess the qualities necessary for carrying out this task. I have the firm hope that I shall at least succeed in forcing the Administration to recognise the people's right to relief."

There was a pause and Zhelyabov went on.

"I know what is in your minds. The coming attempt on the Emperor—do I propose to cancel it? No, most emphatically I do not. I am only asking for a postponement."

There was another pause. No one spoke, but everybody knew what the others were thinking. The party had not the resources to organise a peasant revolt and also to continue the campaign against the Emperor. Postponement might very well mean cancellation.

Zhelyabov waited: but he realised the general feeling, just as well as the others did. Finally he left the room, without putting his proposal to a vote. It was a bitter disappointment to him.

CHAPTER ELEVEN

THE FINAL PREPARATIONS

I

THE first step taken in the new campaign against the Emperor was to ascertain his usual movements. The revolutionaries had no link in the palace who could tell them,* and so Perovskaya was given the task of organising a scouting party. Tikhomirov assisted her at first but soon dropped out. Her team consisted of Natalia Olovennikova, Tyrkov, a student, and three others. They went out in pairs to watch for the Emperor's appearances in the town and to follow his routes. Their task was difficult at first; but after a time they had some idea of when and where to expect him. Perovskaya collated their observations and reported to the Executive Committee.

Meanwhile there was a good deal of discussion as to the actual form of the attack. Zhelyabov was in favour of hand grenades. Kibalchich had recently been experimenting with nitro-glycerine, the possibilities of which were just beginning to exercise the scientific world; this new discovery would facilitate the production of a bomb small in bulk and yet effective in action. The majority of the committee, however, preferred the old idea of a land mine. Early in December Perovskaya and her scouts reported that the Emperor was in the habit of passing through the Malaya Sadovaya. It happened there was a front basement to let in that street, and Zhelyabov went to inspect it. The senior porter was away when he called and the assistant porter had no key. Zhelyabov

---

* One of Zhelyabov's recent Russian biographers in commenting on the party's lack of an intelligence service has suggested that if they had been better informed they would have made their attack on one of the extreme reactionaries, the Crown Prince Alexander or Pobyedonostsev, rather than on the Emperor himself. It is an interesting speculation, but it omits the factor of prestige. They were publicly committed to killing Alexander II.

accordingly could only view the premises from outside. On his return he reported to the committee that he did not think the basement suitable, and that in any case he preferred the use of hand grenades. But he was overruled. It was decided to take the premises, to open a cheese shop there, and to drive a gallery under the road.

Bogdanovich was selected for the part of the cheese merchant and Yakimova to figure as his wife. They assumed the name of Kobozev, and got into touch with the landlord's agent. After some negotiation they agreed to take the basement at an annual rent of 1,200 roubles. They were unable to move in at once as two of the rooms were being plastered; but they signed the lease and paid a deposit of fifty roubles.

The landlord's agent, however, was not entirely satisfied that the young couple were all that they made themselves out to be. Their handwriting, manners and way of speaking were suspiciously good for small tradesmen. He reported the matter to the police. The police enquired at the lodgings where they were staying, and the lodging-house keeper volunteered that they had left a hundred rouble note lying on the table—a most unusual thing for a small shopkeeper to do. The police telegraphed to the police at Voronezh, their alleged town of domicile, to ask if a passport had been issued to a couple named Kobozev. Voronezh wired back that a passport had been issued and gave the correct date and number. So for the time suspicion was allayed. The party had learned by now that when making out false passports it was wiser to make them duplicates of real passports, as the police were apt to refer to the office of issue. It was easy, from time to time, to get hold of a real passport and copy the particulars. There was, of course, a risk of the real Kobozev appearing, but that risk they could afford to take.

In due course the plasterers had finished. The couple moved into their new premises and prepared to open their shop.

II

ON DECEMBER 31 the Narodnaya Volya held their second New Year's Eve party. A rendezvous was arranged in a flat in one of the other suburbs. It was dirty weather—snow and a violent blizzard. As the guests arrived Zhelyabov instructed them that

The Final Preparations

no business was to be discussed that night. In all some twenty came. They all brought something, a bottle of wine or a pie, anything they could afford. At first they were silent and preoccupied. The shadow of the recent casualties hung over the party, and they all were so engrossed in the work that it was hard to find anything else to talk about. But little by little the evening livened up. Sablin was a first-class mimic and was made to do his turn. Then they cleared away the furniture and danced. We hear that Zhelyabov danced with all the girls and "refused to allow anyone present not to enjoy himself." They began by dancing lancers and quadrilles and finished up with Russian country dances. They made such a din that "although it was New Year's Eve, and although nine-tenths of the population of Petersburg were certainly drunk," the people in the flats below came up in alarm to find out what was happening. Finally they sat down to supper and drank to the success of the Revolution and to the death of all tyrants.

III

It is possible that Zhelyabov's advocacy of a bomb attack was partly due to the greater economy of that method, both in money and man power, as compared with a mining venture. Debogori-Mokrievich, who had escaped from the chain gang in Siberia and at about this time was back in Moscow, was struck by the enormous prestige of the Narodnaya Volya. The Cherni Peredel was moribund. All the Moscow students were talking about the terrorists. But he could not help wondering how many of these young people were prepared to act as well as talk, and how many of them were ready to subscribe substantially to the party's funds.

There was still the possibility of a raid on a State Treasury. Frolenko, who had carried through the so nearly successful coup at Kherson in 1879, was authorised to try again at Kishinev. Our knowledge of this attempt is confined to the depositions of Merkulov. According to Merkulov, in December, 1880, he was instructed by Zhelyabov to go to Kishinev to help Frolenko and Lebedeva in an attempt on the State Treasury there. Kolotkevich gave him money for the journey and he went down. Frolenko and Lebedeva had taken a house next to the Treasury, and the idea was to burrow a passage from their cellar to the Treasury cellar. Trigoni at Odessa was also in the conspiracy. But soon the idea was abandoned, and in January Frolenko and Lebedeva shut up the house and returned to Petersburg. That is all that Merkulov told the police, and we can take it that that was all he knew. The authorities were able to confirm that Frolenko and Lebedeva had rented the house in question under the name of Mironenko. But both of them refused to give further details.

We do not know if the attempt at Kishinev was abandoned because of local difficulties there, or because the comrades were needed in Petersburg. It was certainly not because the financial situation had become easier. The cheese shop was proving a costly experiment. On January 1 the Kobozevs had to pay their landlord 250 roubles, which, with the deposit, made up the first quarter's rent in advance. They had a sign made, which cost 35 roubles; and they had to lay in a stock which meant a cash outlay of at least 150 roubles. Zhelyabov made a personal effort to raise the funds and it is significant of the straits the party were in that he even approached Rysakov. Rysakov was a boy of nineteen of a poor family who had managed to scrape enough together to send him to a technical school in the capital. He was a quiet, pious, rather dreamy youth. He joined the revolutionaries and became one of Zhelyabov's assistants in the Workers' Section. His father worked in a timber firm, and had arranged for the firm's Petersburg office to pay out 30 roubles to the boy every month. When Zhelyabov made his appeal Rysakov persuaded the cashier to let him have three months' allowance in advance. Thus he received 90 roubles, and gave 50 to Zhelyabov. All together Zhelyabov collected 600 roubles and the shop was enabled to open.

Mining operations started immediately.

There were three rooms in the basement—the first, with the steps leading down to it, was the shop, the second the storeroom and the third the Kobozevs' living room. The miners drove the gallery from the front wall of the living room straight out under the road. They worked at night, and boarded up the window, so that no light should show from the living room. But the shop window was left unshuttered, and passers-by could look into the shop and see the ikon of St.

The Final Preparations

George with its flickering candle, and round the walls the barrels of cheese. The actual digging was done by Zhelyabov, Kolotkevich, Barannikov, Sukhanov, Isaev, Frolenko, Langans, Sablin, Degaev, and Merkulov, working in shifts. All except the last three were members of the Executive Committee.

IV

EARLY in 1881 a letter was received from Nechaev, now in his ninth year of imprisonment in the Alexis Raveline of the Peter and Paul Fortress. He wrote that the authorities had offered him his liberty if he would turn police informer. On his refusal he had been flogged and placed in solitary confinement. But as the years went by he had succeeded in converting some of his guards to the revolutionary cause. By this means he established touch with Shiraev on the latter's transfer to the Raveline. Shiraev had told him of the latest developments, and had indicated a channel for communicating with the Executive Committee. Nechaev now asked the party to undertake his rescue.

For the members of the committee the receipt of this letter was an exciting and stimulating experience. Most of them had been in their teens when the Nechaev affair had come on. It had given them their first impulse towards the cause of revolution and Nechaev himself had been the hero of their adolescence. Since then his deceptions had been disclosed, and his methods recognised as completely inconsistent with the Narodnaya Volya policy. But for the man himself and for his fighting spirit much of the old glow remained. The meeting at once declared that he must be rescued.

The organisation of the escape, however, was a complicated business. All the resources of the party were taken up with the coming attempt on the Emperor. There is a legend that the committee wrote back asking Nechaev to decide whether or not this attempt should be postponed and that Nechaev magnanimously decided that his own escape must wait. This story is certainly untrue; it is unthinkable that the committee would have put off their attempt for any such reason. But it is agreed that the rescue was put down on the programme for as soon as the Emperor had been dealt with. Zhelyabov suggested that the young Fighting Services' Section should undertake the venture as their introduction to active service.

A number of letters passed between the committee and the Fortress. Zhelyabov handled the correspondence from the committee's end. He made a big impression on Nechaev who even suggested that as soon as the Government was overthrown Zhelyabov should be installed as "Revolutionary Dictator." Given Nechaev's temperament it is remarkable that he should propose anyone but himself for supreme command. However the old spirit of sensational imposture was still strong in him. He put up scheme after scheme: for the issue of a forged ukase ordering the return of the ex-serfs to the possession of their former owners, and another increasing the period of military service; for a forged edict from the Imperial Council abolishing military service and splitting up the big estates; for a forged proclamation from the Holy Synod that the Emperor was insane.

The committee, of course, turned all these proposals down. Their policy was definitely opposed to any form of deception. Nechaev's later letters were concerned more with matters of practical detail. One of them was found on Zhelyabov on his final arrest. It acknowledged receipt of a code, of a copy of the *Narodnaya Volya* and of twenty-five roubles. It went on to recommend three potential recruits for the party. (They were probably ex-warders of the Raveline.) They should, Nechaev wrote, be kept under strict supervision, given no task of importance until they had proved their reliability, and in no circumstances be paid more than twenty-five roubles a month. A letter in similar strain was found on Perovskaya. Both were in cypher, and it was some time before the police could establish the writer's identity.

In the end he was betrayed by a fellow-prisoner, Mirski, the young man who, in 1879, had made the unsuccessful attack on General Drenteln. The guards who had helped to smuggle Nechaev's letters were all arrested, and "the Eagle" himself was relegated to the dungeons for permanent confinement underground. That, in effect, was his death sentence. No news ever came through from him again. There is an unconfirmed story that for his last few months he had one companion—an unidentified lunatic believed to be an officer involved many years previously in a delicate scandal in the Emperor's household and thereafter put away, without a name, to rot. According to the prison records Nechaev died of tuberculosis on May 9, 1883.

V

IT WAS some time in December that Okladski, in prison, began to talk. At first he refused to disclose any names, but he gave two addresses; he did not remember the streets or numbers, but the police sent him out with a plain clothes man and he showed the detective where they were. The police arranged for a permanent watch to be kept on these flats.

Under the old arrangement the party would have heard of this. Searches, arrests, etc., in political cases were instituted by the Third Section and Kletochnikov had access to the papers. But after Loris-Melikov's reorganisation the city police were also empowered to take such action, and the party had no opposite number to Kletochnikov in the city police. We have no evidence of their making any attempt to plant one there. After the arrest of Alexander Mihailov, security arrangements were neglected, and for this much of the responsibility must fall upon Zhelyabov as the outstanding surviving personality in the Executive Committee. Even the liaison with Kletochnikov suffered. Mihailov had rented a special flat for his meetings with Kletochnikov. Maria Olovennikova lived there, and in order to avoid risk of suspicion she led a very quiet life and took no other part in revolutionary activities. At the time of Mihailov's arrest she was ill; when she got well again the committee liquidated her flat and sent her to work in Moscow. Kolotkevich took over the contact with Kletochnikov. The two used to meet in Kolotkevich's room.

On January 25, thanks to one of the addresses indicated by Okladski, the police arrested Barannikov. They looked up the name on his passport in their register of addresses, discovered where he lived, and waited there in ambush. On the following day Kolotkevich walked in and was arrested. The police then proceeded to locate Kolotkevich's lodgings and arranged for a second ambush. Two days later, on January 28, Korba learned of these arrests and went at once to warn Kletochnikov. He was out. She waited, and finally left him a note which he would understand as a warning. But it was too late. Kletochnikov had heard that morning in the office about Barannikov; but the official wheels moved slowly and the report on Kolotkevich had not yet come through. Kletochnikov had hurried off to warn Kolotkevich, and walked straight into the trap.

These three arrests were a major disaster. Kletochnikov was all that was left of the protective organisation so carefully built up by Mihailov. The other two in their way were almost equally irreplaceable. The brains and drive of the Narodnaya Volya as a fighting organisation came primarily from six men: Mihailov, Zhelyabov, Kviatkovski, Frolenko, Barannikov and Kolotkevich. Now only two of them were left. Next came the news that Morozov, returning from abroad, had been arrested on the frontier. Zhelyabov was very depressed. He told Tikhomirov: "We are using up our capital."

It is significant that he did not talk like this at plenary meetings of the Executive Committee. Three months previously he had hesitated; but at this stage he made no suggestion of drawing back. He was a fighter. In the recent arrests the Administration had scored a notable success; the only effective answer was a resolute counterattack. In his view it was the only possible answer. To press ahead might be physical suicide, but to draw back would be moral suicide, the abnegation of all that the party stood for. "We may go down," he told his comrades, "but others will come to take your place."

Members of the Executive Committee on duty in the provinces were summoned to Petersburg for a conference. Olovennikova came up from Moscow and after the meeting Zhelyabov took her aside for a private talk. Olovennikova writes:

"He wanted all possible details about anyone in Moscow who might be worth while considering for the Executive Committee. I think he felt that some of our people were getting off the rails. Talking to me he mentioned, as he had once before, the bad attribute of terrorism: it was apt so to dominate people's minds as to affect their freedom of judgment. I well remember this talk because we went on with it next day. We asked ourselves what was going to happen after the attempt, whether it turned out to be a success or a failure. Zhelyabov did not count on its forcing the Government to grant any important political concessions. The most he hoped for was that the prestige we should gain would make it easier for us to go on with our work, and help us to strengthen our organisation and broaden our basis of support in all sections of society. But that, of course, would only be possible if there survived a sufficient number of really capable members to carry on the party's work. That is why Zhelyabov was thinking so much about Moscow. He was hoping there would be sufficient material to build up a new Executive Committee in Moscow if the old one were wiped out.

"None of the others seemed to be thinking much about the future. Their minds were all too full of the attempt. There was Sukhanov. I remember at one of the meetings he was full of some scheme for bringing the fleet up from Kronstadt and bombarding Petersburg; he firmly believed it was feasible. If anybody objected he would say, 'You just wait.' I cannot forget Isaev either. He had plenty of brains. At one time I had had great hopes of him. Now he could talk about nothing but dynamite. . . .

"I left Petersburg very depressed. One phrase of Zhelyabov's would not come out of my head. 'Mind,' he had said, 'if your Moscow lot don't come on, it's going to be bad.' That showed me how uncertain our position was."

VI

THESE plenary meetings also discussed the possibility of starting a general revolt to coincide with the assassination of the Emperor. It was at once agreed that the party's resources were insufficient to make such a project remotely feasible.

It is impossible to make even an approximate estimate of the numerical strength of the Narodnaya Volya in the early spring of 1881. Yakimova has claimed that there were five hundred adherents who could have been counted on to initiate a rising. But she gives no indication as to how this figure was made up. The Fighting Services' Section numbered, probably, some sixty naval and military officers. This section, however, was in any case only to come into action after the revolution had broken out. The Workers' Section counted at most from four to five hundred members. We have no idea how many of these were actually prepared to come out and risk their lives at the command to march. Finally we have nothing whatever on which to base any estimate of the number of adherents among the students and young intellectuals.

In any case these calculations lead us nowhere. Whether the party numbered fifty, five hundred or five thousand, an attempt to overthrow the colossal machine of the Empire would have been equally futile. There was no prospect of any appreciable support from the peasants. During the winter months there had been progressively less contact with the party's sympathisers among the liberals, who were inclined to pin their hopes on Loris-Melikov: in any case history shows few instances of moderate liberals playing any decisive role in a crisis. The party had no effective allies and was too weak to act alone.

Including all the surviving members of the Executive Committee still at liberty, the number of those who took part in the final attacks on the Emperor was thirty-two, twenty-one young men and eleven girls. It is significant that when the loss of Kolotkevich and Barannikov caused a shortage of workers for the mine the Executive Committee sent for Trigoni, their representative in Odessa. Presumably they had no one in Petersburg whom they regarded as qualified to fill the gap. The trade of a professional revolutionary, still more of a terrorist, is a hard one and highly skilled. During the eighteen months of the party's existence few of the young recruits had been able to complete their apprenticeship.

VII

THE cheese shop in the Malaya Sadovaya was soon in difficulties. The Kobozevs had no experience, little commercial sense and insufficient capital. Figner went in one day to see what the place looked like and was appalled at their meagre stock-in-trade. She felt it must be obvious to anyone that it was not a bona fide business. There was no money to buy more cheese, so Figner did a whip-round on her own and raised another three hundred roubles. With this they laid in more stock and managed to make the shop look more like a shop; but Bogdanovich and Yakimova were still unconvincing as its proprietors. They brought in Merkulov as shopboy. He was so inefficient that he had to go. Neighbouring tradesmen began to talk.

The Final Preparations

One Novikov, himself a cheese dealer, gave evidence at the subsequent enquiry:

"I went round, out of curiosity, to the Kobozevs' and bought half a round of cheese. That was on February 4. Afterwards Kobozev came to my place to collect his money. He seemed to me to be a sort—well, any sort you like but not in the cheese trade. You could tell by his manner. He certainly wasn't one of us. I went back to my shop and said to my people, 'Well,' I said, 'there's something curious about that shop because certainly their competition isn't going to do our business any harm.'"

The actual mining, too, brought its difficulties. The first was in breaking through the concrete wall of the living room. It was not so much the work that was difficult, it was doing it quietly. The Malaya Sadovaya was very still at night and the sound of tapping would at once be noticed and probably reported to police headquarters. Even after they got through the wall and into softer ground they had to post a lookout to watch for the local policeman on his beat, and give a signal to stop work when he approached. When they were under the pavement they came upon an iron watermain. They worked their way round, but a couple of yards farther was a more serious obstacle. It was a big wooden pipe—presumably a drain. They could not drive the gallery over the top because it lay too near the surface of the road. They could not burrow underneath because the city stood on low, marshy ground and they were afraid of getting down to water. Finally they decided to chance it being only half full and cut a sector off the top. They did so and found it was a sewer. Gallery and basement were filled with the stench of Petersburg's middens. The stench was so overpowering that it nearly wrecked the venture. Men could not work in it. Hastily they covered the hole, leaving an aperture between their covering and the roof of the gallery where a man could squeeze through. Even so they had to improvise respirators and put the workers on half shifts. On Sunday, February 15, the Emperor passed along the Malaya Sadovaya; but they were not ready for him.

VIII

UNKNOWN to the revolutionaries, during the winter Loris-Melikov and the Emperor's inner circle of advisers had been engaged in a series of confidential discussions on the delicate task of finding some formula to reconcile modern constitutional progress with autocracy. Count Valuev brought up a project for a measure of popular representation which he had devised as early as 1863, in the era of the great reforms. Another proposal was a very similar one from the Grand Duke Constantine, dated from 1866. Thanks to the jealousy of their rival partisans and to the consistent opposition of the Crown Prince (prompted by Pobyedonostsev,) both these schemes were talked out. "No change," the Crown Prince declared, "should be made in existing arrangements. If popular representatives were elected they would be undesirable tub-thumpers and lawyers and that type of person."

In January Loris-Melikov produced proposals of his own. They were not meant to be far reaching. Loris-Melikov fully realised the limits set by the Emperor's conception of autocracy as a sacred trust. His scheme envisaged the election by the Zemstva of a certain number of delegates to the Imperial Council. But the Council was to receive no executive or legislative authority: it was to remain, as before, a purely consultative and deliberative body. These proposals were approved by the Grand Duke Constantine, and Loris-Melikov succeeded in securing the acquiescence of the Crown Prince. Indeed the latter acted as chairman of a committee appointed to consider the means of putting them into effect. After a month of deliberations the committee produced a draft law enlarging the Imperial Council by fifteen new members representing public opinion. At the same time two commissions were to be established, one to consider financial and the other economic and administrative reforms; and their reports in due course were to be considered by the enlarged Imperial Council. This draft was laid before the Emperor by Loris-Melikov on February 18. The Emperor spent the next few days in making up his mind whether or not to sign.

After the Emperor's death, his young morganatic widow, the Princess Yurievskaya, confided a number of her memories to

The Final Preparations

Victor Laferté, who subsequently published them. His book sheds an interesting sidelight on the atmosphere within the palace at that time. The Princess had no detailed information as to the Loris-Melikov proposals. But she knew that something was being discussed, and she allowed that knowledge to feed her innermost hopes, however slender their real foundations may have been. Laferté writes:

"Having reached an age when a man desires rest and the peaceful enjoyment of family life, the Emperor would have been glad to hand over the sceptre to his heir. But he considered that his civilising mission had not yet been completed and it was his ambition to finish it entirely.

"He wished only to resign the supreme power in favour of his son when, Russia having attained the summit of civilisation and progress, all need of further reforms would be admittedly superfluous. He wished to see Russia set firmly on her peaceful path of progress and prosperity.

"The Princess was eagerly awaiting her husband's abdication . . . the dream which she held in her heart was to see him installed with her in Cairo for a whole winter. She knew how much he liked warmth and sunshine. But this beautiful dream could only be realised on her husband's abdication, and he still felt that such an act would be premature."

IX

WHEN Loris-Melikov submitted his draft law to the Emperor the Executive Committee were making their final plans. March 1 was fixed as the date, and the mine in the Malaya Sadovaya as the main instrument. Zhelyabov again brought up the idea of hand grenades. He had discussed it with Grinevitski, one of his helpers in the Workers' Section, and Grinevitski had been enthusiastic. But the feeling within the committee was still against the project. They had no faith in this new weapon. The matter was referred to Kibalchich, whose expert opinion was that hand grenades were unlikely to be effective. Zhelyabov's only supporter was his old friend Trigoni, now arrived from Odessa. Zhelyabov had always given way to the majority in the past: this time he stuck to his guns. Eventually it was agreed that he might organise a bombing attack with his workmen as a supplement to the main attempt, i.e., he was to be there with his bombers and ready to act in case the Emperor escaped the mine. Then came the question of a third alternative in case the bombers also failed. Trigoni volunteered to go in with a dagger. But, he explained, in view of the Emperor's bodyguard, one single assailant with a dagger would have no chance and he required a force of thirty men to engage the bodyguard. We can assume Trigoni had not yet realised the position at headquarters. His condition made his offer impracticable—the thirty men were not there. Finally Zhelyabov declared that he would undertake the dagger attack, personally and alone. The general outline of the attempt was thus agreed upon.

At once Zhelyabov, to use Rysakov's expression, "gave the word."

Rysakov by now had become an illegal. He had assumed the name of Glazov, changed his lodging and devoted his whole time to the affairs of the Workers' Section. When his own money came to an end Zhelyabov kept him out of the party funds. Zhelyabov now asked him straight out if he would take part in an attempt on the Emperor. The boy was flattered and said he would. He then discovered, with something of a shock, that the attempt was to be made within the next few days.

There was no time to be lost and Zhelyabov's preparations were quick and drastic. It was impossible to continue the normal routine of the Workers' Section while the attempt was in progress. The printing press of the *Workers' Paper* was closed down and the flat where it was housed abandoned. Helfmann told the porter an elaborate story of having to go to Moscow because of illness in the family. The furniture was put in storage. The same day Helfmann herself with Sablin moved into a new flat in the Telezhnaya which was to serve as conspiratorial quarter and general headquarters for March 1. The press and type of the *Workers' Paper* were stored in another flat where Figner was living with Isaev. This flat was also the workshop for the explosive.

On February 20 the four men selected as bomb throwers met for the first time at the flat in the Telezhnaya. They were Grinevitski, aged twenty-four, Timothy Mihailov, a factory hand, aged twenty-one, Rysakov, and Emelianov, a student, both aged nineteen. This was a serious departure from the principle laid down by Alexander Mihailov that important tasks should only be entrusted to tried and mature revolutionaries. But these four were the best available in the youthful Workers' Section. Franzholi was sick and abroad; Kokovski was dying in the Crimea. Afterwards, at the trial, Zhelyabov, when in prison, declared that he had called for volunteers and forty-seven men had offered themselves; this was a lie, intended merely to impress the authorities with the power of the Executive Committee. No such call was made. Zhelyabov approached these four youths, confident that his influence over them would make up for the lack of experience. He was right in so far that while he was there to lead them they would do anything for him. Besides it was expected that there would be no need for the bomb throwers to come into action. Rysakov and Emelianov were brought in to "give them a smell of powder."

Zhelyabov presided over the meeting in the Telezhnaya and Perovskaya and Kibalchich were also present. One object was to give the four grenadiers the chance to get to know each other. So far, except for Grinevitski and Timothy Mihailov, they had not met. Kibalchich also took the opportunity to explain the nature of the bombs. These were to be oval in shape and five pounds in weight. Inside of each were two glass tubes placed crosswise. On the bomb striking a hard object one or other of the tubes would be broken, and the liquid content thus released would set up a chemical action and ignite the detonator.

On February 21 the bomb throwers met again and were given further details of the proposed attack. On the following day Zhelyabov took them to a deserted spot in the Pargolovo Park and they practised bomb throwing with dummies.

X

MEANWHILE the police received an indication that an important revolutionary had arrived, or was shortly expected to arrive, in Petersburg. Their agent could not give the name or any further particulars except that the individual was very dandified, with the manners of a grand seigneur, and the appropriate English nickname of "My Lord." The police made enquiries, and, we assume on the ground of statements by

Okladski (though no procès-verbal has been preserved), arrived at the suspicion that "My Lord" was Trigoni. Trigoni was still a legal. It was thus possible to find out from the register where he was living in furnished lodgings. A police agent was installed as a fellow-tenant in the same house and another was told off to shadow him. One night he was traced to a block of flats in the 1st Rota Ismailovski Polk. This was where Zhelyabov and Perovskaya were living, though the police of course did not know it. One afternoon, on the Nevski, Trigoni stopped and spoke to "a young woman with a big forehead" (Perovskaya). The police agent followed the girl, but she eluded him. Later Trigoni was traced to the cheese shop in the Malaya Sadovaya. Telegrams were sent to the police at Odessa and Simferopol demanding all available information concerning him.

On February 25 Trigoni came to the conclusion he was being watched. His neighbour in his lodgings—a retired naval captain—was so effusively friendly as to be suspicious. It illustrates the carelessness of the revolutionaries after the loss of Alexander Mihailov that either Trigoni did not report his suspicions or else Zhelyabov did not regard them as warranting any special precautions. It must be remembered, however, that special security precautions entail loss of time or loss of manpower, and the revolutionaries were short of both. Late on the evening of the 25th Trigoni went to the Malaya Sadovaya and did his shift as usual. On the 26th Merkulov called at Zhelyabov's flat and was given a bundle of sandbags to take to the cheese shop. These were to be used for packing the charge. Merkulov duly delivered the sandbags and came back. Trigoni was then with Zhelyabov and was complaining about the difficulties. "We haven't finished yet," Zhelyabov was saying. Then he gave Merkulov "a very heavy bottle" to take to the cheese shop. It was the explosive.

The 26th was a busy day. That evening there was another conference of the bombing squad—Zhelyabov, Perovskaya, Rysakov and Timothy Mihailov—in Grinevitski's room. Later in the evening it is almost certain (though the evidence is not entirely conclusive) that Zhelyabov went on to work in the Malaya Sadovaya. He was a glutton at that time for hard physical work as his only chance to give his mind and nerves a rest. In spite of his enormous vitality he was on the verge of a

The Final Preparations

breakdown. He could not sleep. He would prowl up and down his bedroom with his brain a jangle of schemes and day-dreams. He was eating very little and for the first time in his life was subject to fainting fits. He knew himself he was near to collapse. He told his few intimates that all he wanted was to get the attempt over, successfully, and then go off to some village in South Russia and recuperate.

The retired naval captain informed his employers that Trigoni was expecting a visitor on the evening of the 27th and the police lay in wait in an empty flat on the same landing. The subsequent course of events is clear from a statement by Zhelyabov and from Trigoni's memoir. At four o'clock on the afternoon of the 27th Zhelyabov and Perovskaya left their home and took a cab together as far as the Public Library in the Bolshaya Sadovaya. There they paid off the cab and parted. Zhelyabov, walking along the street by himself, found he was being followed by a police agent. He made a detour and shook the man off. He had two or three appointments and when he had finished he went on to Trigoni's lodgings. It was then seven o'clock.

Trigoni had been waiting for him since half past six. Zhelyabov came in and said, "I think you have the police here somewhere." Trigoni went into the passage to look. There was no one about. He called for the servant girl to bring the samovar. At that moment the police came out of the empty flat and pulled him back with them. Zhelyabov waited. Twenty minutes passed and as Trigoni did not return he went out and down the stairs to the main entrance. The door was locked. He was fumbling with the handle when the police came up from behind and caught him. He grabbed for his revolver but the police were too quick and seized it from him. Then they brought Trigoni down and the party went off to the police station.

It happened that the officer on duty at the police station had been concerned, three years before, with the Trial of the 193. He had a good memory for faces and said, "Why, you're Zhelyabov." Zhelyabov laughed and said, "Your very humble servant. But that is not going to help you." The prisoners were searched and led away to separate cells.

CHAPTER TWELVE

KILLING AN EMPEROR

I

WE HAVE it on the authority of Laferté, who, as has been said, obtained these details from Princess Yurievskaya, that on Saturday, February 28, the Emperor got up at eight o'clock, half an hour earlier than was usual. At a quarter to nine he sent a message to his wife, asking her to come with their son (aged eight) to attend Eucharist in the private chapel of the palace. The service lasted till eleven. Then there was breakfast, and the Court doctor arrived to examine the Emperor's health. He found him in excellent spirits; he was particularly pleased at having been able to stand for two hours at the service without fatigue. At noon he went to his study and read the daily report from Loris-Melikov. Twenty minutes later he was in his wife's boudoir.

"I have some news," he said, "and you will not be surprised that I have come at once to share it with you, because I feel that no one takes so real an interest as you do in anything that concerns me."

The news was the arrest of Zhelyabov. Loris-Melikov was not yet completely convinced of his identity, but he was almost certain.

"Both Trigoni," he wrote, "and the individual we believe to be Zhelyabov decline to make any statement. The latter further categorically refuses to state where he lives. I hope shortly to be able to clear up his identity through Okladski, whom I have ordered to be sent from the fortress."

It is easy to understand the relief and satisfaction of the Emperor and of the Princess. The depositions of Goldenberg had made it appear that Zhelyabov was the prime organiser of the terrorist campaign. His arrest removed a constant menace.

Later in the day Loris-Melikov sent in a further report: "Zhelyabov continues to refuse to answer questions, stating that it is merely a waste of time to put them. But the criminal has added that in spite of his arrest the attacks against His Imperial Majesty would be continued relentlessly." Loris-Melikov suggested that in view of this it would perhaps be advisable for the Emperor not to attend the parade in the Manège on the following day. But the Emperor maintained that if all possible precautions were taken there was no reason to change his plans.

We can only presume that this report of Zhelyabov's threat was based on his remark to the police officer, "But that is not going to help you." We have the police records of all his statements under arrest, and no more specific threat occurs in them. It is most unlikely that he would have let his spirit of bravado go so far as to imperil the attempt. But Loris-Melikov was under a heavy responsibility. He could not take the risk of suppressing or minimising any warning signal, however slight.

Usually on a Saturday Loris-Melikov dined at the palace. This particular day, however, he was ill and so was excused. In the afternoon the Emperor went out in his carriage to call on two of the Grand Duchesses. Princess Yurievskaya herself called on Loris-Melikov to enquire after his health and to ask if there was further news. Her visit was encouraging. There had been, she was told, some reports about a certain cheese shop in the Malaya Sadovaya. The place had accordingly been inspected that morning, but nothing suspicious had been found. There was every reason to hope that with the arrest of Zhelyabov any imminent danger had been removed.

That night Emperor and Princess dined alone. He said to her "I am so happy that it almost gives me a feeling of fear." She asked him if he would like company after dinner: but he did not wish to have company. He spent the evening playing with his small son.

On the morning of March 1 the Prefect of Petersburg called together the police officers in charge of districts and congratulated them. Most satisfactory progress, he said, was being made against the revolutionaries. His Imperial Majesty had been especially pleased to hear of the arrest of Zhelyabov.

On that morning, March 1, the Emperor got up at his usual

time, 8.30. He went for a walk in the palace garden with his children. After the walk there was divine service, followed by breakfast with his wife. Loris-Melikov, now somewhat better, called to report. The Emperor informed him that he had decided to sign the new draft law. He handed the document to the Minister. Before leaving for the parade he went to see his wife.

"I have just signed that paper," he told her. "I hope it will make a good impression and that Russia will take it as a proof that I mean to grant everything I can." The Princess was still not entirely happy about the visit to the Manège. She begged her husband to avoid the Nevski and the Malaya Sadovaya and go instead along the Ekaterinski Quay. With the canal along one side of the road and a public square on the other there was little cover for a potential assailant. The Emperor promised he would take that route. He left the palace at 12.55. He was in very good spirits at the parade. He was extremely gracious and talked to a number of officers. From the Manège he went to call on his cousin the Grand Duchess Catherine. On leaving her palace he told his coachman to drive back via the Ekaterinski Canal.

II

To return to the revolutionaries.

On the morning of the 28th they were still unaware of the arrests of the previous evening. At nine o'clock the four bomb throwers and Kibalchich assembled for a final practice. They waited an hour for Zhelyabov. When he still did not appear Kibalchich imagined he must be busy, and decided to carry on without him. He took the young men to the Smolni Monastery. There was no one about in the grounds and they found a disused pit. They practised with the dummies again, and then tried a live bomb. Timothy Mihailov threw it. It was a small sized bomb, and the explosion was not very impressive. Still, it exploded. The bombers then went back to their various homes with orders to report in good time at the Telezhnaya flat the following morning.

Meanwhile the inspection of the cheese shop had been taking place. The initiative had come from the police officer in charge of the district. His suspicions of the shop had been

Killing an Emperor

renewed by "the large number of young men and young women seen going in and out." There were persistent rumours of an impending attempt, and the fact that the Emperor was in the habit of passing down the Malaya Sadovaya made it essential to take every precaution. The police officer requested General Mrovinski of the Corps of Engineers to conduct an examination.

The general arrived at the shop in the guise of a municipal surveyor and accompanied by a couple of policemen. He looked at all three rooms. He asked why the front wall of the living room had been boarded up. The Kobozevs explained that the damp came through the cement. Mrovinski pulled at the boards, but they were fast and for the time he was satisfied. There was a pile of coke in one corner of the storeroom. Mrovinski kicked at it but did not ask for it to be removed. There was also a quantity of straw and it had to be explained to him that the straw was for packing the cheese barrels. In point of fact both straw and coke were used for covering the earth brought out of the gallery, and this would have been at once apparent if the examination had been more thorough. There was more earth packed under the bed. There were a number of barrels and sacks in the storeroom—also filled with earth. The earth was damp and water was oozing out of one of the barrels. Bogdanovich hastily embarked on a long story of how during the carnival they had dropped that particular barrel and stained it, and how soft cheese is apt to sweat. Mrovinski did not ask for the barrels to be opened. But he would not go away. He gave the impression that he himself felt that his inspection so far had been superficial and he was wondering what step to take next. Then the cat came in and rubbed itself against his legs; the general bent down and stroked it, and Yakimova—remembering no doubt stories of Perovskaya at Moscow—started off on the animal's intimate history. Mrovinski was amused and the atmosphere thawed. Finally he bade them good morning and went off with his policemen. Once again a conspiratorial cat had saved the day.

That same morning Sukhanov made an attempt to get into touch with Trigoni at the latter's lodgings and thus became aware of the catastrophe of the night before. He was overwhelmed. Hurriedly he passed the news to his colleagues and by three o'clock all available members of the Executive Committee were gathered at Figner's flat. These were Figner herself, Sukhanov, Perovskaya, Frolenko, Tikhomirov, Korba, Isaev, Grachevski, Langans and Lebedeva. It was a desperate meeting. The mine was not yet charged. The shop was under suspicion. The bombs were not yet made—indeed it was uncertain whether they would be effective, as there had been no opportunity to make a proper test. They had lost their main leader. But the feeling was unanimous that they must go ahead with the mine attempt on the following day. Then Perovskaya volunteered to lead the bombers as a second line of attack. This was approved.

Isaev went straight from this meeting to the cheese shop to charge the mine. Sukhanov went to the flat in the Ismailovski Polk to remove anything incriminating before the police came to make their search, which sooner or later they were obviously bound to do. So far Zhelyabov had succeeded in keeping his address undisclosed, but the police were already suspicious of the place because of Trigoni's visit there. In point of fact, they sent orders to the house porter to let them know as soon as the "male occupant" returned. This message reached him soon after Sukhanov had left. Not long after that Perovskaya returned to have a last look round. The porter reported that the girl was back: the police replied he must keep on the watch and report at once when the man came. The porter went up to the flat and asked Perovskaya where her brother was. She told him he was at work.

"I must know as soon as he comes in," he informed her. "I have a form from the police for him to sign. Ask him to come and see me as soon as he comes in."

Perovskaya promised and the porter went back to his den. She finished her tidying up, but she was too agitated to do it thoroughly. When the police eventually came they found traces of explosive and bomb-components, also a number of cheese labels. Perovskaya left the flat shortly before eight and went to Figner's. There she found Figner, Kibalchich, Sukhanov, and Grachevski who had been busy working on the bombs since five. Perovskaya set to and helped, but at eleven o'clock they made her go and lie down to get some rest for the next day. The others went on working. Figner mixed the chemicals for Kibalchich, and cut up paraffin cans for Sukhanov to make the containers. By two o'clock there was nothing

Killing an Emperor

more that she could do and she went to bed. When the two girls got up at seven next morning the three men were still working. Two of the bombs were ready. Perovskaya took them and left in a cab for the Telezhnaya flat. Kibalchich was to follow on with the other two bombs as soon as they were finished.

III

THAT morning, March 1, the bomb throwers were up betimes. Before leaving home Grinevitski composed a farewell letter to his comrades:

"Alexander II must die. His days are numbered. . . . The near future will show whether it is for me or another to strike the final blow. But he will die and with him we shall die, his enemies and executioners. What of the future? I, with one foot already in the grave, am afflicted by the thought that after me there will be many further victims. It will not be my lot to take part in the final battle. Fate has allotted me an early death. I shall not see one day, not one hour of our triumph. But I believe that by my death I am doing all that I have in my power to do, and that no one on earth can demand more of me. . . ."

Rysakov was also up early. His landlady said afterwards that he had seemed strangely elated. He came to her room and talked to her, a thing he had never done before. She asked why he was up so early on a Sunday and he explained he had to go to work that day. She gave him some tea before he left.

All four were assembled by the time Perovskaya arrived. She showed them the bombs. She had nursed them in her lap all the way in the cab for fear a jolt on the cobbles might set them off. She explained the other two bombs would be along as soon as ready. She broke the news of Zhelyabov's arrest and then proceeded to explain the plan of action. They had a map of Petersburg on which Zhelyabov had marked the positions. But the scale was small, and to make things clearer Perovskaya drew a rough plan on the back of an envelope.

The assumption was that the Emperor would take the normal route from the palace to the Manège, i.e., via the Nevski, Malaya Sadovaya and Bolshaya Italianskaya. Accordingly "Kotik" (Grinevitski) and Timothy Mihailov were to take up positions at the two corners where the Malaya Sadovaya joined the Italianskaya. The other two men were to stand farther down the Malaya Sadovaya, towards the Nevski. All were to be at their posts by twelve noon. Perovskaya herself would be on watch at the corner of the Nevski. The bombers were to wait for a loud explosion and then move in towards the sound; if the Emperor were still alive they should attack at once. Rysakov hitherto had no knowledge of the mining venture. Grinevitski, who was in Zhelyabov's confidence, had known about it for some time. The other two knew vaguely that something was on foot.

There was, however, the possibility that the Emperor would not take the expected route. In that case Perovskaya was to walk down the Malaya Sadovaya and give the bombers a signal. (Historians have described her as waving a handkerchief. This is incorrect. In any case it would not have been feasible with the streets full of detectives. Perovskaya blew her nose.) On receipt of this signal the four men were to leave the Malaya Sadovaya and proceed to positions along the Ekaterinski Canal, at intervals of some thirty yards between the corner of the Inzhenernaya and the Teatralni Bridge. Perovskaya herself would wait on the other side of the canal at a spot from where she could look at the Inzhenernaya. When she saw the Emperor coming she would repeat the signal.

At ten o'clock Kibalchich turned up in the Telezhnaya with the other two bombs. One hour later they all left the conspiratorial quarter, carrying their bombs wrapped up in paper. They had plenty of time. Perovskaya, Grinevitski and Rysakov went to a café and had coffee and cakes.

IV

THE preparations for the mine had already been completed. Isaev had laid the charge and fixed up the firing apparatus. There was no more actual work to be done. Frolenko had been allotted the honour of pressing the lever. They had placed a table by the window in the living room: Frolenko would thus be able to stand on the table and watch for the exact moment to make the connexion. Of the other conspirators only the two Kobozevs were allowed in the shop that day, and they were to be out of the way before the explosion took place. Bogdanovich left at eleven. Yakimova remained on to serve any customers. As zero hour approached she was to watch for the arrival of the imperial procession at the corner of the Nevski, warn Frolenko to get ready, and then leave at once. Frolenko was to get away as best he could in the general confusion, always supposing that he was not blown to bits by the back-fire.

Of the others Helfmann and Sablin were on duty at the Telezhnaya flat, and Figner had been instructed to stay at home, at any rate until 2 P.M., to give shelter, if need be, to the cheese-shop party. At ten in the morning she received a visit from Frolenko, who produced a bottle of red wine from one pocket and half a loaf and some sausage from the other and proceeded to make a substantial meal. Figner, who was all on edge, asked him how he could possibly have an appetite at such a time. Frolenko solemnly replied that it was just because the moment was so decisive that he had to maintain all his force and all his faculties.

Frolenko went on to the cheese shop. At two o'clock he was standing on the table in the basement living room with the connecting gear in his hand and watching through the window. Presently he called out to Yakimova that they were a long time coming. Yakimova went out and walked up to the street corner. She came back with the news that the imperial party had gone round by the canal. Frolenko packed up his gear and left the shop.

It was a dreary afternoon. Dirty snow lay piled up in the streets and piled in heaps along the sidewalks. Kibalchich, wearing as always his old top hat, was hanging about in the neighbourhood to see the result of the explosion. When he discovered the route the Emperor was taking he took it for granted the attempt had failed and went back to his lodgings. He had little faith in the bombing project, and was worn out after his seventeen hours of continuous work the previous night. He knew nothing of the events of the day until he saw the newspapers next morning.

While the parade was in progress Perovskaya hung about within sight of the entrance to the Manège. She saw the Emperor leave, watched the direction his carriage was taking and hurried off to give her signal to the bombers. Fifteen

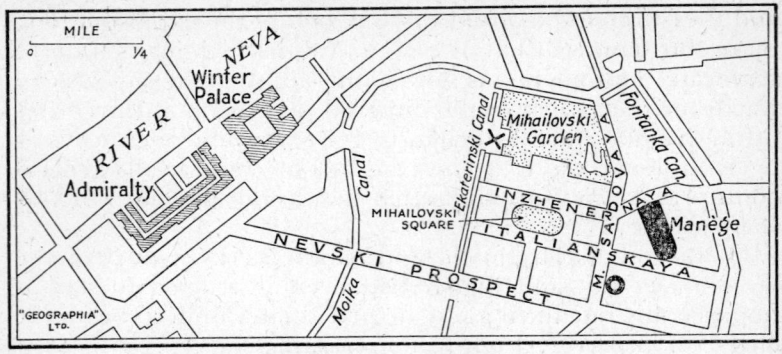

THE ATTACK OF MARCH 1

O The cheese shop. **X** Scene of the bomb attack.

minutes later the Emperor left the Grand Duchess. The convoy moved at full speed down the Inzhenernaya—mounted Cossacks in front and on the flanks, the Emperor's own carriage, then a sleigh with Colonel Dvorzhitski and his personal staff, then a second sleigh with Captain Koch of the police and another officer. At the bottom of the Inzhenernaya the party turned to the right along the quay. Timothy Mihailov should have been posted at this spot; but he had cold feet at the last moment and edged out of his place. Fifty yards farther was Rysakov who threw his bomb. It exploded under the back axle of the Emperor's carriage. One of the Cossack escort fell. So did a small boy who had stopped to watch the procession; he was badly hurt and screamed incessantly. The back axle of the imperial carriage was damaged, but the carriage held together. The horses bolted, and the coachman (who had private orders from Princess Yurievskaya to drive on fast in any emergency) whipped them forward. The Emperor ordered him to stop, and he pulled up in about eighty yards. Colonel Dvorzhitski alighted and opened the carriage door. The Emperor was seen to limp as he got out; possibly he had been hit by a splinter. Dvorzhitski suggested driving straight on to the palace but the Emperor wished to see what had happened. Rysakov had been caught by this time and a small party of police and soldiers were holding him. Captain Koch went through his pockets and found a revolver. All around was porter out for cigarettes. The latter was on his way downstairs when he met a big young man coming up. He asked him where he was going. The young man said to flat No. 12. There was no flat No. 12 in the block but the porter had his instructions and told him to go up. In due course the young man, who was Timothy Mihailov, arrived in flat No. 5 and found himself surrounded by police. They asked him what he wanted. He said he was looking for a cab-driver, a friend of his, who had told him he lived there. The police told him to sit down and wait. After a short time he got up to leave and when they made a move to stop him he pulled out a revolver and began to shoot. Two policemen were wounded before Mihailov was disarmed and overpowered. The police sat down to wait for the next caller.

It was Kibalchich who first discovered what had happened at the Telezhnaya flat. He warned the Executive Committee that same morning. There was another hurried and desperate meeting. Zhelyabov's fears were justified. Obsessed as they had been with the idea of the attempt they were completely unprepared for its consequences. The raid came as a rude reminder of realities. It was obvious that someone was talking: they could not yet tell who it was but they suspected Rysakov. It seemed probable that the next development would be a further investigation at the cheese shop. The Kobozevs, therefore, must leave while they could. Bogdanovich caught the midday train to Moscow. As before, Yakimova stayed on to divert suspicion: if the shop were closed or deserted during working hours the police would be sure to be notified and take action at once. Evening came and Yakimova shut the shop. She tidied up and left some money on the table with a note to say the money was for the butcher and would he please remember to feed the cat. Then she slipped out and took the night train via Smolensk. It was now to be assumed that the direct Petersburg-Moscow trains were being watched so she took the roundabout route. She left just in time. Early next morning the shop was inspected again and the mine discovered. The news was at once telegraphed to the provincial newspapers, and all the way from Smolensk to Moscow people in Yakimova's compartment were talking of nothing else. The printed accounts of "Madame Kobozeva" were especially lurid. She was, apparently, an incessant smoker of cigarettes and had the unbourgeois habit of staying out at night. Incidentally, all reports agreed that she was extremely beautiful. Yakimova, who was entirely without personal vanity, found this last somewhat embarrassing.

III

By March 4 the Executive Committee had little trace left of their former exuberant optimism. The initiative was no longer in their hands. Their organisation was crippled. They had no immediate policy and no leader who could formulate and impose one. Tikhomirov was wearing deep mourning for the Emperor, and spent most of his time attending memorial services. Sukhanov "seemed completely lost without the iron hand of Zhelyabov to control him." Of Perovskaya we have several accounts, one of them from Tyrkov of her scouting party, whose care and devotion during the last few days of her liberty ultimately led to his own arrest.

Tyrkov writes:

"I was often with Perovskaya after March 1. On February 27 Zhelyabov was arrested, the person who was the most important to her. She herself was ill. Sometimes she could hardly walk. It was a time of great strain for her. But she kept her feelings well under control; outwardly she was quiet, sensible, composed. On March 3, I think it was, I was with her on the Nevski. The paper boys were calling out a new edition with 'fresh revelations about the crime' and we bought a copy. There we read that Zhelyabov had declared he was the organiser of March 1. Up till then it had been possible to hope that he would not be implicated. Of course there was a good deal against him in his police dossier, but there could not have been any evidence as regards the actual assassination. But it was clear from the paper that now his fate was definitely sealed. It was a terrible moment for Perovskaya. She did not lose her self-control. She walked on slowly with her head bent and the paper dangling from one hand. She said nothing and I did not want to speak. I knew she was in love with Zhelyabov. At last she said something. I asked: 'Why did he do it?' She said: 'He is right. It was necessary. . . .'

"She kept talking about rescuing Zhelyabov. Of course the

idea was impossible. But she could not or would not see that; she could not keep still, she had to try every possibility. She was anxious to establish some contact in the District Court where we thought the trial was going to be. Then we went round together looking for empty flats near the Third Section in the Panteleimonovski; her idea was to establish a lookout post there, and when they brought Zhelyabov out, to make an organised mass attack on the guards and carry him off. She had all sorts of other plans. It would have been hopeless to try and discourage her. She would only have tried to go through with it all by herself. She seemed to have lost all sense of realities. She had become quite irresponsible. So I made a point of agreeing with everything she said and going with her wherever she wanted to go. People said, 'Sonia has lost her head.' It was quite true. They tried to make her leave Petersburg and go into hiding for a time. She would not hear of it. She was like a bird who sees a hawk above her head, a hawk that had stolen her young."

Stepniak (Kravchinski) has recorded an account by Rina Epstein, the girl who had shared Perovskaya's flat in the Ismailovski Polk before Zhelyabov joined her there. Epstein was not a member of the party, but she sympathised with their aims and did them small services when the opportunity arose. She was in Petersburg for a few days at the end of February. She had then one interview with Perovskaya who appeared completely worn out. She was very concerned over funds: she had just been to collect a subscription of one hundred roubles but the money had not been forthcoming. Epstein offered to lend her the sum, but Perovskaya refused as she could not guarantee repayment.

Epstein went on to Gatchina. She was there when news came of the Emperor's death, but she had no inkling that Perovskaya had any hand in it. On the following Thursday (March 5) she returned to the capital and found an atmosphere of gloom and panic. The whole city was hung with black flags and crêpe; there were detachments of police and Cossacks at every corner; at every hour of the twenty-four house searches and arrests were taking place in every street. Epstein was profoundly relieved to receive a message from Perovskaya, making an appointment for that evening. It was a proof that she was still at liberty, and Epstein, who had some experience of smuggling revolutionaries over the frontier, determined to persuade her to leave the country.

When Perovskaya arrived, however, she would not listen to any suggestion of escape. She was in a mood of extreme exaltation and full of the wildest schemes for exploiting the party's "great victory." (It is significant of Perovskaya's state of mind at this time that she alternated between extreme exaltation and blank despair.) She was, however, anxious to ascertain exactly what admission Zhelyabov had made to the authorities: at the moment she was eagerly persuading herself that he had not become irrevocably incriminated. Perovskaya was still in indirect touch with a certain high official who was in a position to know the details of the preliminary examination. She wished Epstein to call on him and hear what news he had. She then was full of funds: she offered Epstein the money to buy a new dress for her visit.

Epstein made her call, and later in the evening arranged a rendezvous with Perovskaya.* In the meantime a reaction had set in. Perovskaya turned up three hours late. Her face was white with black rings under the eyes. She said she was tired. The people of the house brought tea in a samovar and left the two girls together. Epstein's account is as follows:

"I told her what His Excellency had said. I did not see her face because she was looking at the ground. When she raised her eyes I saw she was trembling. She took my hands and sank down and buried her face in my lap. She stayed like that for several minutes. There were no tears but I felt her trembling. Then she got up and tried to compose herself. But suddenly she caught my hands again and gripped them so hard as to hurt."

The two girls talked confusedly, playing with words to keep back the pressure of feeling. They spoke of writing to Zhelyabov's family in the South but neither of them knew the address. Then Epstein had to repeat her story of Zhelyabov's self-assurance and defiance under examination. For a time Perovskaya's colour came back again.

* It is possible that Tyrkov's or Epstein's dates are incorrect, and that Perovskaya first heard of Zhelyabov's confession while Epstein was paying her call on the high official.

"It could not be otherwise," she said again. "The trial of Rysakov alone would have been too colourless."

They talked about the other prisoners, and Perovskaya kept maintaining they would none of them disclose the party's secrets. She was proud of them all. The two girls talked for over three hours. When it was time to go Perovskaya had scarcely the strength to stand.

We have other glimpses of Perovskaya at this time. One evening she called at Vera Figner's flat. Figner writes:

"She asked me, 'Vera, may I spend the night here?' I said, 'How can you ask me that?' She said, 'I ask, because if they make a raid and find me here you will be hanged.' 'I have a revolver,' I told her, 'and if they come I will shoot, whether you are here or not.'"

Tyrkov again writes:

"She told me some of Zhelyabov's special friends among the workmen had come to ask her what they could do to rescue their Zahar. 'What could I say to them?' she asked me. Indeed what could she have said to them?"

A "Madame B" writes:

"She knew that those she cared for most were going to die, and she did not wish to survive them."

She was arrested five days after her last interview with Epstein. Copies of her photograph had been distributed to the Petersburg police, but it was recognised that the likeness was not a good one* and the authorities employed the woman who kept the dairy shop where Perovskaya used to buy milk. This woman spent several days accompanying a detective to places where it was thought Perovskaya might be found. On March 10 they saw her driving down the Nevski in a cab. They gave chase and caught her. Perovskaya had a fifty rouble note which she offered to the detective to let her go. But he would not take it.

IV

THE Imperial Police archives enable us to follow in some detail the course of events within the prison.

---

* This photograph has come down to us, and is most unflattering. All who knew Perovskaya agree that she was very good looking.

Within twenty-four hours of his arrest Zhelyabov made the following statement:

"My name is Andrei Ivanovich Zhelyabov, peasant, of the village of Nikolaevka. My occupation is to work for the liberation of my country. I have a father, a mother, sisters and brothers living in the Feodosia district. I am married and have one son. I do not know the whereabouts of my wife and child; they are probably with my father-in-law Yahnenko in the province of Kherson. I was involved in the Trial of the 193 and was acquitted. I have been living on funds collected for the liberation of our country. I have lived under various pseudonyms which I do not propose to disclose. I admit my adherence to the Narodnaya Volya party. I admit that I organised the attempt at Alexandrovsk and that I pressed the lever of the apparatus—i.e., in the attempt to blow up the imperial train. I then lived under the name of Cheremisov. I am not prepared to give my present address in Petersburg or the names of any of my friends. On my arrest they took from me a loaded Smith & Wesson revolver, some spare cartridges and a sealed envelope containing two sheets written in a cypher which I am not prepared to disclose. They also took a key.

ANDREI ZHELYABOV."

General Komarov of the police, in his covering letter, reported:

"After considerable hesitation the individual arrested with Trigoni admits not only to be the peasant Andrei Zhelyabov but also to have organised the attempt on the Sacred Person of His Majesty the Emperor at Alexandrovsk in November, 1879, and states that he himself pressed the lever. He still resolutely refuses to disclose his Petersburg address, presumably to give his mistress Anna Yakimova [sic] the chance to escape. Steps are being taken to discover his quarters."

One of Zhelyabov's Soviet biographers has described his confession of his part in the Alexandrovsk attempt as "attempted suicide"; he pictures Zhelyabov as suffering from nervous breakdown and anxious to put an end to his life by confessing to a capital crime. This interpretation seems unnecessary and far fetched. Zhelyabov knew perfectly well that the police had obtained from Goldenberg the details of his role at Alexandrovsk, and there was no point in trying to hide his identity once he had been recognised by the officer at the police station. It might perhaps have been wiser to have made no statement of any kind. But here we come up against the Narodnaya Volya temperament. "The heroic spirit was too strong."

At 2 a.m. on the night of March 1–2, Zhelyabov was waked, taken to the prison office and confronted with Rysakov. He made no attempt to deny the acquaintanceship, and the police were struck by his obvious friendship and affection for the younger man. The two shook hands. When Rysakov had been removed Zhelyabov asked why he had been disturbed in the middle of the night. They then informed him of the Emperor's death. His delight and triumph at the news were unconcealed. That day, he informed the officials, would be a memorable one for the cause of liberty and for the whole Russian nation. He went on to say that he had been listening all the afternoon for the sound of an explosion. Owing to the late Emperor's fondness for parades it was easy to foresee his movements on a Sunday, and that day was the obvious choice for the assassination.

The officer on duty asked if he would care to make a written statement, and he wrote as follows:

"The attack can only have been made by the Fighting Groups of the Executive Committee. But I have no knowledge of the individuals involved, except Rysakov with whom I have now been confronted and who is known to me as a devoted revolutionary of high calibre. I took no physical part in the attempt, but that was due merely to the accident of my arrest. My moral participation is unquestionable. I have for some time been acquainted with the idea of hand grenades, but I do not know which type of grenade was used today. That question was decided by the committee's technical experts after my arrest."

That night he made one further declaration. The police had by now, apparently, established the fact that for the last few months he had been using the duplicated passport of one Slotvinski. There was therefore no longer any purpose in denying this alias; in any case Perovskaya had had ample time to clear out of the flat in the Ismailovski Polk. Zhelyabov's conscience demanded that he should do what he could to clear the real Slotvinski of suspicion. "I do not know him," he declared, "and he had nothing whatever to do with the duplication of this document."

During the night he had the chance to think things over, and decided to make a more definite statement. On the following morning, March 2, he called for pen and paper and composed his memorable note to the public prosecutor:

"If the new Emperor, having received his sceptre from the hands of the revolutionaries, intends to follow the established tradition and to execute Rysakov, then it would be a grave injustice to spare my life. I have on many occasions made attempts on the life of Alexander II. It was by pure chance that I took no physical part in his death. I demand to be associated with the act of March 1, and if necessary I will make such disclosures as may be required to implicate me. I demand that this statement be followed by appropriate action.

Andrei Zhelyabov."

"P.S.—I am disquietened at the possibility of the authorities rating legal formalities higher than real justice, and adorning the Crown of the new Monarch with the corpse of one young hero merely for lack of formal evidence against myself, a veteran of the revolution. I protest against such flagrant injustice. It would only be cowardice on the part of the authorities to erect one gallows and not two."

The last sentence of Zhelyabov's postscript reveals his motive. It had become, as we have seen, a tradition of the revolutionaries to regard a political trial as the supreme opportunity to proclaim their message to the world. The proceedings in connection with the death of the Emperor Alexander II would be an event of universal, not merely Russian, interest, and it was essential to exploit the opportunity to the uttermost. The prestige and with it the whole future of the party were at stake. The task would be one of great difficulty. The prosecution, and the court itself, would employ all the resources of invective, obstruction and intimidation to discredit the revolutionary cause. At that moment the interests of the party demanded that their most redoubtable champion should be in the dock. Perovskaya well realised where the issue lay. "The trial of Rysakov alone would have been too colourless."

There was also no doubt the motive of personal loyalty. It was Zhelyabov who had engaged Rysakov in the venture. He then felt for him all the affection of a leader for one of his most promising recruits. It would have been hard for him to leave the lad to pay the penalty alone.

All that day, March 2, Zhelyabov was in the best of spirits. He made no further written depositions, but was perfectly willing to talk to the senior officials who saw him. He explained to Plehve that the lull in terrorist activity during the summer and autumn had been due to the hope that Kviatkovski and Presnyakov might be spared: the moment they were hanged, however, the days of Alexander II had been numbered. He had another long interview with General Komarov. The general was a serious and devoted officer, whose insistence on referring to Alexander II as "the Sacred Person of His Late Imperial Majesty" seems to have aroused Zhelyabov's flippancy. "Our plans," he told him, "depended largely on the object of our attack. The place, for instance, depended on the object's movements." Komarov was also interested in the nature of the bombs, but here again he could not elicit much information. "In answer to my enquiries," he reported, "the prisoner replied that the bombs might be of various shapes. Some were oval or spheroid, and some were rectangular. But he did not appear to know what was inside them."

V

It is an interesting illustration of the cumbersome working of the Russian administrative machine that, although Zhelyabov's "confession" was in the Petersburg papers on March 3, on March 4 Captain Paleolog of the Kiev Gendarmerie was still unaware of his arrest. On that day the captain submitted to Petersburg his proposals for apprehending Zhelyabov. He pointed out that Zhelyabov's wife was then living with her child on one of her father's properties in South Russia. It was to be assumed that both "for natural reasons" and in order to have access to her money Zhelyabov was still in touch with her. Accordingly by establishing a close watch on Olga Semenovna's movements, visitors and correspondence, it should soon be possible to trace her husband.*

---

* There is, of course, no basis for the assumption that Zhelyabov was in touch with his wife. Shortly after this date Olga Semenovna, at the insistence of her family, renounced the name of Zhelyabov both for herself and her son and resumed her maiden name of Yahnenko. We have no record of what subsequently became of either of them.

VI

Rysakov, described by the *Times* correspondent as "a thick-set, short-necked, repulsive-looking dark man, very resolute in his refusal to answer questions," had been examined shortly after his arrest on March 1. He had then declined to make any statement likely to implicate his associates. On March 2 he was examined again. This time it was Dobrinski who handled him—the same Dobrinski who had elicited the disclosures of Goldenberg and who was the most brilliant and experienced official of the Imperial Russian Police for this particular work. Rysakov was nineteen years old, ignorant, weak, credulous and frightened. The contest was unequal. During that examination of March 2 Rysakov said enough to enable the police to identify the flat in the Telezhnaya. That was the beginning of the shipwreck of the Narodnaya Volya, and of the moral shipwreck of Rysakov himself which was not the least tragic part of it. For the next month Rysakov was under examination nearly every day.

The original intention of the authorities had been to try Rysakov by court martial on March 3 and hang him on March 4. It is possible that some inkling of this may have determined Zhelyabov to write his note to the public prosecutor. In any case after his declaration of March 2 Loris-Melikov recommended to the Emperor that Zhelyabov and Rysakov should be tried on the 4th and hanged on the 5th. Alexander III wrote on the margin of this recommendation: "Am entirely of your opinion." However, on the 3rd, thanks to Rysakov's disclosures, came the raid on the Telezhnaya flat with the consequent discovery of a number of further clues and the arrest of Timothy Mihailov. The following day, March 4, the mine at the cheese shop was discovered. On that same day Zhelyabov was confronted with Sablin's body. He said he did not know him. Zhelyabov was then subjected to a further examination but all he would say was that he was himself an "agent of the Executive Committee of the Third Class," and that when he had asked for volunteers to kill the Emperor forty-seven young men had come forward. The authorities then seem to have concluded that little of value was likely to be obtained from Zhelyabov and they transferred him from the Provisional Detention Prison to a cell in the Trubetskoi Bastion. (From that time till his execution he was never left by himself; there was a sentry posted on duty inside his cell day and night. The same precautions were taken with other prisoners who were brought to trial with him.) Rysakov, however, proved to be more amenable. He identified Sablin as the occupant of the Telezhnaya flat. He identified Helfmann as the housekeeper there, and he identified Timothy Mihailov as one of his fellow-bombers. This last, of course, was of great interest to the police and they held a further examination of Zhelyabov. Zhelyabov for the first time realised what Rysakov was doing, and began his attempt to save young Mihailov's life. He demanded to make a further written statement:

"I certainly engaged Rysakov," he wrote. "But Rysakov is entirely incorrect in his account of the part played by Timothy Mihailov. There is no truth whatever in Rysakov's story that proposals were ever made to Mihailov to participate in the attack."

The authorities, however, were satisfied that Rysakov was speaking the truth. At the same time, in the light of these new revelations, it was obvious that the original arrangements suggested for the trial would have to be modified. Fears were expressed lest the executions might give rise to disturbances in the streets and it was particularly desired there should be no disorders during the funeral of the late Emperor. It was therefore decided that the trial should be postponed until a complete case was established against all the individuals implicated.

The authorities redoubled their precautions. Thousands of Cossacks were drafted into the town. All the surrounding roads were picketed. Restrictions were so severe that there was serious interference with the normal supply of foodstuffs. Police activities were intensified. Whole streets were blocked while house-to-house searches were made in every flat. We hear of one woman, completely innocent of any connection with the revolutionaries, who was arrested five times within a week. Private individuals were completely in the dark as to what either the authorities or the revolutionaries were about to do next. Business was at a standstill. The reactionary group at Court purposely exaggerated the gravity of the position so as to be the better able to oppose any concessions to liberal opinion along the lines of Loris-Melikov's reforms. The young Emperor was taken out of the city to the comparative safety of his palace at Gatchina. Even at Gatchina deep trenches were dug round the imperial residence to guard against the danger of mining operations. Alexander III sat there a virtual prisoner, spending his time over the police reports that reached him every few hours. His marginal comments are still preserved in the State Archives. On the final report on the mine of the Malaya Sadovaya he wrote: "This only shows how carelessly the first inspection must have been conducted." * Sablin's body was finally identified by his brother, a serving officer; and the Emperor wrote: "Nice to have a brother like that."

Meanwhile within the Provisional Detention Prison Dobrinski continued his sessions with Rysakov. On March 10 Perovskaya was arrested. Rysakov identified her as the blonde in command of the bombing party. Perovskaya admitted her complicity, but refused to give names or details and consistently denied that Timothy Mihailov had been concerned. Of Zhelyabov she would only say: "In September last he came to live with me in my flat. That is all." Timothy Mihailov professed complete ignorance and could not be shaken. Helfmann was equally adamant. But the wretched Rysakov "already felt the rope round his neck." He repeated all that he had heard of Perovskaya's scouting party. On March 14 the police laid their hands on Tyrkov and Natalia Olovennikova. Three days later they arrested Kibalchich and Frolenko. Rysakov identified Kibalchich as the bombers' technical expert. Frolenko, however, he had never met.

The authorities decided that a charge of tsaricide could now be established against Zhelyabov, Perovskaya, Kibalchich, Rysakov, Helfmann and Timothy Mihailov, and the trial was arranged to take place before the Senate at the end of the month. That this trial was confined to individuals connected with the bombing party was due to the fact that the prosecution was based on the depositions of Rysakov, who had no details to disclose about the cheese shop.

* General Mrovinski was subsequently tried for negligence and banished to the province of Archangel.

VII

PEROVSKAYA obtained permission to write from the prison to her mother. Her letter has been preserved. She entreated her mother not to grieve; her own life, she wrote, had been spent as she had wished to spend it. She herself had nothing to regret except the pain she was now causing her family.

She finished:

". . . Buy me some cuffs and collars—the collars rather narrow and the cuffs with buttons. They do not allow studs here. I shall have to mend my dress before the trial. Goodbye till we next meet. Once more I beg you not to grieve. My fate is not such a sad one after all and you must not worry.

Your own
SOPHIA."

Madame Perovskaya hurried up from the country and sought an interview with Loris-Melikov to ask for permission to visit her daughter. Her son has left us her account of this interview. She was kept waiting in the anteroom. When she was finally admitted Loris-Melikov said:

"I am to inform you that it is His Imperial Majesty's desire that you should induce your daughter to disclose the names of her accomplices."

The old lady answered: "It is impossible for me to persuade my daughter to do anything against her own convictions."

Madame Perovskaya was allowed to see her daughter twice before the trial. On each occasion the sentry and a police officer were present. Few words passed. Sophie knelt by her mother with her head in her lap and asked her to remember that she was not the only child and that there were the rest of the family to be cared for.

CHAPTER FOURTEEN

THE TRIAL OF THE SIX

I

SOME days before the trial took place Pobyedonostsev, whose influence was considerable now that his former pupil had ascended the throne, warned the young Emperor that public opinion was "disquietened by rumours of the possibility of the lives of the tsaricides being spared." Alexander III said: "Do not be alarmed. No one would dare approach me with such a proposal. I can promise you that all six will be hanged."

Shortly after this, on March 25, Zhelyabov addressed a memorandum to the authorities:

"As our activities have been directed solely against the Administration, the Court of the Senate, being composed of members of the Administration, is an interested party and therefore not competent to judge the issue. . . . The sole tribunal competent to adjudicate is the nation, acting by means of a national plebiscite or referendum, or else through a freely elected Constituent Assembly. . . . Failing that, the social conscience might be able to make itself felt in a trial by jury. I accordingly request and require a trial by jury. I have no doubt that this would lead to our acquittal as it led to the acquittal of Zasulich."

This was a warning to the authorities, if such were needed, of the attitude that Zhelyabov was likely to adopt at the trial. They had experience of the tendency of political prisoners to launch out on indictments of the Administration. The necessary precautions had already been taken. Arrangements had been made for the censorship of accounts of the proceedings in the Russian press, and to ensure that only carefully selected individuals, officials for the most part, should be admitted to the court. None the less there was still a certain danger of leakage. Accordingly Fuchs, who had been appointed president of the court, was approached in turn by Loris-Melikov, by Nabokov (the Minister of Justice) and by Pobyedonostsev, who informed him that His Imperial Majesty would prefer to see the proceedings made as short as possible; it would be undesirable for the accused to be allowed to make long speeches, or for Zhelyabov to be given the opportunity to expound his political views.

II

THE proceedings opened at 11 A.M. on March 26. The court consisted of ten persons, including Fuchs, the president, and representatives of the Estates of the Empire. The merchant class was represented by the Mayor of Moscow and the peasants by one Helker, a rural district headman. The prisoners sat in a row: Rysakov, Mihailov, Helfmann, Kibalchich, Perovskaya and Zhelyabov, in that order. The arrangement was intentional. The more malleable prisoners came first, and Zhelyabov last, so that he would not be able to give a lead to the others. All were represented by counsel except Zhelyabov. Apart from Rysakov the prisoners were calm and in good spirits. From time to time Zhelyabov whispered to Perovskaya until he was stopped by an officer of the court.

Each of the accused was called upon to give his name, age, and religion. When it came to Zhelyabov's turn he objected to the form in which the charge had been communicated to him and required an answer to his memorandum demanding a trial by jury. His objections were overruled and the formalities proceeded.

"Name?"

"Andrei Ivanovich Zhelyabov."

"Age?"

"Thirty."

"Religion?"

"I was baptised into the Orthodox Church but am no longer a member. At the same time I admit the teaching of Christ to be the basis of my moral convictions. I believe in truth and justice. I consider religion without deeds to be of no value. I hold it to be the duty of a sincere Christian to fight on behalf of the weak and oppressed; and, if need be, to suffer for them. That is my faith."

"Address and occupation?"

"My last place of residence was in the Ismailovski Polk. I have lived at various addresses as ordered by the Executive Committee. My sole occupation has, for several years, been the liberation of my fellow-countrymen."

The clerk of the court read the charge against the prisoners: "That they did enter into a secret society calling itself the Russian Social Revolutionary party and having as its aim to overthrow by force the form of government and the social structure at present existing in this Empire; and that they did undertake a series of attempts against the Sacred Person of His Late Imperial Majesty . . ." The twenty-four counts of the charge covered the attack on the Ekaterinski Quay, the mine in the Malaya Sadovaya, and (this last concerned Zhelyabov alone) the attempt on the railway at Alexandrovsk.

The prisoners were told to plead.

Zhelyabov, when it came to his turn, said:

"I admit I am a member of the Narodnaya Volya, in accordance with my convictions. I have acted as agent of the Executive Committee. At one time I devoted several years to peaceful propaganda. I was forced to abandon that form of activity. By the time I came to settle in Petersburg I had become convinced that the main enemy of the Russian social movement was the Russian bureaucracy."

The President: "I will not permit expressions of that nature."

Zhelyabov: "I do not plead guilty of belonging to a secret society composed of the six persons here and a few others. Some of them have taken a leading part in revolutionary activities, but they do not form a secret society in the terms of the charge. In any case Mihailov had nothing whatever to do with the matter at issue."

Muraviev, the acting public prosecutor, informed the court that he proposed to read the depositions of Colonel Dvorzhitski and of two other witnesses who had been wounded by the explosion and were unable to attend in person; also that he proposed to read the depositions of Goldenberg. Counsel for the accused raised no objection. Zhelyabov announced that he wished to call Kolotkevich and Kurshunikov (Barannikov). To this the prosecution objected in view of a rule that the evidence of other political prisoners was not to be accepted

The Trial of the Six

in political trials as their "natural inclination would be to distort rather than to clarify the issue." Zhelyabov replied that in that case he objected to the depositions of Goldenberg. There ensued a legal argument; finally Zhelyabov's objection was overruled on the grounds that, as Goldenberg was dead, the rule did not apply to his case. Zhelyabov then demanded proof of the death of Goldenberg, and the court pronounced that sufficient evidence of his death had been produced at the Trial of the Sixteen.

This concluded the preliminaries and the trial began.

III

THE trial lasted for three days. The court sat from eleven in the morning till half past two, and again from eight in the evening till after midnight. There was no ventilation in the courtroom and the atmosphere became oppressive as the evening wore on. Very few of the public stayed till the end. Elaborate precautions were taken to prevent the prisoners from communicating with each other. They were carefully watched while in the dock, and were at once removed to separate cells whenever the court rose.

A large number of witnesses were called. There were nineteen of them, all officials or military, to testify to the actual attack on the Ekaterinski Quay. Police Captain Koch in the course of his evidence declared he had been forced to use his weapons to defend Rysakov from the fury of the mob. Zhelyabov at once challenged this statement and extorted the admission that the captain had drawn his sword but as there was no occasion to use it he had put it back into its sheath. He was incessantly on the alert for any weakness in the prosecution's evidence. Rysakov's landlady was called to identify visitors to the boy's room. Zhelyabov contested her competence to do so. Rysakov's table with his samovar, he explained, was against the far wall and the guests sat up to it: when the landlady came to the door she could therefore see only their backs. From time to time he intervened to claim for himself the responsibility on some particular count. There was the marked map of Petersburg found in the Telezhnaya flat. "These marks," he declared, "were made by me. I am not prepared to explain their significance." He watched for the opportunity to puncture a dramatic moment in the prosecution's case. A witness had been describing the removal of the dying Emperor.

Zhelyabov: "May I ask for guidance on a matter of procedure?"

President: "Well?"

Zhelyabov: "Am I supposed to stand or to sit when addressing the court?"

President: "When addressing the court you should stand."

It was only Zhelyabov who made the attempt to harry the prosecution. Perovskaya, Helfmann and Mihailov were content to answer the questions put to them. As to Rysakov, Count Milyutin, the Minister of War, who was present, has recorded that he seemed like "a small schoolboy facing his examiners." One of the witnesses called was a woman with whom he had lodged as a child.

"He was always well behaved," she said. "I felt like a mother to him. He never played rough games with other boys. He was quiet and industrious. He used to like to go to church."

President: "He had a weak character?"

Witness: "He had a certain obstinacy, but one could do much by being kind to him."

President: "He was more susceptible to kindness than to logic?"

Witness: "Yes."

Kibalchich confined himself to insisting upon meticulous accuracy in matters that concerned his own province. The military experts who were called gave their opinion that the explosive content of the hand grenades had been imported from abroad.

"I must protest," said Kibalchich, "against the allegation of the experts that this substance was imported. It was made in our own laboratory. The necessary formulæ for its composition may be found in Russian scientific literature. I refer you to the *Russian Artillery Journal* for August, 1878."

There was the question of the mine in the Malaya Sadovaya. The chief expert, General Fedorov, suggested that the crater would have been some fifteen to twenty feet in diameter. Windows in the neighbouring houses, he added, would all have been broken, the plaster would have been torn off the walls and the stoves shattered. The walls of the nearest houses would have been cracked. All pedestrians on the pavement and all persons at windows in the lower stories would have been killed by the explosion. There was also the danger from flying fragments of asphalt and stones.

Kibalchich objected. "Taking," he said, "the diameter of the crater as twenty feet, the effective zone of the explosion would have been very local. In view of the appreciable distance between the edge of the crater and the edge of the pavement, there would, in my opinion, have been no very serious danger to pedestrians. There would, of course, be fragments of asphalt: but these would be thrown vertically into the air. The sole danger would be from falling fragments. It is probable that windows in the immediate neighbourhood would be broken. But in my opinion serious damage to stoves and ceilings is unlikely. I would ask the experts if they can quote me any authority in scientific literature pointing to the probability of eighty pounds of dynamite exploded under these conditions producing a zone of destruction similar in extent to that which they now suggest. I maintain that the destruction occasioned would have been less than that caused by the two hand bombs. To sum up, anything located within the area marked by the circumference of the crater, that is the carriage and the escort, would have been destroyed; but nothing else."

IV

THE hearing of the witnesses occupied two whole days and, to ensure that the trial should be concluded on the third, proceedings were resumed at ten in the morning. Muraviev started his speech for the prosecution:

"Gentlemen, called as I am to undertake the prosecution in this most appalling of crimes ever committed upon Russian soil, I feel overwhelmed by the immensity of my task. Before the fresh-filled grave of our adored Monarch, amid the universal tears of a great Empire mourning the so unexpected and so terrible end of its Father and Reformer, I fear lest my weak powers . . ."

It must be remembered, in justice to Muraviev, that this somewhat florid style was the fashion of his day. It must be remembered, too, that it was not his main task to establish the facts. The facts were largely admitted. Muraviev was required by his position to testify, "as a Russian, as a devoted subject, as a citizen and as a man," to the majesty and might of the imperial autocracy and to the impotence and perversity of its opponents. This task he fulfilled to the complete satisfaction of his authorities. Count Milyutin records that he proved himself "an orator in the full sense of the word." Appreciation in higher quarters took a more concrete form and he was subsequently appointed to be Minister of Justice. In any case his speech was a remarkable *tour de force*. It was immensely long and pulsated with emotion. He screamed, he gesticulated, he shuddered, he wept.

"This is not a mere fact. This is history. It is with the profoundest grief that I evoke once more the memory of the assassination of our Martyred Emperor. But lo, from out that bloody fog that lowers over the Calvary of the Ekaterinski Canal, there loom the grim figures of the Tsaricides—"

Zhelyabov laughed. The prosecutor paused.

"Here," he continued, "I am interrupted by Zhelyabov's laugh—that amused or ironic mirth that has been his throughout the whole course of the preliminary proceedings, that mirth with which he greets the shattering picture of the First of March. . . . But I shall not hesitate once more to expose the Mourning of a Nation to that mockery. For so it should be. When men weep, then Zhelyabov laughs. . . ."

Muraviev went on to describe the actual events of the assassination.

". . . Thus he fell, a warrior at his Imperial post of danger, fell in the battle for God, for Russia and for Russia's Peace, in mortal combat with the enemies of Justice, of Order, of Morality, of Family Life, of all that is strong and holy in human society, of all that without which man cannot live.

"When the first bitter pangs of national grief and horror have abated, when stricken Russia may at last compose her thoughts, there can be but one question: Who is guilty of this dreadful deed? On whom shall fall a Nation's Curse? Russia needs know them, and, through the united voice of her true-hearted sons, demands their due punishment. I count myself happy that to this solemn question of my Country, I can boldly answer, here before this Court and before my fellow-subjects. You wish to know the Tsaricides? They are there!"

The Trial of the Six

He pointed with a sweep of the arm to the bench where the accused were sitting. He went on to repudiate any attribution of power and influence to the revolutionaries. He maintained that in recent Secret Police reports the same half dozen names were always cropping up. Zhelyabov was always one of them. He had, of course, associates. "I do not suggest there is only one Zhelyabov; there may be ten of them." But there was no Revolutionary party, and the mysterious Executive Committee was a myth created in view of the supposed need of the Russian masses for firm leadership. Muraviev went over the statements of the accused in their preliminary examinations. He emphasised the credibility of Rysakov as compared with Zhelyabov and "his alter ego" Perovskaya, who both had seemed mainly concerned with cheating the gallows of Timothy Mihailov. He dealt with the former careers of the accused. He described Zhelyabov as a "bandit chief." He went back to the Lipetsk conference. He enlarged on the revolutionaries' hostility to the Established Church. He read extracts from a brochure on terrorism which Morozov had written while abroad, a copy of which had been found on Zhelyabov. He quoted the Programme of the Workers' Section. He described the socialist peril that was threatening from Western Europe. Finally he returned to the accused:

"Cast out by man, accursed of their Country, may they answer for their crimes before Almighty God! And Peace and Calm will be restored. Russia, humbling herself before the Will of that Providence which has led her through so sore a trial, will march on, filled with new strength, with new and burning faith in her Glorious Future. Such was not the aim of the black conspirators of March 1. But their bloody thoughts and deeds beat in vain against the loyal Russian breast. Conspiracy with treacherous blow may cut the span of human life, even, by God's will, of the life of the Great Lord of Russia. But Conspiracy has ever been and ever will be impotent to shake the eternal devotion of the Russian people to their Throne and to their present system of government. The Russian People will root out these venomous weeds from Russian soil, and follow fearlessly their One, their Invincible, their Holy Hope, their August Leader now succeeding to the Throne."

After Muraviev came the speeches of the counsel for the

defence. They are not impressive. The counsel had been appointed by the court. They realised the nature of the trial and the effect on their subsequent careers if they showed a tendency to make trouble. It was natural for them to emphasise their reluctance at being put in a position where they were forced to speak on behalf of the accused and they confined themselves to appeals for such mercy as the court might feel inclined to show. A striking exception was Gerard, who defended Kibalchich.

Gerard stood up to the prosecution. "I well appreciate," he said, "the emotion which animated the prosecutor . . . but your duty, gentlemen of the court, is to keep your judgment free from emotion." Gerard's main concern was to explain the circumstances in which Kibalchich had become a revolutionary. He told the court of Kibalchich's arrest on account of the *Tale of Four Brothers;* of his three years in prison awaiting trial; of his frustrated attempt to resume his normal studies. He exposed the whole story of the Trial of the 193 and of the police measures that had preceded and accompanied that trial. Again and again the president called him to order. "The actions of our administrative authorities," the president declared, "are not a subject for consideration by this court."

V

ZHELYABOV had refused the services of counsel and was therefore entitled to make a speech in his own defence. This, in spite of the precautions taken to avoid publicity, was a matter of some concern to the authorities. The bureaucracy continued to be intensely suspicious of any court of law. After the first day of the trial Count Baranov, the prefect of Petersburg, had complained to the Minister of Justice of the "weakness" of Fuchs in face of the accused. According to a report which there seems no reason to doubt, on the morning of the 28th the president received a personal message, purporting to come from the Emperor, which pointed out the "extreme undesirability" of allowing Zhelyabov to speak at all. Fuchs was thus in a difficult position. But he was a man of integrity, and, in any case, to refuse Zhelyabov his legal right might well entail consequences quite other than those intended. Zhelyabov was allowed to make his speech, but only within limits that were strictly defined.

The following is the account that appeared in the *Times:*
"The speeches of Zhelyabov, Mihailov, and Kibalchich were all more or less explanatory of the unhappy conditions of society and government in Russia. Although the Procuror in his case for the Crown went fully into the whole question of Socialism and Nihilism at home and abroad, and particularly dwelt upon the aims of the Russian Revolutionary Party, in order to explain the heinous character of the prisoners' views and aims, yet the prisoners referred to, as well as their advocates, were frequently requested to confine themselves to the circumstances of the crime of the first of March, and not to go into the general questions upon which the prosecution dilated at such length. The speech of Zhelyabov was the most remarkable of all. With an air of assurance, changing to one of defiance when interrupted by the Court or the disapproving murmurs of the audience, Zhelyabov tried to lay bare the state of things and the social conditions which had made him and his fellow-conspirators what they are now. When the incidents just referred to occurred, and he glared round the Court like a wild beast at bay, there stood the wiry type of the fierce and unyielding demagogue."

The *Times* correspondent goes on to describe how Zhelyabov exposed the distress of the peasantry and the misdeeds of officials "who did everything for themselves and nothing for the people." There is nothing of this in the official stenographic account of the proceedings which has come down to us. It has been suggested that the court records were subjected to a secret censorship. Be that as it may, we must turn to the official account for all we can know of the one occasion accorded to Zhelyabov to attempt a public declaration of his faith.

Zhelyabov: "Gentlemen of the court, a sincere worker in any cause will hold his cause dearer than his life. Today our cause has been more grossly misrepresented than our own personal actions; and so it is our duty to explain our party's aims and methods. I maintain that the picture drawn by the prosecutor was false, and this I intend to prove by the documents and evidence on which he based his speech. The Programme of the Workers' Section served as basis for allegations that we do not recognise ordered government. Relying on the text of this programme I maintain that we are adherents of ordered government, not anarchists. It is an old story that we are anarchists. We affirm that as long as there are common interests it will be necessary to maintain a government. I would like to explain our principles—"

President: "No. The law allows you only to dispute those statements of fact on the part of the prosecution which you consider untrue."

Zhelyabov: "Then I will keep to the points of the indictment. We are not anarchists. We stand for Federal Government. We advocate a Constituent Assembly. How can we then be regarded as anarchists? Further, we criticise the existing economic system, and we maintain—"

President: "You are now using your right of defence in order to advance theories. Economic and social theories are not matters for consideration by this court."

Zhelyabov: "The prosecutor remarked that the event of March 1 was not a mere fact but was history. I agree; and accordingly this event must be considered in the light of the factors concerned."

President: "The crime of March 1 is a historical fact. But our business now is to consider your personal participation, and you are entitled to speak on that only."

Zhelyabov: "The prosecutor lays the responsibility for March 1 on the whole party, not merely on the accused here in court. It is therefore only logical to refer to the aims and methods as laid down in the party's publications."

President: "You have merely the right to deal with your personal participation. This court does not regard you as authorised to speak on behalf of the party, and, for the purposes of this court, the party has nothing to do with the question of your guilt. The prosecutor referred to your party, and in view of this you have the right to deal with any views attributed by the prosecutor to the party which you yourself do not hold. But I warn you that this is no place for the airing of political theories; further that I will not allow anything to be said derogatory to the law, to the authorities or to religion. That is my duty as president and I intend to fulfil it."

Zhelyabov: "My original plan for my defence was very

different. I had intended to say only a few words. But, as the prosecutor has devoted five hours to misrepresenting facts which I had considered to be clear, I submit that a defence within the limits you now set me is inconsistent with the freedom you allowed to the prosecution."

President: "My attitude is dictated by the nature of the crime with which you are charged. Within these limits and so far, but only so far, as you can do so without offence to the law and to the existing social order you may use that freedom."

Zhelyabov: "I shall confine myself to the evidence called by the prosecutor. He has produced various documents, a brochure by Morozov and a lithographed manuscript found in my possession. He considers that these are evidence. On what grounds? Because they were in my possession. Now they are in his. Have I the right to say they represent his convictions because he has them? How can he maintain that they represent mine? As to Morozov's pamphlet, I have not read it, but I know of its contents. As a party we disapprove of its line of argument, and we have asked our émigré friends abroad, so long as they are abroad, not to express views on the tasks of the party in Russia. Now, apparently, we are to be held responsible for the views of Morozov because at one time in the past certain members of the party, like Goldenberg, took the attitude that our whole task was to clear our way by a series of political murders. At present terrorism is only one among a whole row of other means designed to secure the amelioration of our national life. I—as the prosecutor said of himself—have also the right to call myself a Russian."

(*A murmur among the public: Zhelyabov turned and glowered at them and then continued.*)

"So much for the aims of the party. Now for its methods. I wish to make a short historical sketch, as the prosecutor did. Every social phenomenon must be regarded in the light of its past. To understand our present methods of struggle you must understand our history. For we have a history, short in years but rich in experience. Gentlemen of the court, if you were to look into the records of political trials, that open book of the past, you would find that the Russian Peoples' party did not always use bombs, and that we, as a party, have had our youth, a youth of radiant dreams. If this is now all past and gone it is through no fault of ours."

President: "You are exceeding the limits which I laid down. Restrict yourself to your own personal activities."

Zhelyabov: "I am coming to that. We looked for means of helping the people, and the means we chose was to take up positions as common working men and women with a view to the peaceful propagation of socialist ideas. This surely was harmless. What happened? Those concerned were imprisoned or sent into exile. An entirely peaceful movement, opposed to violence, opposed to revolution, was crushed. I took part in this movement, and this the prosecutor lays to my charge. I have to explain its character, as an integral part of my defence."

President: "But you were acquitted."

Zhelyabov: "None the less the prosecutor lays it to my charge."

President: "Confine yourself to facts directly connected with the matter in hand.

Zhelyabov: "I wish to point out that in 1873, '74, and '75, I was not a revolutionary as the prosecutor alleges. My aim was to work for the good of the people by the spread of socialist ideas. I did not approve of violence, I was not concerned with political matters—my companions even less so. In 1874, as far as we had political ideas, we were anarchists. To this extent I agree with the prosecutor. Indeed, there is much truth in what he says. But fragments of truth, taken from different periods and put together again in a purely arbitrary manner, are apt to form, to use his own expression, 'a bloody fog.' "

President: "Is this with reference to yourself?"

Zhelyabov: "It is. I say that all I wished to do was to work in a peaceful manner among the people. I was put in prison. There I became a revolutionary. I now pass to the second stage of the socialist movement. This stage—no, possibly I should cease trying to defend my principles and instead merely request that the prosecutor's speech be printed word for word as he said it, and published for the world to judge.* Well, perhaps after all I will make the attempt. This temporary movement to the people showed our ideas to be impracticable and doctrinaire. But we found that there was much in Russian popular tradition that we could build on. Because of

---

* Muraviev's speech (like the rest of the proceedings) was not published until 1906.

The Trial of the Six

this and because the authorities made it impossible for us to spread our ideas by peaceful means we socialists became Narodniks. We decided to work on the needs and desires of which the people were already conscious. That is the distinguishing mark of Narodnichestvo. From dreamers we became workers. We took to deeds, not words. Action meant some use of force. But force was not used to any great extent. So things went on up to 1878. In that year, as far as I know, there first appeared the idea of more radical action, of cutting the Gordian knot. The movement that culminated in the event of March 1 began to take shape in the winter of '77–'78. The year 1878 was a transitional year, as can be seen from the pamphlet 'A Death for a Death.' The party had not yet grasped the significance of the political front, although circumstances were forcing it into open war against the political system."

President: "Now you are talking of the party again—"

Zhelyabov: "I was one of its members."

President: "Speak only of yourself."

Zhelyabov: "Circumstances were forcing me, among others, to declare war against the existing political structure. All the same I spent the summer of 1878 in a village, propagandising peacefully. In the winter 1878–79 there seemed to be no solution. I spent the spring of 1879 in the South. For me it was a time of anxiety and distress. I knew that my comrades were feeling the same perplexities, especially in the North, and that in the North there had come a split in the Zemlya i Volya society. Some of its members held the same views as myself and a few of my friends in the South. We eventually joined forces at Lipetsk. There we drew up a new programme and policy. But the Lipetsk conference did not cover so narrow a field as the prosecution makes out. The basic principles of the new policy were as follows: the political structure—"

President: "I will not allow you to continue, as you refuse to obey my directions. You are now indulging in a historical dissertation."

Zhelyabov: "I am accused of taking part in the Lipetsk conference."

President: "No. You are accused of taking part in the attempt at Alexandrovsk, which was a consequence of the Lipetsk conference."

Zhelyabov: "If I am merely accused of participation in the

Alexandrovsk attempt and the event of March 1, then all I have to say is 'Yes' as the facts have been proved. But a bald affirmation is not a defence."

President: "We are considering the question of your motive."

Zhelyabov: "In that case I submit that an explanation of the development of my ideas—"

President: "I will admit an explanation of your personal convictions as far as they concern the events under consideration. But I will not admit an account of the views of the party."

Zhelyabov: "I do not understand the distinction."

President: "I am asking you to confine your remarks to your own physical and moral participation in these events."

Zhelyabov: "I answered this question at the beginning of the proceedings. If I may add nothing further, then I must merely draw the court's attention to my previous statements."

President: "If you have nothing to add—"

Zhelyabov: "I have given the bare outlines, the skeleton. I wished now to give the soul."

President: "Your own soul, not that of the party."

Zhelyabov: "Yes, mine. I took part in the Lipetsk conference. This conference led to a series of events as the result of which I am here in the dock. I must therefore explain the decisions taken at Lipetsk. According to the prosecutor the task we then set ourselves was to attempt to kill. This is untrue. The task we set ourselves was not so narrow. Our basic principle—my basic principle if you will—was that the Social Revolutionary party should bring about a revolution. To this end we were to organise revolutionary forces on the widest possible scale. Up till then I had not seen the necessity of organisation. Like other simple socialists I had felt that certain matters, the supply of prohibited literature for instance, should be organised. Otherwise I had relied on individual initiative. But once we had set ourselves the task of carrying out an armed revolution it was obviously necessary to establish a strong, centralised machine, and we—myself included—devoted vastly more time and effort to this work than to preparing assassinations. After Lipetsk I became a member of the body at the head of which stands the Executive Committee, and I devoted all my powers to the creation of a strong centralised organisation, consisting of a number of semiautonomous groups working on a common plan and inspired by a common idea. My personal task, the object of my life, had been to work for the common good. I tried first to do this by peaceful means. Later on I was forced to turn to violence. I would willingly abandon violence if there were the possibility of serving my ideals by peaceful means—of peacefully expounding my views and organising those of my way of thinking. I repeat again as my last word, to avoid any misunderstanding, a peaceful solution is possible. I myself would at once abandon terrorist activity if the conditions—"

President: "You have nothing more to say in your defence?"

Zhelyabov: "In my defence, nothing. But I wish to correct an earlier statement. In the interests of justice I drew the attention of the court to the part played by Timothy Mihailov, that is, to the fact that Mihailov was in no way involved either in the bomb attack or in the Malaya Sadovaya mine. I now understand that my attempt to prevent a miscarriage of justice has wounded the feelings of Timothy Mihailov. I accordingly wish to declare that should this matter be raised again I would not repeat my statement. I hasten to add that we, the accused and the prosecutor, conform to very different moral standards."

VI

AFTER the conclusion of the speeches for the defence, and before pronouncement of verdict and sentence, the accused had the right to give their "final word." They were called upon one by one. Rysakov said:

"I do not belong to the terrorist section as the prosecutor said. I deny having worked for it. This is true, because I do not approve of terrorism as a method of struggle. I only heard of it here in this court . . . I do not approve of open warfare with the authorities. I am convinced that no good would come of violent action . . . And I am not the only one to oppose terror. Goldenberg did the same." *

Timothy Mihailov said:

"I have not the education to explain myself . . . I belong to the Social Revolutionary party, but a party for protecting the workers, not for starting revolutions, at least as far as I

* Dobrinski seems to have made full use of Goldenberg's depositions in order to make Rysakov talk.

could understand ... It is difficult to make my meaning clear because I am uneducated."

Helfmann confined herself to correcting police statements of her previous history. "I wish to point out" she said, "that when I came back to Petersburg (as an 'illegal' in 1879) it was not in order to escape the police but because I had devoted myself to the service of that cause which I had been and have been serving."

Kibalchich recapitulated the prosecutor's theories regarding social unrest in Russia. He then said:

"There now comes the question of how to prevent the repetition of regrettable events such as that with which we are here concerned. He (the prosecutor) appears to believe that the one sure method is to make no move towards conciliation and to rely entirely upon the gallows and the firing squad. I regret that I cannot agree with the prosecutor that the methods he suggests will lead to the result desired."

Kibalchich went on to a matter with which he had been deeply occupied during the ten days of his detention.

"There is one thing more. I have drafted a project for a flying machine. I am of the opinion that my invention is practicable. My draft contains full details, and the necessary designs and calculations are attached. It now appears unlikely that I shall have the opportunity of discussing my invention with qualified experts, and as the possibility exists of my plans being exploited by unauthorised persons, I wish now publicly to declare that my project and sketch are to pass into the sole possession of my counsel, M. Gerard."

Perovskaya said:

"The prosecutor has made a number of charges against us. With regard to his statements of fact I have dealt with these in my preliminary examination. But I and my friends are also accused of immorality, brutality and contempt for public opinion. I wish to say that anyone who knows our lives and the circumstances in which we have had to work will not accuse us either of immorality or of brutality."

Zhelyabov said:

"Only this. During the preliminary examination I said little, knowing that any statement of mine would merely be used by the prosecution for their own ends. Now I regret having said what I have said here in court. That is all."

It was now midnight. The court retired to consider the verdict and the prisoners were removed. Those of the public who sat on in the dim and musty court for the trial to drag to its inevitable conclusion have confessed to a feeling of unreality and utter weariness. At 3 A.M. the prisoners were brought back and the court returned. The president read out the twenty-four counts against the prisoners. On twenty counts the individuals concerned were found guilty. Rysakov, Mihailov and Helfmann were found not guilty of participation in the mine in the Malaya Sadovaya. As to the remaining count the court ruled that it was not necessary to decide the question of whether Timothy Mihailov was member of a society aiming at the overthrow of the existing social structure, or merely at the embitterment of relations between employers and employed.

The prosecutor demanded the death sentence. There followed a legal argument upon the submissions of Rysakov's counsel as to the applicability of the death penalty to minors. The court retired again to consider sentence. There was another long wait. Many of the public left. Most of those few who remained went to sleep in their seats. The grey morning light began to show at the windows. At half past six the court came back and the president read the long, formal sentence. All six prisoners were condemned to be hanged. As Perovskaya was of the class of the nobility her sentence would be submitted to the Emperor for confirmation. Appeal might be lodged up to 5 P.M. on March 31.

CHAPTER FIFTEEN

THE END

I

ON APRIL 11 (New Style) the ageing Marx in London wrote to his daughter Jenny: "Have you been following the trial of the assassins in Petersburg? They are sterling people through and through, *sans pose mélodramatique,* simple, businesslike, heroic. Shouting and doing are irreconcilable opposites . . . they try to teach Europe that their *modus operandi* is a specifically Russian and historically inevitable method about which there is no more reason to moralise—for or against—than there is about the earthquake in Chios."

II

THE *Times* correspondent in Petersburg telegraphed:
"It was not expected even by the public present at the State trial that all the accused would be indiscriminately condemned to be hanged."
On the same day he reported:
"It is rather strange that on Friday night Professor Soloviev in the course of his lecture to the University of St. Petersburg took occasion to state that the Emperor ought to pardon all the political prisoners then being tried; that, as Our Lord preached mercy, so ought the Emperor to exercise it. Great applause accompanied his remarks, many officers, however, immediately leaving the room. The Professor then went on to the general question of abolishing capital punishment altogether, of which he was in favour. He evidently saw what a mistake he had made in referring to the political prisoners then being tried and thus endeavoured to get out of the difficulty. His hearers however cheered him wildly and at the

end of his discourse followed him out into the street. The consequence is that the Professor is being subjected to a course of domiciliary arrest." *

III

NONE of the prisoners lodged an appeal, though Mihailov and Rysakov petitioned the Emperor for reprieve. Rysakov wrote:
"Your Imperial Majesty and All Merciful Ruler:
"Fully aware of the horror of the crime which, under the influence of others, I committed, I have decided most humbly to beg Your Imperial Majesty to spare my life so that I may unceasingly attempt to atone for my appalling deed. The august court, against whose sentence I dare not formally appeal, will testify that even the prosecutor did not consider me an unmitigated monster: I was turned to crime accidentally, through the evil influence of others, whom my immaturity and ignorance of life and men were unable to oppose.
"In asking for reprieve I call upon God as witness—God in whom I have always believed and believe today—that I am not thinking of the momentary pain of death. During the month of my arrest I have grown familiar with that prospect. But I am terrified to appear before the Awful Tribunal of God on High before I have had the chance to cleanse my soul by a long penitence. I do not beg you to grant me life, but to postpone my death . . ."

This petition, as also that of Mihailov, was rejected. On March 31 Kibalchich made two requests, firstly, to be allowed to interview a scientific expert to discuss his flying machine, secondly, to see Perovskaya and Zhelyabov. Both requests were refused. On the same day Helfmann reported that she was pregnant. This was confirmed by a medical commission appointed to examine her and her death sentence was commuted to one of imprisonment for life.

A story became current that between March 31 and April 3 the prisoners were tortured in order to extort information as to their associates still at liberty. The story is based on the three-day interval between the expiry of the right of appeal

---

* Soloviev was a distinguished philosopher and not, as the *Times* implies, a university lecturer. Incidentally an appeal on behalf of the prisoners was also made by Leo Tolstoi to Pobyedonostsev.

and the execution; on the refusal of any permission to visit the prisoners on those three days; on some words of Rysakov on his way to the gallows; and on an entry in the diary of the wife of a General Bogdanovich who moved in well-informed circles. This entry runs: "I have heard very confidentially that after the trial they are going to try and make Zhelyabov give the details of his organisation. This is essential for the public safety. I hope to God they torture him. I am not a cruel woman, but it is necessary." Later in the summer Tkachev's émigré newspaper *Nabat* gave a sinister and circumstantial story of how the normal prison guards were removed for a couple of hours while a party of mysterious visitors spent some time in each of the prisoners' cells.

But there is no confirmation whatever of the *Nabat* story either in police archives or in disclosures by former prison officials. The same holds good of the rumour that reached Madame Bogdanovich. By April 3 the wretched Rysakov had become completely irresponsible. There are a number of natural causes to account for the delay in the execution. The refusal to allow visits to the prisoners is on a par with the "strong line" that the authorities were then adopting. Taken individually all the arguments supporting the theory of torture are flimsy; and their cumulative weight does not inspire conviction.

On April 2, the eve of the execution, Kibalchich made his will, formally leaving all rights to his lawyer Gerard.* On the same day Rysakov made one last attempt to save his life. He addressed a letter to General Baranov, the prefect of Petersburg. "Terrorism," he began, "must be brought to an end." He went on to speak of the terrorist leaders still at large, naming in particular Isaev and Figner. He assured the prefect that he would be able to bring about their arrests. He suggested that he should be sent to Moscow to track them down: two expeditions, of course under police supervision, ought to be sufficient. Or perhaps it might be preferred that he should work for a year at police headquarters. "God Himself," he wrote, "can witness that it is in no cynical spirit that I ask

---

* The authorities paid no attention to this bequest. Kibalchich's project, which was based on an ingenious application of the rocket principle, remained for forty years filed away in the archives of the Imperial Police, and was only discovered some time after the Revolution.

for employment with the police. It is urgent and sincere desire, in the hope that I may thus expiate my sin. This last month in prison has formed my character and raised my moral level. A spiritual development is more possible for me now than in the days of my pride and self-will . . . I am ready to do all in my power to eradicate terrorism, and I would not dare to try to impose conditions."

It was of no avail. The authorities had no further use for Rysakov. In any case Isaev had already been arrested.

IV

AT EIGHT O'CLOCK on the evening of April 2 five Orthodox priests were admitted to the prison and taken to the cells of the five condemned prisoners. Rysakov made his confession and received the Sacrament. Timothy Mihailov confessed but would not take communion. Kibalchich held a long discussion with the priest but did not make his confession or take the Sacrament. Perovskaya and Zhelyabov refused to see a priest.

According to the sentries posted in the cells the prisoners all lay down to sleep between eleven and midnight. Before doing so Mihailov, Kibalchich and Zhelyabov wrote letters to their parents. These letters have not come down to us.

At six o'clock on the morning of April 3 the prisoners were called and given tea. When they had dressed they were brought to the prison waiting room and there changed into the black clothes prescribed for condemned criminals. Perovskaya was the first to come down. She was very distressed. Timothy Mihailov who came next said, "Cheer up, Sonia," and she pulled herself together.

The five were then taken to the prison yard and bound to their seats on the tumbrils. These last were heavy springless carts on which platforms had been erected so that the prisoners sat twelve feet above the level of the road. They sat with their backs to the horses, strapped by the waist to an iron bar behind them. They were handcuffed and their feet were fettered. Each bore a placard attached by a cord round the neck with the word "Tsaricide" in large letters.

At 7.55 the prison gates were opened.* The first cart to

---

* The legend that Madame Perovskaya was waiting outside is not supported by serious evidence.

come out carried soldiers and police, then came the tumbril with Zhelyabov and Rysakov, then the second tumbril with Mihailov, Perovskaya and Kibalchich—Perovskaya sitting in the middle between the two men. There followed the priests, the cart with the coffins, and the remainder of the military escort. Level with the tumbrils were detachments of drummers beating a muffled roll. Their task was to counter any attempt on the part of the prisoners to address the crowd; they had instructions to beat loud enough to drown the voices if the prisoners began to speak. There were troops lining the streets and formed up in the Semenovski Square around the scaffold. All together, 12,000 troops were paraded, besides police and detectives.

There was a big crowd in the streets. One girl who saw the cortège pass wrote afterwards that the prisoners "rode by like conquerors." This, given the circumstances, seems most unlikely. Revolutionary writers maintain that the general feeling of the crowd was one of sympathy for the prisoners, but it is agreed that certain spectators who waved to them were set upon by their neighbours. Official assurances of the solemn satisfaction of the public at this triumph of justice sound equally hollow. Figner is more convincing when she records the gleam of unnatural excitement in the eyes of a well-dressed young man who sat next to her in a tram that morning. There is little variation in the effect of a public execution upon any crowd.

It is agreed that apart from Rysakov the prisoners showed great self-control. Throughout the ride Rysakov's eyes were fixed on his companion, but Zhelyabov would not speak to him and deliberately avoided his glance. Kibalchich was the most self-possessed of all. Half way the hitherto silent Mihailov began to shout to the bystanders. The drums beat up and drowned his voice, but he continued shouting all the way in a vain attempt to make himself heard. It was a long journey. The road was uneven and the prisoners on their platforms were swung and shaken as the carts lurched over the potholes.

It was a fine morning, with intermittent glimpses of a pale spring sun. The thaw was beginning and there were puddles round the snow piled up in the gutters. Over eighty thousand people were assembled in the Semenovski Square. Those with connexions in high quarters had privileged tickets affording access to the scaffold when the proceedings were over. There had been a big demand for these tickets, in view of the superstition that it is lucky to possess a piece of the rope used in an execution. The scaffold had been erected in the middle of the square. It was a wooden platform with a balustrade thirty feet by twenty-four and painted black. A flight of six steps led up to the platform. The gallows consisted of two supports and a long crossbeam in which were six iron rings. The sixth ring had been intended for Helfmann. Behind the gallows, at the back of the platform, were three tall posts with chains and manacles. In front of the scaffold was a low platform for the officials. A regiment of Foot Guards was drawn up on each side of the scaffold and detachments of Cossacks were in position at various points around the square.

Frolov, the executioner, and his assistants were at their post by half past seven. They waited for the prefect of Petersburg and the other officials and then began to prepare the ropes. Next came the carriages with the priests and the coffins, which had taken a shorter route. At half past eight the tumbrils with the prisoners arrived and a murmur went up from the crowd.

The drummers, still beating their roll, formed up in two rows in front of the scaffold. The prisoners were unstrapped and taken down. Zhelyabov, Perovskaya and Mihailov were chained to the posts at the back of the scaffold, and Kibalchich and Rysakov to the railing of the balustrade in line with them. The prefect reported to the representative of the Minister of Justice that all was ready. The drums were muffled down and an official of the court read out the sentence. It was a lengthy document and the reading took several minutes. While this was in progress Zhelyabov was seen to lean towards Perovskaya and speak to her.

The priests mounted the scaffold each with a cross which they held out to the prisoners. All five prisoners kissed the cross. The priests blessed them and withdrew. Frolov then unchained them from the posts and the railing. They were still handcuffed and their legs fettered. Zhelyabov kissed Perovskaya goodbye, Kibalchich and Mihailov did the same. Rysakov came to her but she turned away from him. Frolov then led them to their places under the gallows and he and his assistants enveloped them in the prescribed white cowls. The cowls were provided with a slit in the neck to admit the rope.

At 9.20 Frolov took off his coat and began his work. Each prisoner was led up onto a small portable stand with three steps; the rope was then drawn tight and the stand removed. Kibalchich came first. The *Times* correspondent reported: "With the exception of an accident to one of the ropes which broke twice the sad proceedings passed off without difficulty." He had been allotted a privileged ticket and seems to have been anxious not to offend the authorities. Count Milyutin noted in his diary: "They did not even know how to hang them." The reference is to Timothy Mihailov, the second victim. He had been hanging for nearly a minute when the noose slipped and he fell with a crash on the platform. The crowd roared. Frolov readjusted the noose, and Mihailov climbed up on the stand again. The stand was once more removed and he hung for a minute and a half. Then the noose slipped again. The crowd burst into a frenzy and tried to fight past the troops and get at the scaffold. Mihailov was by now too weak to move unaided. The executioners had to haul him up. He had been hanging for the third time, for some three minutes, when there came again a surge and a howl from the crowd; Mihailov was a big man and his weight was pulling the ring out of the crossbeam. Frolov took a ladder and ran a second rope to the hook intended for Helfmann. All this time Perovskaya was waiting her turn. Zhelyabov came fourth. To avoid another accident with this second heavy man Frolov put a double knot in the noose. This delayed strangulation and the convulsions lasted for some minutes. The military doctor on duty protested in disgust, and Frolov, furious and sodden with vodka, turned round and cursed back at him. Meanwhile the drumming continued. Last of all came Rysakov. He struggled and tried to cling to the stand with his feet till they pulled it from him.

At 9.30 all was over. The bodies hung still. The drums stopped. The coffins were brought up on the platform and the bodies let down and packed into them under the supervision of the doctor. Then they were loaded on the carts and driven to the railway station en route for the prisoners' burial ground in the Preobrazhenskoe cemetery. It is not known if they were buried separately or in a common grave. Twenty-five years afterwards, when such a pilgrimage no longer entailed the likelihood of arrest, a little party of sympathisers set out to visit the graves of Perovskaya and Zhelyabov. The ancient caretaker took them to the back of the burial ground and vaguely indicated a corner overgrown with weeds and rubbish.

The carts with the coffins drove off at 9.50. Ten minutes later the prefect gave the order for the demolition of the scaffold. The crowd began to disperse. The troops were marched back to barracks with the exception of a small detachment who remained to help the police keep all but the privileged ticket holders away from the work of demolition.

A REVOLUTIONARY WHO'S WHO

THIS is not a complete list of the leading Narodovoltsi, far less of the Russian revolutionaries of the time. It is included merely as an appendix to this life of Zhelyabov, and covers only those who figure more or less prominently in the book. It is primarily intended for any readers who may want to know what happened to those of Zhelyabov's associates who survived him. It may also be of help to those of us who are apt to be bewildered by long strings of unfamiliar names.

ARONCHIK, *Isak Borisovich:* Born 1856 of a family of small tradesmen in Gomel in Central Russia. Member of Narodnaya Volya party. Participated in the railway attempt at Moscow 1879, and in the preparations for the attack of March 1, 1881. Arrested same month. Tried in Trial of the Twenty 1882. Died same year in Peter and Paul Fortress.

BARANNIKOV, *Alexander Ivanovich (Kurshunikov):* Born 1858 of a family of gentry in the Kursk province. Entered Pavlovski Military Academy as cadet; left 1876. An active revolutionary and an "illegal" from 1877. Participated in attack on Mezentsev 1878. Member of Zemlya i Volya. Attended Lipetsk and Voronezh conferences. Member of the Executive Committee of the Narodnaya Volya. Participated in the railway attempts 1879, in the attempt at the Kamenni Bridge 1880 and in the mine in the Malaya Sadovaya. Arrested January, 1881. Tried in the Trial of the Twenty 1882. Died 1884 in Peter and Paul Fortress.

BOGDANOVICH, *Yuri Nikolaevich (Kobosev):* Born 1849, son of a landowner near Pskov. Entered State Land Survey Department 1869. Dismissed 1871 for political undesirability. Attended School of Medicine 1873. Member of Chaikovski Circle. Participated in arranging the escape of Kropotkin from prison in 1876, and other escapes. Called by Figner to Petersburg 1880. Member of the Executive Committee of the Narodnaya Volya. Acted as proprietor of the cheese shop for the mine in the Malaya Sadovaya 1881. Arrested March, 1882. Tried in the Trial of the Seventeen 1883. Died in Schlusselburg Fortress (tuberculosis) 1888.

A Revolutionary Who's Who

BRESHKOVSKAYA, *Ekaterina Konstantinovna Breshko:* Born 1843. Daughter of an army officer. Married 1868. Engaged in revolutionary activities from 1873. Arrested 1874. In prison until 1878. Sent to Kara penal station 1879. Escaped 1881. Re-arrested one month later. For the next forty years her life was a continuous succession of imprisonments, escapes and re-arrests. When George Kennan, the American journalist, was in Siberia in 1888 he met Breshkovskaya, who said to him: "We shall die in exile, and our children and perhaps our children's children, but in the end something will come of it." History moved more quickly than she had feared. But the "Grandmother of the Revolution" fell foul of the Soviet regime. She died in Czechoslovakia in 1935.

DEBOGORI-MOKRIEVICH, *Vladimir Karpovich:* Born 1848, son of a small landowner near Kamenets-Podolsk. Attended Kiev University. Became "illegal" 1873. Member of the Kiev group. Participated in the Chigirin affair and in the escape of Stefanovich and associates from prison. Arrested February, 1879. Sentenced to 14 years' hard labour. Transferred to Siberia autumn, 1879. Escaped November. Spent 14 months at large in Siberia. Returned to Moscow January, 1881, and two months later went abroad. Engaged in literary work in various European countries and in the U.S.A. Eventually settled in Bulgaria and died there 1926. His memoirs are the literary masterpiece of the revolutionary movement of his time.

DEUTSCH, *Lev Grigorievich:* Born 1855, son of a Jewish merchant in South Russia. Associated with the revolutionary movement in Kiev from 1873. Arrested 1875. Escaped 1876. Participated in the Chigirin affair. Arrested in September, 1877. Escaped May, 1878. Member of Zemlya i Volya and, after the split, of the Cherni Peredel. Went abroad 1880. Arrested in Germany 1884, extradited to Russia and imprisoned. Escaped 1901. Arrested 1906 and escaped the same year. Was for some time associated with Plekhanov, Zasulich and Lenin in the Social Democratic party. Had various differences with the orthodox Communists, but returned to live in the U.S.S.R. for the rest of his life.

EMELIANOV, *Ivan Panteleimonovich:* Born 1861, son of a deacon in a village in Bessarabia. From the age of 9 brought up by his grandfather who was employed at the Russian Embassy in Constantinople. Attended a technical school and granted a scholarship to complete his studies abroad. Deeply influenced by accounts in the foreign press of the Trial of the Sixteen, returned to Russia December, 1880. Member of the Narodnaya Volya. Participated as bomb thrower in the attempt of March 1, 1881. Arrested April.

Tried in Trial of the Twenty 1882. Sentenced to hard labour for life in Siberia. Released 1905. Died at Kharborovsk 1916.

FIGNER, *Vera Nikolaevna (Filipova)*: Born 1852. Daughter of a senior forestry official stationed near Kazan. Married 1870. Attended Zurich University with her husband. Returned to Russia 1875. Divorced 1876. Thereafter a whole-time revolutionary. Attended Voronezh conference 1879. Member of Executive Committee of Narodnaya Volya. Took part in the attempts at Odessa in 1879 and 1880. Assisted in the attack of March 1, 1881, and in the arrangements for the assassination of Strelnikov in 1882. By the end of that year she was sole surviving and active member of the Executive Committee, which she attempted to revive by co-opting officers of the Fighting Services' Section. Betrayed by Degaev and arrested 1883. Was the outstanding personality of the Trial of the Fourteen 1884. Imprisoned in Schlusselburg till 1905. Died in Moscow during the Second World War.

FROLENKO, *Mihail Fedorovich*: Born 1849 near Stavropol (Caucasus). Son of an army sergeant-major. Attended the Petrovski Academy for Land Survey in Moscow. In 1874 implicated in revolutionary activities and became an "illegal." Associated with the Kiev group. Member of the Zemlya i Volya. Participated in the rescue of Stefanovich, Deutsch and Bokhanovski from Kiev prison, and in the attempt on the Kherson State Treasury. Attended the Lipetsk and Voronezh conferences. Member of the Executive Committee and of the Administrative Council of the Narodnaya Volya. Participated in the attempt at Odessa 1879, in the attempt on the Kishinev State Treasury 1880–81, and in the mine in the Malaya Sadovaya. Arrested March, 1881. Tried in the Trial of the Twenty. Imprisoned in the Peter and Paul Fortress and in Schlusselburg. Released 1905. Died in Moscow during the Second World War.

GOLDENBERG, *Grigori Davidovich*: Born 1856. Son of a Jewish merchant from near Kiev. Involved in revolutionary activities, and exiled to Archangel province April, 1878. Escaped June, 1878. Associated with the early Kiev terrorists. Assassinated Prince Kropotkin at Kharkov, February, 1879. Attended Lipetsk conference. Participated in preparations for the Moscow attempt. Arrested November, 1879. Was induced by the police authorities to make far-reaching revelations implicating a large number of his associates. Committed suicide in prison July, 1880.

GRACHEVSKI, *Mihail Fedorovich*: Born 1849, son of a deacon from near Saratov. Attended ecclesiastical seminary. Engaged in socialist propaganda 1871. Arrested 1873. Released the same year.

A Revolutionary Who's Who

Re-arrested 1875. Tried in Trial of the 193. Sentenced to three months' imprisonment. Released 1878. Re-arrested in the autumn of that year. Escaped early in 1879, re-arrested, and escaped again. Adhered to the Narodnaya Volya early 1880. Member of Executive Committee. Participated in the attempt at the Kamenni Bridge and in the preparations for the attack of March 1. Arrested 1882. Tried in the Trial of the Seventeen 1883. Committed suicide in Schlusselburg 1887.

GRINEVITSKI, *Ignati Ioakimovich (Kotik):* Born 1856, Catholic, son of small landowner near Grodno. Attended secondary school in Byelostok and Technological Institute in Petersburg. Mixed in revolutionary circles, both Polish and Russian. Member of the Narodnaya Volya 1880. Associated with Zhelyabov and Petrovskaya in the organisation of the Workers' Section. Acted as bomb thrower in the final attempt on March 1, 1881. It was his bomb which killed the Emperor, and he himself died of his wounds a few hours later.

HARTMANN, *Lev Nikolaevich:* Born 1850 in the Archangel district. Parents were artisans of German extraction. Arrested for revolutionary activities in 1876. Released one year later. Member of Executive Committee of the Narodnaya Volya. Took leading part in the attempt at Moscow 1879. Escaped abroad. Arrested in Paris 1880, at the instance of the Russian Government, but after considerable publicity and polemic his extradition was refused. Visited England and U.S.A. Was in touch with Marx and Engels, and acted to some extent as the Executive Committee's foreign representative. Did not return to Russia. Died 1913.

HELFMANN, *Gesya Mironovna (Jesse):* Born 1855, daughter of small Jewish tradesman from near Kiev. Associated with the revolutionary movement 1874. Arrested 1875. Tried in Trial of the Fifty. Imprisoned till 1879 and then confined to a fixed residence by police order. Escaped the same year. Member of the Narodnaya Volya party. With Sablin in charge of the conspiratorial quarter for the attempt of March 1. Tried in Trial of the Six. Death sentence suspended in view of her pregnancy. Daughter born September, 1881, and sent to an orphanage as being of "parents unknown." Helfmann died in prison February, 1882. (The father of her child was Kolotkevich.)

ISAEV, *Grigori Prokofievich:* Born 1857, son of a postman, near Mogilev. Expelled from secondary school in 1875 for distributing subversive literature. Attended Petersburg University and later the School of Medicine. Engaged in revolutionary agitation from 1877. Member of the Executive Committee of the Narodnaya

Volya. One of the party's technical experts. Participated in the railway attempts 1879, in the attempt at Odessa 1880, and in the preparations for the final attempt of March 1, 1881. Arrested April, 1881. Tried in the Trial of the Twenty 1882. Died in prison 1884.

IVANOVA, *Sophia Andreevna:* Born 1857. Daughter of an army officer. Involved in the demonstration in the Kazan Square at Petersburg and arrested December, 1876. Tried 1877. Exiled to Archangel province. Escaped spring of 1879. Member of the Executive Committee of the Narodnaya Volya. In charge of the party's printing press. Arrested January, 1880. Tried in the Trial of the Sixteen 1880. Sentenced to 15 years' imprisonment. Died Moscow 1927.

KHALTURIN, *Stepan Nikolaevich:* Born 1857. Peasant's son from near Viatka. Learned trade of joiner and from 1875 employed in various Petersburg factories. Engaged in subversive activities from 1875. Organised Northern Workers' Union 1878. Escaped arrest on its betrayal by Reinstein. Member of the Executive Committee of the Narodnaya Volya. Carried out the attempt in the Winter Palace, February, 1880. Participated in assassination of Strelnikov in Odessa, March, 1882. Arrested on the spot and executed a few days later.

KIBALCHICH, *Nikolai Ivanovich:* Born 1853, son of a parish priest, near Chernigov. Attended Petersburg Engineering College from 1871 and School of Medicine from 1873. Arrested 1875 for lending a prohibited book to a peasant. In prison till 1878, tried in Trial of 193 and sentenced to two months' imprisonment. Shortly after release became an "illegal." Member of the Narodnaya Volya party, and acted as the party's chief technical expert for the preparation of explosives. Arrested March, 1881, tried in the Trial of the Six; executed April, 1881. Count Todtleben said afterwards it was a mistake to hang men of the calibre of Kibalchich; he should have been shut up somewhere with a library of books and given scientific problems to work on. A pioneer of jet propulsion.

KLETOCHNIKOV, *Nikolai Vasilievich:* Born 1848 at Penza. Government official. Attended Moscow and Petersburg Universities, but unable to take final examinations because of ill health. Came in touch with Alexander Mihailov in Petersburg, and under his guidance obtained post in Third Section. Member of the Narodnaya Volya. Served as the party's intelligence agent within the Administration. Arrested January, 1881. Tried in the Trial of the Twenty 1882. Died in Peter and Paul Fortress 1883.

A Revolutionary Who's Who

KOKOVSKI, *"Valentin":* Born about 1860. Son of a parish priest near Kiev. Attended Kiev and Petersburg Universities. Member of the Narodnaya Volya 1880. Associated with Zhelyabov in the organisation of the Workers' Section. His health broke down in January, 1881. Sent by Zhelyabov to a doctor who found him suffering from advanced tuberculosis. Zhelyabov then ordered him to the Crimea to recuperate. Died there the following September.

KOLOTKEVICH, *Nikolai Nikolaevich:* Born 1851, of a family of landowners near Chernigov. Attended Odessa and Kiev Universities. Engaged in revolutionary activities from 1875. In touch with the Kiev group. Participated in the Chigirin conspiracy 1877. Attended Lipetsk and Voronezh conferences. Member of the Executive Committee of the Narodnaya Volya. Participated in the preparations for the attempt at Odessa 1879. Associated with Zhelyabov in organisation of Fighting Services' Section. Worked in the mine in the Malaya Sadovaya. Arrested January, 1881. Tried in the Trial of the Twenty 1882. Died in prison 1884.

KORBA, *Anna Pavlovna Pribyleva:* Born 1849, daughter of a landowner. Member of Narodnaya Volya 1879, and of Executive Committee 1880. Arrested 1882. Tried in Trial of the Seventeen 1883. In prison at Kara (Siberia) till her release in 1902. Died in Russia 1930.

KRAVCHINSKI, *Sergei Mihailovich (Stepniak):* Born 1851. Son of an army doctor. Attended Military Academy and then Artillery School; Second Lieutenant in the Artillery 1870. Resigned 1871. Attended Petersburg Forestry Institute 1872. Member of Chaikovski Circle. Went to the Balkans 1874, to assist revolt of Southern Slavs against the Turks. Returned to Russia 1878. Member of Zemlya i Volya. Carried out the assassination of Mezentsev, August, 1878. Went abroad again two months later. Engaged in literary activities in various European countries and the U.S.A. One of the founders of the Friends of Russian Freedom and the Russian Free Press in London. Run over by a train in London in 1895.

KVIATKOVSKI, *Alexander Alexandrovich:* Born 1853, in Tomsk, of a family of gentry. Attended the Tomsk Technological Institute. Arrested 1874 for being in possession of illegal books. Provisionally released 1876. Became an "illegal." Wanted for the Trial of the 193 but avoided arrest. Associated with the Kiev group. Member of Zemlya i Volya. Attended Lipetsk and Voronezh conferences. Member of Executive Committee of Narodnaya Volya.

Participated in the attempt in the Winter Palace. Arrested January, 1880. Tried in Trial of the Sixteen. Hanged November, 1880.

LANGANS, *Martin Rudolfovich:* Born 1852, at Kherson. Prussian subject. Attended Petersburg Technological Institute. Arrested 1874 for subversive activities. Acquitted. Arrested at Kiev 1879 and expelled from Russia. Returned 1880. Member of the Executive Committee of the Narodnaya Volya. Participated in the attempt of March 1. Arrested April, 1881. Tried in the Trial of the Twenty 1882. Died in Peter and Paul Fortress 1884.

LEBEDEVA, *Tatiana Ivanovna:* Born 1853, daughter of a government official near Moscow. Member of the Executive Committee of the Narodnaya Volya. Participated in the attempt at Odessa 1879, and assisted in the party's explosive laboratories. Arrested September, 1881. Tried in the Trial of the Twenty 1882. Died in prison at Kara (Siberia) 1887.

LIZOGUB, *Dmitri Andreevich:* Born 1850, wealthy landowner from near Chernigov. Attended Petersburg University. From 1874 engaged in various revolutionary activities. Member of Zemlya i Volya. Financed the revolutionary party, and initiated steps to liquidate his properties and so devote his whole fortune to the cause. Arrested at Odessa, August, 1878. Tried August, 1879, and executed four days later.

MERKULOV, *Vasili Apollonovich:* Born 1861. Son of a soldier. Worked as carpenter in Odessa, where he became acquainted with Zhelyabov. Member of Narodnaya Volya party 1880. Participated in the attempt at Odessa 1880, the attempt on the Kishinev State Treasury 1880–81, and in the preparations for March 1. Arrested February, 1881. Tried in the Trial of the Twenty 1882. Gave evidence against his former associates and entered the service of the Secret Police. Assisted in the arrest of Figner. Died about 1905.

MIHAILOV, *Alexander Dmitrievich:* Born 1857, of a family of gentry at Kursk. Attended the Technological Institute in Petersburg. Involved in student disturbances in 1875, visited Kiev and thereafter became a revolutionary. Member of Zemlya i Volya. Leader of the Death or Freedom group. Concerned in the assassination of Mezentsev 1878, with the attempt on Drenteln by Mirski, and with Soloviev's attack on the Emperor 1879. Principal initiator of Lipetsk conference, which he attended, and also conference at Voronezh. Member of Executive Committee and also of Administrative Council of the Narodnaya Volya. Participated in the attempt at Moscow 1879. Arrested November, 1880. Tried in the

A Revolutionary Who's Who 251

Trial of the Twenty 1882. Died in prison 1883. Has been described as the ideal Minister of the Interior for a Revolutionary Government.

MIHAILOV, *Timothy Mihailovich:* Born 1860. Son of a peasant near Smolensk. Came to Petersburg and was employed as metal worker in various factories. Member of the Workers' Section of the Narodnaya Volya. Participated as bomb thrower in the attack of March 1, 1881. Arrested March 3. Tried in Trial of the Six. Executed April, 1881.

MOROZOV, *Nikolai Alexandrovich:* Born 1855 (illegitimate); son of a landowner near Yaroslavl. Expelled from secondary school on grounds of subversive activity. Tried in Trial of the 193. Became "illegal." Co-editor of *Zemlya i Volya* newspaper. Attended Lipetsk and Voronezh conferences. Member of Executive Committee of Narodnaya Volya. Co-editor of *Narodnaya Volya* newspaper. Participated in attempt at Moscow 1879. Visited Western Europe 1880. Arrested on return to Russia, January, 1881. Tried in Trial of the Twenty 1882. Imprisoned in the Peter and Paul Fortress and in Schlusselburg. Released 1905. Settled in Leningrad. The latest news of him (winter of 1943–44) is that he is still alive and at work.

MYSHKIN, *Ippolit Nikitich:* Born 1848. Son of a non-commissioned officer. Started a secret illegal printing press in Moscow 1873. From 1874 an "illegal." Attempted rescue of Chernishevski 1875. Arrested same year. Tried in the Trial of the 193. Sentenced to ten years' imprisonment. Continued his activities among fellow-prisoners in Siberia, and in 1880 his term was increased by another 15 years. Escaped 1882. Re-arrested. Transferred to Peter and Paul Fortress 1883, and to Schlusselburg 1884. Attacked a prison inspector, was tried by court martial and executed January, 1885.

NECHAEV, *Sergei Gennadievich ("The Eagle"):* Born 1847. Son of a serf from near Vladimir. Attended lectures at Petersburg University 1868. Formed revolutionary circle 1869, and staged bogus escape the same year. Joined Bakunin in Switzerland. Returned to Russia, August. Founded new revolutionary circle and murdered Ivanov, November. Escaped to Switzerland again. Arrested and extradited to Russia 1872. Tried 1873. Imprisoned in Peter and Paul Fortress. Conducted revolutionary propaganda among his warders. In touch with the Executive Committee 1881. His activities were shortly afterwards betrayed by a fellow-prisoner and he was removed to the dungeons where he died 1883.

OKLADSKI, *Ivan Fedorovich:* Born 1858, artisan, of Novoshev near Pskov. Carpenter. From 1872 employed in factories at Petersburg. From 1876 engaged in revolutionary activities, and became an "illegal." Member of the Narodnaya Volya. Participated in the attempt at Alexandrovsk. Arrested July, 1880. Tried in Trial of the Sixteen. Entered the service of the Secret Police and was released from prison. Worked as police agent in the Caucasus and in Petersburg. Tried by the Soviet Court as an agent provocateur in 1925 and sentenced to ten years' imprisonment. Has since died.

OLOVENNIKOVA, *Maria Nikolaevna (Oshashina):* Born 1850. Member of Zemlya i Volya. Attended Lipetsk and Voronezh conferences 1879. Member of Executive Committee of Narodnaya Volya. Acted as link with Kletochnikov. Transferred by the Executive Committee to Moscow, December, 1880. Escaped abroad 1882. Died in Paris 1897.

OLOVENNIKOVA, *Natalia Nikolaevna:* Born 1856. Member of the Narodnaya Volya 1880. Member of Perovskaya's scouting party for the attack of March 1. Shortly afterwards suffered a nervous breakdown and took no further part in the party's affairs. Died 1924.

OSINSKI, *Valerian Andreevich:* Born 1853, son of a wealthy landowner near Taganrog. Attended Engineering Institute in Petersburg. Appointed to a post on the railways 1873. Dismissed for political undesirability 1876. Became "illegal" and participated in revolutionary activities. Arrested 1877 for distributing forged tickets for the Trial of the Fifty. Released soon after. Moved to Kiev and became main leader of local revolutionaries. Instituted terrorist reprisals against police spies and officials from 1878. Organised the escape of Stefanovich, Deutsch and Bokhanovski from Kiev prison. Arrested January, 1879. Tried at Kiev in May and executed that same month.

PEROVSKAYA, *Sophia Lvovna (Sonia):* Born 1854. Father was Governor General of Petersburg. Took part in revolutionary activities from 1872. Member of the Chaikovski Circle. Arrested 1874 and released on bail. In Trial of the 193. Acquitted 1878. Re-arrested, but escaped while being conveyed to place of exile. Became an "illegal." Attended the Voronezh conference 1879. Participated in the attempt at Moscow 1879. Member of the Executive Committee of the Narodnaya Volya. Participated in the attempt at Odessa 1880. Associated with Zhelyabov in the organisation of the Workers' Section. Assumed charge of the bombing attack on March 1, 1881. Arrested ten days later. Tried in Trial of the

Six. Executed April, 1881. The inevitable heroine of the history of the Narodnaya Volya.

PLEKHANOV, *Georgi Valentinovich:* Born 1857 of a family of gentry near Tambov. Attended Petersburg University. Associated with the revolutionary movement from 1876. Member of Zemlya i Volya. Attended Voronezh conference. Leader of Cherni Peredel party. Emigrated 1880. Was subsequently associated with Lenin in the Social Democratic party and became an outstanding figure in the international Left Wing movement. Returned to Russia 1917, but had by then split with Lenin. Died in Finland 1918.

PRESNYAKOV, *Andrei Korneevich:* Born 1856, son of an artisan of Oranienbaum. Attended Teachers' Institute at Petersburg, but left (1875) and worked as joiner in various factories. Engaged in revolutionary activities. Killed a Secret Police agent 1877; arrested; escaped April, 1878; went abroad to Paris and London. Returned to Russia, March, 1879. Member of the Executive Committee of the Narodnaya Volya. Participated in the railway attempts. Arrested July, 1880. Tried in the Trial of the Sixteen. Executed November, 1880.

RYSAKOV, *Nikolai Ivanovich (Glazov):* Born 1862, artisan from Tikhvin. Attended a technical school in Petersburg. Became associated with the Workers' Section of the Narodnaya Volya. Participated as bomb thrower in the attack of March 1, 1881. Arrested same day. Tried in Trial of the Six. While under arrest made voluminous depositions implicating a number of his associates. Executed April, 1881.

SABLIN, *Nikolai Aleksievich:* Born about 1854. Son of a landowner. Attended Moscow University. Engaged in revolutionary activities from 1873. Went to Zurich 1874. Returned to Russia in March, 1875. Arrested the same month. In prison till the Trial of the 193. Found guilty January, 1878, but shortly afterwards released in view of his long preliminary confinement. Member of Narodnaya Volya 1880. Participated in the Odessa attempt 1880, and in preparations for March 1. Committed suicide in course of police raid on the Telezhnaya conspiratorial quarter March 3, 1881.

SHIRAEV, *Stepan Grigorievich:* Born 1857. Peasant from near Saratov. Attended Veterinary Institute at Kharkov. Participated as a very young man in various revolutionary activities. Emigrated 1876. Worked as factory hand in Paris and London. Returned to Russia. Attended Lipetsk conference. Member of the Executive

Committee of the Narodnaya Volya. Participated in the attempt at Moscow. Arrested December, 1879. Tried in the Trial of the Sixteen. Imprisoned with Nechaev in the Peter and Paul Fortress. Died there August, 1881.

SOLOVIEV, *Alexander Konstantinovich:* Born 1846, son of a government official near Petersburg. Attended Petersburg University. Took post as a school teacher 1867. Resigned 1874. Engaged in revolutionary activities in various country districts. Returned to Petersburg December, 1878, with intention of assassinating Alexander II. Made his attempt April 2, 1879. Was apprehended, tried, and hanged on May 28.

STEFANOVICH, *Jacob Vasilievich:* Born 1854. Son of parish priest in the Ukraine. Associated as a very young man with the Kiev revolutionaries. Chief organiser of the Chigirin affair. Arrested 1877. Escaped from Kiev prison 1878. Member of Zemlya i Volya. On the split in the party at first joined the Cherni Peredel, but came over to the Narodnaya Volya after the assassination of Alexander II. Member of the Executive Committee. Arrested 1882. Tried in the Trial of the Seventeen 1883. Served term of imprisonment and exile in Siberia. Died in South Russia 1915.

STEPNIAK (*see* KRAVCHINSKI).

SUKHANOV, *Nikolai Evgenievich:* Born 1853, son of a doctor in Riga. Attended Naval Academy. Midshipman 1873. Posted to Vladivostock. Denounced his commanding officer for defalcations in connexion with the supply of coal. His allegations were confirmed by the Court of Enquiry, but as certain influential persons were involved the court's decisions were quashed and the captain reinstated. Sukhanov was promoted lieutenant 1879. Transferred to Kronstadt. Put in charge of Naval Electrical Institute in Petersburg 1880. Came in touch with the revolutionaries. Member of Executive Committee of the Narodnaya Volya 1880. Helped with organisation of the Fighting Services' Section. Took part in preparations for March 1, 1881. Arrested in April. Tried in Trial of the Twenty, and executed by firing squad at Kronstadt, March, 1882.

TETERKA, *Makar Vasilievich:* Born 1854, artisan of Odessa. No education. Involved in workers' revolutionary movement in Odessa 1877. Member of Narodnaya Volya. Participated in the attempt at the Kamenni Bridge 1880. Looked after the party's carriage and horses. Arrested January, 1881. Tried in the Trial of the Twenty 1882. Died in the Peter and Paul Fortress 1884.

TIKHOMIROV, *Lev Alexandrovich (Starik)*: Born 1850 in the Don province. Associated in revolutionary activities from the early 'seventies. Member of the Zemlya i Volya. Attended Lipetsk and Voronezh conferences. Member of the Executive Committee and of the Administrative Council of the Narodnaya Volya. Offered resignation, which was refused, 1880. Co-editor of the *Narodnaya Volya* newspaper. Escaped abroad 1882. Published biographies of Zhelyabov, Perovskaya and Kibalchich, and engaged in other revolutionary literary work. Recanted 1888. Was subsequently amnestied and returned to Russia where he attained a prominent position as an extreme Right Wing reactionary journalist. Died 1922.

TIKHONOV, *Jacob Tikhonovich:* Born 1852, peasant of Smolensk. Subsequently became weaver and then carpenter. Arrested 1875 for subversive propaganda. Exiled 1877. Escaped the same year. Re-arrested in Moscow November, 1878. Escaped again March, 1879. Member of the Narodnaya Volya. Participated in the attempt at Alexandrovsk. Arrested November, 1879. Tried in Trial of the Sixteen. Died of tuberculosis in prison at Kara in 1883.

TRIGONI, *Mihail Nikolaevich ("My Lord"):* Born 1851, in the Crimea, son of a general. Companion of Zhelyabov both at school at Kerch and at Odessa. Remained "legal" but took part secretly in various revolutionary activities. Member of the Executive Committee of the Narodnaya Volya. Participated in the mine in the Malaya Sadovaya. Arrested (with Zhelyabov) February, 1881. Tried in Trial of the Twenty. Imprisoned in Peter and Paul Fortress and in Schlusselburg till 1905. Died in the Crimea 1917.

TYRKOV, *Arkadi Vladimirovich:* Born 1860, in Petersburg of a family of gentry. Attended Petersburg University. Member of Narodnaya Volya 1880. Member of the scouting party for the attack of March 1, 1881. After the attack he devoted himself to looking after Perovskaya. His arrest followed closely on hers. Suffered a nervous breakdown in prison and was transferred to Siberia by administrative process. Amnestied 1905, and returned to the family estate near Novgorod. After the Revolution was allotted a pension by the Soviet Government. Died in Russia 1925.

YAKIMOVA, *Anna Vasilieva (Bashka):* Born 1856. Daughter of a parish priest near Viatka. Attended teachers' training school. Implicated in subversive activities and tried in the Trial of the 193, 1878. Ordered by the court to reside in her place of birth.

Ran away February, 1879. Member of Zemlya i Volya; member of Executive Committee of the Narodnaya Volya. Participated in the attempts at Alexandrovsk 1876 and Odessa 1880. Was the "Madame Kobozeva" of the cheese shop in the Malaya Sadovaya. Arrested April, 1881. Tried in the Trial of the Twenty 1882. In prison till 1905. On release joined up immediately with the "Battle Organisation." Betrayed by an agent provocateur and rearrested.

In 1925 a play on the subject of March 1 was produced at a Moscow theatre and the surviving veterans, including Yakimova, were invited to attend. *Izvestia's* dramatic critic referred rather patronisingly to the gratification Yakimova must feel at seeing herself portrayed on the stage. This provoked a spirited reply from the old lady in which both play and critic were effectively trounced.

Settled in Leningrad and died during the Second World War.

ZASULICH, *Vera Ivanovna:* Born 1852. Daughter of a small landowner near Smolensk. Associated with Nechaev 1868. Arrested 1869. Imprisoned till 1871, subsequently exiled till 1873. In touch with the Kiev group 1875. In consequence of the flogging of the student "Bogolyubov" at the orders of Trepov in July, 1877, Zasulich called on the latter on January 24, 1878, and severely wounded him with a revolver. Tried by jury and acquitted. Rescued by crowd from attempts of the police to re-arrest her. Member of the Cherni Peredel. Associated with Plekhanov and Lenin in the Social Democratic party, but had split with Lenin by the outbreak of the Revolution. Died 1919.

ZHELYABOV, *Andrei Ivanovich (Tarass, Zahar, Borodach):* Born 1850 in the Crimea, son of a house serf. Attended school at Kerch. Admitted University of Odessa 1869, expelled 1871. Member of Volkhovski Circle. Arrested three times 1874, subsequently released on bail. Tried in Trial of the 193. Acquitted 1878. Became "illegal" 1879. Attended Lipetsk and Voronezh conferences. Member of the Executive Committee of the Narodnaya Volya. Took part in the attempts at Alexandrovsk, in the Winter Palace, and at the Kamenni Bridge. Chief organiser of the Workers' and Fighting Services' Sections. Main organiser of the attack of March 1, 1881. Arrested February 27. Tried in Trial of the Six. Executed April 3, 1881. Was considered by Lenin to be the ideal revolutionary leader.

ZUNDELEVICH, *Aaron Isakovich:* Born 1855, son of a small Jewish merchant of Vilensk. Became a revolutionary 1875. Fled abroad to avoid arrest, returned to Russia under false name. Member of Zemlya i Volya. Member of Executive Committee of the Narodnaya Volya. Arrested in the Public Library at Petersburg October, 1879. Tried in Trial of the Sixteen. Sentenced to hard labour for life. Released 1905. Eventually settled in England where he died in 1923.

BIBLIOGRAPHICAL NOTE

ALL phases of the Russian revolutionary movement have inspired a vast literature of varying reliability and interest. In the case of the Narodnaya Volya the zeal and piety of surviving revolutionaries and the publication of the Imperial Archives provide an almost unique opportunity of studying a secret society both from inside and as seen by the authorities. It is, however, a fact that the greater part of this material has for various reasons been completely neglected or ignored by Western historians. In any case much of it is out of print or otherwise not easily available.

What follows has no claim to be an exhaustive bibliography of the revolutionary movement of the period. It is merely a list of those works which the writer has found to have direct or indirect bearing on the lives of Zhelyabov and his associates. To those who wish to pursue the matter further a word of warning may perhaps be given, obvious though it may seem. Militant revolutionary activities take place in an atmosphere of acute physical danger and of high nervous and emotional strain. Participants and eyewitnesses who subsequently write about them are seldom without some conscious or unconscious incentive to distort, to omit or to interpolate. Contradictions and inconsistencies are almost inevitable in any two accounts of the same happening. To get near the truth—and if we do not get near the truth we are wasting our time—we must check every item from every available angle; and above all we must pay regard to what we know of the human element.

Biographies, etc., of Zhelyabov

Andrei Ivanovich Zhelyabov (Zhelyabov's autobiographical fragment with a foreword by Vera Figner). Moscow 1930.
Asheshov, N., *Andrei Ivanovich Zhelyabov*. Petrograd 1919.
Dragomanov, M., *K Biografii A. I. Zhelyabova*. Geneva 1892.
(Tikhomirov, L.), *Andrei Ivanovich Zhelyabov*. Geneva 1899.
Voronski, A., *Zhelyabov*. Moscow 1934.
Zaslavski, D., *A. I. Zhelyabov*. Moscow 1925. (Of these Voronski's work is the most complete, but, like all the others, it is out of print.)

The Trials

Bogucharski, V. L., *Protsess 20ti Narodovoltsev*. Rostov-on-Don 1906.
Burtsev, V. L., *Protsess Shestnadtsati Terroristov*. St. Petersburg 1906.
Deutsch, L., *Dyelo 1 Marta, 1881*. St. Petersburg 1906. (The foreword by Deutsch contains some interesting personal reminiscences.)
Protsess 1 Marta, 1881. St. Petersburg 1906.
Yakimova, A. V. and Pribylev, A., *Narodnaya Volya Pered Tsarskim Sudom*. Moscow 1930.

Historical Reviews

Byloe. London 1903–4; St. Petersburg 1906–7; Paris 1908–12; Petrograd 1917–26; Paris 1933.
Katorga i Ssylka. Moscow 1921–35.
(Both of these are essential for the study of our subject. They contain memoirs of eye-witnesses and participants and also extracts from the Imperial Archives. Most of the individual numbers contain at least one and often several articles with direct bearing on the revolutionary movements of the 'seventies and 'eighties. Of special interest are the contributions by Yakimova, Korba, Figner, Frolenko, Morozov, Tyrkov and Trigoni.)

Revolutionary Brochures, Articles, Etc.

Bogucharski, V., *Revolyutsionaya Zhurnalistika Semidesyatih Godov*. Rostov-on-Don 1906? (A useful compilation.)
Bogucharski, V., *Literatura Partii Narodnoi Voli 1879–84*. St. Petersburg 1907. (A collection of the party's publications during this period.)
Borisov, I., *Nachalo Kontsa*. Geneva 1881.
Burtsev, V. L., *Za Sto Lyet*. London 1897. (In addition to the collection of documents this book contains an exhaustive chronological table.)
Kravchinski, S. (Stepniak), *Smert za Smert* (with foreword by Petrovski). Petersburg 1920.

The Revolutionaries and the Revolutionary Movement

Aptekman, O. V., *Iz Istorii Revolyutsionavo Narodnichestva*. Rostov-on-Don 1907.
Asheshov, N., *Sofiya Perovskaya*. Moscow 1921.

Aschenbrenner, M., *Voennaya Organizatsia Narodnoi Voli*. Moscow 1924.
Bogucharski, V., *Iz Istorii Politicheskoi Borby v 70-ıh 80-ıh XIX Vyeka*. Moscow 1912. (Valuable.)
Branfoot, A. I. S., A Critical Survey of the Narodnik Movement. Ph. D. thesis, London 1926. (The only full-length study of this subject in English. Consulted by courtesy of the London University authorities.)
Byelokonski, I. P., *Dan' Vremeni*. Moscow 1928.
Debogory-Mokriewitsch, W., *Erinnerungen Eines Nihilisten*. German translation, Stuttgart 1905. (Of great interest. I have unfortunately not been able to locate a copy of the Russian issue —Debogori-Mokrievich, *Vospominania*. St. Petersburg 1906.)
Figner, Vera, *Zapechatlenni Trud*. Moscow 1921. (A vivid account of the history of the Narodnaya Volya by one of its leading members.)
Frolenko, M., *1881 God*. Moscow 1925.
Kruzhok Narodovoltsev, *I Marta 1881 Goda*. Moscow 1933.
Kupczanko, Gregor, *Der Russische Nihilismus*. Leipzig 1884.
Lavigne, E., *Introduction à l'histoire du Nihilisme Russe*. Paris 1880.
Mihailov, A. D., *Vospominania* (with notes by personal acquaintances). Geneva 1903.
Mihailovski, N. K., *Vospominania*. Berlin 1906.
Morozov, N. A., *Povesti Moei Zhizni*. Leningrad 1928. (The autobiography of "the herald of the terrorist movement.")
Narodovoltsi, *Sbornik III*. Moscow 1931.
Perovski, V. L., *Vospominania o Sestre*. Moscow 1927.
Plekhanov, A., Introduction to the Russian translation, published Geneva 1903, of Thun's *Revolutionären Bewegungen* mentioned below.
Serebriakov, E. A., *Obshchestvo Zemlya i Volya*. London 1902.
Stepniak, S. (Kravchinski), *Podpolnaya Rossia*. London 1893.
Thun, Alfons, *Geschichte der Revolutionären Bewegungen in Russland*. Leipzig 1883. (The notes and bibliography are of interest.)
Tikhomirov, L., *Nikolai Ivanovich Kibalchich* (with a memoir by Breshkovskaya). St. Petersburg 1906.
Tikhomirov, L., *Sofiya Lvovna Perovskaya*. Geneva 1899.
Zhukovski-Zhuk, I. I., *Valerian Andreevich Osinski*. Moscow 1926.
Zilliacus, Konni, *The Russian Revolutionary Movement*. English translation, London 1905.

Alexander II

Laferté, Victor, *Alexandre II—Détails inédits sur sa vie et sur sa mort.* Basel 1882.
Tatishchev, S. S., *Aleksander II: Evo Zhizn i Tsarstvovanie.* St. Petersburg 1903. (The standard work on the subject.)

Background

Burtsev, V. L., *Borba za Svobodnyu Rossyu.* Berlin 1923.
Carr, E. H., *Bakunin.* London 1937.
Cambridge Modern History, Vol. XI, Cambridge 1909; Vol. XII, Cambridge 1920.
Deutsch, L., *Za Pol Vyeka.* Berlin 1923.
Gertsen (Herzen), A. I., *Byloe I Dumy.* Berlin 1921.
Kennan, George, *Siberia and the Exile System.* London 1891.
Kropotkin, P., *Memoirs of a Revolutionist.* London 1899.
Lenin, N., "Chto Dyelat?" (In Vol. IV of *Collected Works.*) Moscow 1929.
Leroy-Beaulieu, R., *L'Empire des Tsars et les Russes.* Paris 1890. (The outstanding general work on the Russia of the period.)
Marx-Engels, *Selected Correspondence.* London 1936.
Milyukov, P. N., *Histoire de Russie.* Paris 1933.
Mirski, D., *Russia.* London 1931.
Pares, Sir Bernard, *Russia and Reform.* London 1907.
Pobyedonostsev, K., *Reflections of a Russian Statesman.* English translation, London 1898.
Pokrovski, M., *Brief History of Russia.* English translation, London 1933.
Svatikov, S. G., *Obshchestvennoe Dvizhenie v Rossii.* Rostov 1905.
Slovtsov, R., "Dnevnik D. A. Milyutina," in *Poslednia Novosti.* Paris, June 22, 1939.
Steklov, Y., *Mihail Aleksandrovich Bakunin.* Moscow 1927.
Stepniak, S. (Kravchinski), *Russia under the Tsars.* London 1885.
London *Times.* 1881.
Wallace, D. Mackenzie, *Russia.* London 1905.

Reference

Bolshaya Sovietskaya Entsiklopedia. Moscow 1926.
Deyateli Revolyutsionnavo Dvizhenia v Rossii—Bio-Bibliograficheski Slovar. Moscow 1934. (This most comprehensive work, which is not yet complete, gives full bibliographies, including specific references to individual articles in *Byloe, Katorga i*

Ssylka and other periodicals, for each participant of any consequence in the Russian revolutionary movement.)
Entsiklopedicheski Slovar. St. Petersburg 1890.
Russki Biograficheski Slovar. St. Petersburg 1905.

INDEX

ADLERBERG, Count, 126
Alekseev, 66–67
Alexander I, 6
Alexander II, vii, viii, 12, 14–17, 18, 34, 62, 63, 82–84, 92, 93, 94, 107, 112–119, 126, 130, 131, 133, 136, 137, 138, 171 n., 181, 182, 183, 184, 188–191, 193, 196–200, 202, 212, 213
Alexander III (Crown Prince up to 1880), ix, 37, 62, 137, 138, 156, 171 n., 182, 202, 203, 214, 216, 217, 218, 225, 235
Alexandrovsk (Zaporozhe), 112–119, 122, 124, 127, 132, 139, 140, 149, 210, 220, 231
Alexis Raveline, 175–176
Apraxin Dvor, 17
Aptekman, 103
Aronchik, 120, 121, 245
Aschenbrenner, 53, 163
Azev, 151 n.

BAER, 32
Bakunin, 23–26, 40, 42, 43–44, 57
Barannikov, 81, 87, 100, 114, 116, 143, 144, 147, 153, 157, 169, 175, 177, 178, 180, 220, 245
Baranov, Count, 226, 238
Bardina, 66
"Batishkov." See Khalturin
Battenberg, Prince of, 137
Ben Ami, Rabbi, 29
Blanc, Louis, 22
Bogdanov, 136
Bogdanovich ("Kobozev"), 172, 174, 180, 181, 191, 194, 195, 200, 205, 245
Bogdanovich, Madame General, 238
Bogishich, Professor, 31–34, 49
Bokhanovski, 62, 64, 74–78
"Borodach." See Zhelyabov
Bosnia-Herzegovina revolt, 52
Braddon, 155
Brandtner, 97, 98, 99
Breshkovskaya, 49, 56, 88, 246
Burtsev, 54 n., 158, 202 n.
Byron, 29

CAIRO, 183
Cat, conspiratorial, 122, 191, 205

Catherine II, 5
Catherine, Grand Duchess, 190
Chaikovski Circle, 42
"Cheremisov." See Zhelyabov, A. I.
Cherkassi, 61
Chernavskaya, 120–123
Chernigov, 83, 84, 85, 96
Cherni Peredel, 31, 107, 114, 120, 130, 145, 153, 158, 159, 173
Chernishevski, 39, 40, 68
Chigirin, 61
Chudnovski, 29
Clemenceau, 159
Constantine, Grand Duke, 17, 182
Crimean War, 9, 10, 16, 64
Crown Prince. See Alexander III
Cooper, Fenimore, 20

DEATH or Freedom. See Troglodites
Debogori-Mokrievich, 43–46, 49, 62, 72–78, 97–99, 173, 246
Decembrist revolt, 6, 19
Degaev, 72 n., 165, 175
Deutsch, 62, 64, 74–78, 105, 106, 107, 114, 246
Dickens, 29
Directive Committee, 101, 102
Disorganizing Group, 59, 71, 105
Dobrinski, Captain, 139, 140, 214, 216, 233 n.
Dolgoruki, Princess. See Yurievskaya
Dolgoruki, Prince, 126
Dostoevski, 21
"Dove," The, 74–75
Dragomanov, 159
Drenteln, General, 91, 93, 176
Drigo, 96 and n.
Dvorzhitski, Colonel, 196–198, 220
Dyelo, 160

EKATERINSKI Canal and Quay, 143, 190, 194–199, 203, 220, 221, 224
Elizavetgrad (Kirovo), 123, 124
Emancipation, Act of, 12–13, 14, 15, 66
Emelianov, 184, 199, 246
Engelson, 9
Epstein, 154, 207, 208
Executive Committee, 101, 102, 108, 114, 118, 119, 120, 126, 130, 131, 135,

Red Prelude

Executive Committee (*Continued*)
137, 138, 139, 141–142, 144, 145, 147, 149, 151, 152, 153, 158, 159, 160, 161, 164, 165, 167–169, 175–180, 183, 185, 202, 203, 204, 205, 206, 211, 214, 220, 225, 232

FEDEROV, General, 222
Feodosia, 2, 11, 35
Fighting Services' Section, 164–165, 176, 179, 201
Figner, E., 128, 129
Figner, Vera, 21, 40, 72 n., 101, 103, 105, 107, 112, 113, 119, 141–142, 151, 152, 157, 158, 160, 165, 184, 192, 193, 195, 200, 209, 238, 240, 247
Franzholi, 161, 185
Frolenko, 75–78, 95, 96, 100, 101, 102, 103, 112–113, 157, 169, 173, 174, 175, 178, 192, 194–195, 216, 247
Frolov (executioner), 166, 241–242
Frolov (serf), 1, 2, 10, 11
Frolova, Lyuba, 10, 11
Fuchs, president of the court, 218–235

GATCHINA (Krasnogvardeisk), 207, 216
Geneva, 22, 23
Gerard, 226, 234, 238
"Glazov." *See* Rysakov
Gogol, 152
Going to the People. *See* Narodnichestvo
Goldenberg, 90–92, 101, 113, 114, 120, 121, 123–124, 139–141, 144, 145, 159, 165, 166, 188, 210, 214, 220, 221, 229, 233 n., 247
Golden Charter, 62, 63
Golos, 82
Goncharov, 39
Gorinovich, 66, 71
Grachevski, 68, 192, 247
Grinevitski, 161, 162, 183, 184, 185, 186, 193, 194, 197, 198, 199, 200, 202, 248

HARTMANN, 120–124, 159, 248
Haxthausen, 38
Heiking, Captain, 74
Heine, 29
Helfmann, 161, 162, 184, 195, 204, 215, 216, 219–235, 237, 241, 242, 248
Helker, 219
Herzen, 9, 20, 24, 26, 39
Hood, 31
Hugo, Victor, 29, 159

"IMPERNICKEL." *See* Nicholas I
Irkutsk, 68
Isaev, 87, 88, 107, 116, 121, 141, 143, 147, 153, 157, 169, 175, 179, 184, 192, 200, 238, 239, 248
Italianskaya, No. 45, 141–142
Ivanov, 25–26
Ivanova, 87, 101, 105, 128, 129, 134, 135, 165, 249
Ivichevich, 73, 95

KAMENETS-PODOLSK, 86
Kamenni Bridge, 143, 144, 164
Karakozov, 18, 20, 24, 41, 146
Kashki-Chekrak, 2, 10
Kazan, 13
Kedrin, 199
Kerch, 2, 12, 21, 35, 51, 53
Khalturin, 89, 90, 131–137, 249
Kharkhov, 78, 79, 80, 83, 85, 90, 91, 113, 114, 115, 124, 161, 166
Kherson, 97, 210
Kibalchich, 55–56, 87, 88, 107, 112, 116, 123, 124, 135, 153, 167, 171, 185, 190, 192, 193, 194, 195, 205, 216, 219–235, 237–243, 249
Kiev, 43, 44, 45, 59, 60, 61, 62, 63, 64, 65, 66, 71–77, 80, 90, 92, 95, 97, 213
Kishinev, 173, 174
Kletochnikov, 88–90, 134, 139, 141, 156, 177, 178, 249
Knoop, Colonel, 33, 51
Kobilianski, 91
"Kobozev." *See* Bogdanovich
"Kobozeva." *See* Yakimova
Koch, Captain, 196, 198, 221
Kokovski, 148, 149, 151, 161, 162, 185, 250
Kolotkevich, 95, 100, 101, 103, 112, 157, 160, 163, 164, 169, 173, 175, 177, 178, 180, 220, 250
Komarov, General, 210, 213
Korba, 147, 148, 149, 153, 157, 169, 177, 192, 250
"Kotik." *See* Grinevitski
Kotlyarevski, 72, 73, 74, 76
Kovalskaya, 106
Kovalski, 80, 81, 95
Kravchinski, 39, 43, 72, 80, 81, 87, 96, 207, 250
Kremenchug, 78
Kremlin, 125
Kronstadt, 163, 165, 179
Kropotkin, Prince D., 90, 91, 123, 140
Kuritsin, 139
"Kurshunikov." *See* Barannikov

Kursk, 107, 114, 126
Kviatkovski, 1, 87, 92, 100, 101 n., 105, 128–133, 135, 140, 157, 165–167, 178, 213, 250

LAFERTÉ, 183, 188, 198
Lampsi, 2
Langans, 68, 169, 175, 192, 251
Lavrists, 42, 43, 48, 49
Lavrov, 40–43
Lebedeva, 112–113, 157, 173–174, 192, 251
Lenin, vii, 110
Lermontov, 29
Leshern, 98, 99
Lesnoy, 105, 107
Lipetsk, 95, 97, 99–107, 140, 147, 166, 225, 231, 232
Listok Zemli i Voli, 87, 92, 94
Livadia, 107, 118, 157
Lizogub, 96–97, 251
London *Times*, 9, 214, 227, 237 n., 242
Longfellow, 29
Lorentsov, 2, 10, 11, 20, 146
Loris-Melikov, Count, 138, 139, 145, 156, 167, 177, 180, 182, 183, 188–190, 214, 216, 217, 219
Luludaki, 21, 27, 30, 35

"MADAME B," 209
Makarevich, 50, 51
Malaya Sadovaya (mine), 171–172, 174–175, 180–181, 186, 189–195, 204, 205, 216, 220, 222, 233, 235
Manège, 189–190, 193, 195
Marx, 40, 159–160, 162, 236
Merkulov, 141, 142, 143, 151 n., 173–174, 175, 180, 186, 251
Mezentsev, General, 80–82, 87
Michael, Grand Duke, 197
Mihailov, Alexander, 58–61, 65, 80, 81, 83, 87–90, 92, 93, 94–96, 99, 100, 101, 102, 103, 106, 120, 131, 143, 144, 147, 149, 152, 153, 157, 163, 167–168, 177, 178, 185, 186, 251–252
Mihailov, Timothy, 184, 185, 186, 190, 193–194, 196, 200, 205, 214–216, 219–235, 237–243, 252
Mihailovski, 160, 202 n.
Miller, Major, 134–135
Milyutin, Count, 222, 224, 242
Mironenko. *See* Frolenko and Lebedeva
Mirski, 92, 176
Mlodetski, 139
Morozov, 87, 92, 94, 100–102, 106, 107

and n., 121, 135, 146, 158, 178, 225, 229, 252
Moscow, 21, 25, 65, 66, 83, 90, 101, 114, 116–126, 128, 129–130, 132, 140, 153, 154, 161, 165, 173, 177–179, 205, 219, 238
Mrovinski, General, 191, 216 and n.
Muraviev, acting public prosecutor, 220–234
Myshkin, 68–69, 78, 252

NABAT, 238
Nabokov, 70, 218–219
Narodnaya Volya newspaper, 101, 108, 109–111, 128–129, 158, 160–161, 163, 176
Narodnaya Volya party, vii–ix, 54 n., 87, 107–111, 113, 120, 128–131, 137, 138, 139, 144, 145, 147, 150, 157–165, 172–173, 175, 176–180, 202–203, 210, 211, 214, 220
Narodnichestvo, 42–48, 54, 57–58, 61, 62, 65–69, 85, 95, 103–107, 231
Narodovoltsi. *See* Narodnaya Volya
Natanson, Mark, 58
Natanson, Olga, 58, 60
Nechaev, 21–27, 41, 61, 72, 175–177, 252
Nelidov, 2, 11–12
Nicholas I, 6, 9, 15, 19, 38, 130
Nihilist movement, 19, 72
"Nikitin," Madame, 97
Nikolaev, 165
Nikolaevka, 210
Nikonov, 71
Northern Workers' Union, 90, 131
Novorossisk University (Odessa), vii, 21, 30–36
Novikov, 181
Novobelgorod, 166

OBLOMOV, 39
Obolenski, Prince D. D., 124–126
Odessa, vii, 27–35, 48–53, 66, 80, 81, 85, 86, 95, 96, 112, 113, 123, 124, 127, 128, 140–143, 146, 153, 157, 161, 163, 165, 180, 186
Ogpu (N.K.V.D.), 149
Okladski, 114–119, 144, 149, 151 n., 165, 177, 185–186, 188, 253
Old Believers, 60, 120, 122
Olovennikova, Maria (Oshashina), 100, 157, 167, 177–179, 253
Olovennikova, Natalia, 171, 216, 253
Osinski, 59, 65, 66, 69, 71–78, 80, 83–86, 90, 92, 95, 97–99, 146, 253
Otechestvenne Zapiski, 160

PAHLEN, 46, 47, 57, 70
Paleolog, Captain, 213
Pargolovo Park, 185
Parnell, 160
Pavlov, 199
Perovskaya, vii, viii, 41, 42, 68, 78–80, 103–108, 120–123, 129–130, 141, 142, 147, 153–155, 157, 158, 161, 162, 164, 167, 169, 171, 185, 186, 191–195, 199–201, 206–209, 211, 212, 216–217, 219–235, 237–243, 253–254
Perovskaya, Madame, 41, 217, 239 n.
Perovski, General, 41
Peter the Great, 99
Peter and Paul Fortress, 54 n., 80, 175
Petersburg (Leningrad), 7, 17, 22, 25, 33–36, 41, 51, 55, 58–61, 67, 69, 79–82, 87, 88–91, 103, 105–107, 115, 120, 121, 125, 128, 129–130, 131, 132, 142–145, 152, 153, 161, 165, 173, 174, 180, 181, 189, 204, 205, 207, 210, 213, 220, 221, 236, 238
Petrotski, Corporal, 133, 136
Petrovski Park, 143
Petrovna, 51
Petrunkevich, 83–85
Pisarev, 39, 40
Plehve, 213
Plekhanov, 58, 65, 87, 92, 94, 95, 103, 105–108, 153, 254
Pobyedonostsev, 8, 37, 171 n., 182, 218–219, 237 n.
Podolskaya, 135
Polish revolt, 17, 18, 39
Popko, 74
Popov (of Kazan), 13
Popov (revolutionary), 92
Preliminary Detention Prison, 65, 67, 215, 216
Preobrazhenskoe cemetery, 120–126, 242
Presnyakov, 101, 114, 116, 117, 118, 143, 144, 157, 165–168, 213, 254
Pribyleva-Korba, Anna. See Korba
"Ptashka" (Lubkin), 129, 134–135
Pugachev, 40
Pushkin, 12, 29, 30

RABOCHAYA GAZETA, 161–162, 184
Razumovski, 136
Red Cross, Revolutionary, 150
Reid, Mayne, 20
Reinstein, 90, 92
Romanovs, 7, 15 n., 16, 37
Rostov-on-Don, 71, 161
Rusanov, 204

Rysakov, 151 and n., 161, 165, 174, 184, 186, 193–200, 205, 209, 211–216, 219–235, 237–243, 254

SABLIN, 141, 142, 173, 175, 184, 195, 204, 214, 215, 216, 254
Sagaidak, 115, 119, 139
Sapernaya printing press, 128–129, 134–135, 144, 165
Samara (Kuybyshev), 169
Saratov, 60, 169
Schechter, 30, 31
Schlusselberg, 54 n.
Semenovski Square, 240–243
Semenyuta, 52, 86
Sevastopol, 10
Shakespeare, 29
Shelgunov, 160, 204
Shiraev, 87, 88, 100, 103, 107, 123, 124, 129, 157, 165, 175, 254
Simbirsk (Ulianovsk), 28
Simferopol, 2, 68, 79, 107, 113, 114, 116, 117, 124, 186
Slotvinski, 211–212
Smolensk, 205
Soloviev, A. K., 91–93, 94, 140, 255
Soloviev, Professor, 236–237 and n.
Stefanovich, 44–46, 49, 61–64, 74–78, 105, 255
Stein, 1, 2
Stenka Razin, 5
"Stepniak." See Kravchinski
Strelnikov, 139
Sudeikin, 71 n., 139
Sukhanov, 88, 151, 163–165, 175, 179, 191–192, 201, 206, 255
Sukhorukov. See Hartmann
Sultanovka, 2, 10, 11
Sviridenko, 97, 98, 99

"TARASS." See Zhelyabov
Telezhnaya (conspiratorial quarter), 184–185, 190, 193–195, 204, 205, 214, 215, 221
Terentieva, 97
Teterka, 143–144, 255
Thackeray, 29
Third Section, 8, 18, 28, 80, 82, 89, 91, 94, 139, 156, 159, 177, 207
Tiflis, 165
Tikhomirov, 53, 87, 100, 101, 105, 108, 115, 131, 149–150, 152, 154, 160, 161, 167, 171, 178, 192, 202 and n., 206, 256
Tikhonov, 114–119, 165, 256
Tkachev, 22, 41, 238
Todtleben, Count, 113, 142, 249

Index

Tolstoi, Count D., 14, 19, 30, 33–34, 83, 156
Tolstoi, Leo, 237 n.
Trepov, 65, 67, 69, 70, 72, 80
Trial of the Six, 218–235
Trial of the Sixteen, 165–166, 221
Trial of the Fifty, 65, 66
Trial of the 193, 65, 67, 68, 69, 78, 80, 85, 91, 153, 187, 212, 226
Trigoni, 20, 142, 174, 180, 183, 184, 185–188, 191, 210, 256
"Troglodites," 87, 90, 91, 94–96, 100, 101, 142, 174, 180, 186–188, 210, 256
Troitski Pereulok, 161–162
Trubetskoi Bastion, 215
Tula, 124–125
Turgeniev, 15
Turkish War, 64, 138
Tver (Kalinin), 42
Tyrkov, 171, 200, 201, 206, 208 n., 209, 216, 256

UNGERN-STERNBERG, Baron, 113

VALUEV, 138, 182
Varvar, 81
Verne, Jules, 20
Vilyuisk, 68
Volkhovski Circle, 48, 49, 161
Voloshenko, 97, 98, 99
Voronezh, 94, 96, 103–105, 107, 153, 172

WINTER PALACE, 129, 131–133, 135–138, 145

Workers' Section, 148, 160–162, 174, 179, 183, 184–185, 225, 227–228
World Revolutionary Alliance, 23, 24, 25
Wormwood Scrubs, 54 n.

YAHNENKO, 49, 50, 52, 53, 210, 213
Yakimova, 68, 87, 101, 114–118, 119, 149, 157, 167, 169, 172, 179, 180–181, 191, 195, 199, 200, 205, 210, 256–257
Yurievskaya, 15, 182–183, 188–190, 196, 198, 199–200

"ZAHAR." *See* Zhelyabov
Zasulich, Vera, 22, 69–70, 72, 80, 105
Zemlya i Volya, 58–59, 60, 65, 79, 80, 81, 87, 92, 96, 103, 105, 107, 128, 144, 231
Zemstva, 17, 83, 84, 85, 156, 182
Zhelyabov, A. I., vii–3, 10–12, 13, 19–21, 27–36, 48–53, 54, 67, 69, 85–86, 90, 95, 99, 100–107, 112–119, 130, 135, 137, 139, 141–144, 146–155, 157–164, 167–170, 171–179, 183–187, 188–192, 193, 202, 206–216, 218–235, 237–243, 257
Zhelyabov, I, 1, 2, 3
Zhelyabova, Olga (nee Yahnenko), 49, 50, 52, 53, 95, 213 and n.
Zlatopolski, 141, 169
Zundelevich, 92, 101, 129, 140, 157, 165, 257–258
Zurich, 40, 42

MAR 6 1989